addressing
challenging behaviors
in early childhood settings

addressing challenging behaviors in early childhood settings

A TEACHER'S GUIDE

by

Dawn M. Denno, Ed.D.
Cincinnati Children's Hospital Medical Center
Cincinnati, Ohio

Victoria Carr, Ed.D.
University of Cincinnati
Cincinnati, Ohio

and

Susan Hart Bell, Ph.D.
Georgetown College
Georgetown, Kentucky

·P A U L·H·
BROOKES
PUBLISHING Cº ®

Baltimore • London • Sydney

Paul H. Brookes Publishing Co.
Post Office Box 10624
Baltimore, Maryland 21285-0624
USA

www.brookespublishing.com

Typeset by Integrated Publishing Solutions, Grand Rapids, Michigan.
Manufactured in the United States of America by
Versa Press, Inc., East Peoria, Illinois.

The individuals described in this book are composites of real people whose situations have been masked and are based on the authors' experiences. Names and identifying details have been changed to protect confidentiality.

The cartoons in this book are reprinted with permission: Giangreco, M.F. (2007). *Absurdities and realities of special education: The complete digital set [CD]*. Thousand Oaks, CA: Corwin Press.

Library of Congress Cataloging-in-Publication Data

Denno, Dawn M., 1951–
    Addressing challenging behaviors in early childhood settings : a teacher's guide / by Dawn Denno,
        Victoria Carr, Susan Hart Bell.
        p.   cm.
    Includes bibliographical references and index.
    ISBN-13: 978-1-55766-984-1 (pbk.)
    ISBN-10: 1-55766-984-8 (pbk.)
    1. Behavior modification.   2. Early childhood education.   3. Classroom
        management.   I. Carr, Victoria M. E.   II. Bell, Susan H.   III. Title.
    LB1060.2.D46 2010
    372.139'3—dc220   2010002822

British Library Cataloguing in Publication data are available from the British Library.

2014

10   9   8   7   6   5   4   3   2

Contents

CD-ROM Contents

About This CD-ROM

Chapter 1: Habitual Ways of Responding to Situations and People
Child Temperament Assessment
Strategies for Support (Temperament) Tool
Child Skill Assessment
Strategies for Support (Skill Development) Tool
Child Preference Observation Tool
Child Preference Parent Interview Tool

Chapter 2: Attitudes and Beliefs about Behavior in Educational Settings
Family Eco-map Tool
Brief Parenting Style Assessment Tool
Parent Interview–Sibling Rivalry Tool
Parent Conference Documentation Tool
Parent Communication Note
Tool for Communicating Across Child Care Settings

Chapter 3: Feelings of Safety and Belonging
Center Safety Plan
Separation Anxiety Assessment
Naptime Behaviors Assessment
Strategies for Supporting Naptime Behaviors Tool

Chapter 4: Designing the Physical Classroom Space
General Survey of Classroom Elements
Time Sample of Types of Groups in the Classroom
Ground Rule Discussion Tool
Interest-Focused Parent Discussion Tool
Time Sample of Classroom Areas Used
Levels of Sensory Stimulation Scale
Brief Event Sample with Stimulation Levels

Chapter 5: Using Responsive Curriculum to Support Behavior
Anecdotal Observation of Activity Tool
Monthly Summary of Anecdotal Observations
Time Sample of Individual Participation in General Content Areas
Tolerance Levels Rating Scale
Checklist for Guiding Engagement
Event Sample of Time Engaged
Event Sample of Teachers' Questions
Event Sample of Child's Questions
Language Support Plan
Dramatic Play Planning Tool

Chapter 6: Using Routines and Schedules to Support Positive Behavior

Planned and Actual Classroom Schedule
Wait Time Event Sample
Plan for Decreasing Wait Time
Waiting List
Analysis of Choice Time Tool
Schedule with Intentional Transitions

Chapter 7: Centerwide Support

Request for Collaborative Centerwide Support
Classroom Modifications to Support Behavior Tool
Centerwide Professional Development Needs Tool

Chapter 8: Teachers' Reactions to Children's Behaviors

Temperament Scale to Determine Goodness of Fit
Reflection Questions to Focus on Reframing Perceptions

Chapter 9: Teacher Language

Brief Reflection Tool
Intentional Instruction Tool
Teacher Managerial Tool
Positive Relationship Building Tool
Reflective Listening Checklist
"I" Message Checklist
Teacher–Child Interactions in Challenging Situations Tool
Script Template

Chapter 10: Peer Culture

Helping Children Enter Play Tool
Strategies to Reduce Challenging Behaviors

Chapter 11: Developing an Individualized Behavior Plan

Tool for Assessing Challenging Situations
Sample Script to Prevent Biting
Sample Script for Preventing a Child from Running Away

Chapter 12: Evaluating and Revising Behavior Plans

Frequency Tally of Targeted Behavior
A Picture of Progress
Tool for Tracking the Frequency and Duration of Targeted Behavior
Acceptability of Scripts Tool
Developing a Hypothesis Tool
Evaluation of Plan Quality

About the Authors
Software License Agreement

About the Authors

Dawn M. Denno, Ed.D., is Director of Early Education and Care at the Cincinnati Children's Hospital Medical Center in Cincinnati, Ohio. Dr. Denno received a master of science in early childhood education and an education doctorate in special education. Dr. Denno spent 10 years as an early education classroom teacher. She has served as a Head Start director, a child care licensing specialist, and an administrator of Montessori and traditional child care programs. Dr. Denno previously worked for the Ohio Department of Education, where she facilitated quality improvement initiatives and assessment in early education programs across the state. Dr. Denno's areas of interest include school readiness, literacy, assessment, language development, and supporting children with challenging behavior. Her publications include articles on early intervention, outcome measurement, and behavior support.

Victoria Carr, Ed.D., is Director of the Arlitt Child and Family Research and Education Center and Associate Professor in Early Childhood Education, University of Cincinnati. She is Executive Director for the Arlitt Head Start program and Executive Producer for Arlitt Instructional Media. For many years, Dr. Carr's work has focused on children who have challenging behaviors. Her current research is on nature and children. She collaborates with the Cincinnati Nature Center to lead The Cincinnati Playscape Initiative. Dr. Carr holds a bachelor of science in elementary education and learning and behavioral disorders, a master of science in gifted education, and a doctorate in early childhood special education.

Susan Hart Bell, Ph.D., is Professor of Psychology and Coordinator of Child Development at Georgetown College in Georgetown, Kentucky. Dr. Bell received a master of science degree in clinical psychology from Eastern Kentucky University and a doctorate in school psychology from the University of Cincinnati. She has coordinated an interdisciplinary team serving preschool children with disabilities in Raleigh, North Carolina, and consulted with preschools in the Greater Cincinnati area. Dr. Bell directed the Ohio Early Childhood Intervention Project at the University of Cincinnati. With David Barnett and Karen Carey, she coauthored the book *Designing Preschool Interventions: A Practitioner's Guide* (The Guilford Press, 1999). She coauthored a second book, *Challenging Behaviors in Early Childhood Settings: Creating a Place for All Children* (Paul H. Brookes Publishing Co., 2004), along with Victoria Carr, Dawn Denno, Lawrence Johnson, and Louise Phillips. Dr. Bell and her husband, Jeff, have two children, Sarah and Chad, and one grandchild, Elijah Chad.

Acknowledgments

I am deeply grateful for the teachers in the Department of Early Education and Care at Cincinnati Children's Hospital. They field-tested all of the tools in this book and provided practical advice for revisions, which made the tools much more meaningful and useable.

I am particularly grateful for the leadership of the Department of Early Education and Care, Shelly Bowers and Kathy Haders. Shelly and Kathy have a commitment to finding the most respectful and effective methods for supporting all children. They engender a culture of respect and openness to new ideas.   —DD

I am grateful for the opportunity to work with such a stellar early childhood preschool staff at the Arlitt Child and Family Research and Education Center. The opportunities to see what works and what does not creates learning venues for many. I have great respect for Connie Corkwell, the administrative leader for children's progams at Arlitt. She grounds us all in philosophy, respect, and collaboration.   —VC

I acknowledge the generous support of Georgetown College and Provost, Dr. Rosemary Allen, in allowing me to continue to pursue research and publication in the areas of school psychology and early childhood. In addition, I wish to thank my amazing colleagues in the psychology department, Dr. Karyn McKenzie, Dr. Regan Lookadoo, Dr. Jennifer Price, Dr. Rebecca Singer, and Dr. Jay Castaneda, for their friendship and encouragement. Finally, I would like to thank a continuing succession of excellent school psychology students who make me so grateful to have been part of their lives—most recently fellow researchers Brooke Reed, Ashleigh Gray, and Ashley Perkins.   —SHB

Introduction

*Dawn M. Denno, Victoria Carr,
and Susan Hart Bell*

All children have delightful moments. Young children are spontaneous, creative, and active by nature. Yet, the timing, intensity, and duration of these actions in group settings can create challenges for teachers. For many teachers, challenging or concerning classroom behavior of young learners generates a cycle of actions and conversations that requires much time and focus.

Challenging behaviors in the early childhood classroom create havoc for all when left unchecked, addressed in unsystematic ways, or when educators do not receive guidance and support with regard to classroom dysfunction and child-related disruptions. Most of these challenges can be addressed through organizing the classroom environment, managing daily activities proactively, and positively and consistently responding to behavioral challenges. However, some children need more concrete supports.

To provide positive support, it is necessary to expand one's working knowledge of prevention and response. Building on pedagogical research and practice in early childhood education, this book contains practical strategies and tools for addressing challenging behaviors that commonly occur in early childhood classrooms. It is designed to support educators who work with young children in group settings whose professional practices and philosophical orientations vary across early childhood experiences. Teachers are encouraged to use the information and forms presented to make positive changes in early childhood settings.

This book is guided by four fundamental principles. These principles provide a philosophical framework for the strategies presented.

1

Principle One: Most Concerning Behavior Can Be Prevented When We Start with the Basics

To create harmony, teachers must first understand the tenets of a developmentally and individually appropriate curriculum and engaging learning environments. They must create a learning environment that encourages children to regulate themselves and solve conflicts with others. Effective classroom organization and management skills are crucial to creating a place for all children to thrive.

Challenging behaviors can often be prevented by designing engaging curricula. When children are interacting in learning experiences that are of interest and are geared toward their learning needs, problems decrease. Careful assessment and observation of all children are fundamental to positive participation.

Supportive, caring relationships provide the basis for appropriate behavior. Teachers must get to know children and their families. And, families must know that their views are welcome. This knowledge becomes a resource that will be helpful over the long term.

All of the actions described thus far will address challenging behaviors in the classroom as a whole. However, there are some situations which require more intense, specific thought and action. This book addresses these specific strategies and levels of intensity needed by some children.

An overview of what constitutes a developmentally and individually appropriate curriculum and engaging learning environment is specifically outlined in Section II, but these concepts are embedded throughout the book. The focus is on factors under the control or influence of the teacher with regard to preserving harmony by taking action to address challenging behaviors.

Principle Two: In Order to Support Real Change, We Must Understand All Influencing Factors

The contexts under which challenges arise are multifaceted. These factors that interact with one another are unique to each individual. All factors taken together provide the *ecological context* of the behavior. For the purposes of this book, the ecological context has been divided into three sub-contexts—the *environmental, transactional,* and *intrapersonal.*

- Section I describes intrapersonal factors. Intrapersonal factors are those which stem from inside the child.

- Section II describes environmental factors. Environmental factors include all aspects of the child's relationship to peers, family, and the environment.

- Section III describes transactional factors. Transactional factors refer to those contexts that change as children interact with peers and adults.

These factors may represent relationships and circumstances outside of the classroom. Factors may also reflect circumstances that took place in the past. Although some children may need mental health or behavioral interventions, there are numerous actions that educators can take to plan for a harmonious classroom, respond to behaviors that are challenging, and influence the development of social skills that foster positive engagement in early childhood settings. It is important that educators understand their roles in providing effective proactive interventions (when warranted) to assure that all children and adults in the environment are working to preserve a sense of harmony that fosters learning and creativity for children as well as a sense of professionalism for educators.

Principle Three: No Matter How out of Control We Feel, There Is Always Something We Can Do

Sometimes the factors influencing behavior are many. And, often, those factors are not under teachers' control. The following charts provide an overview of what elements are and are not under the control or influence of the educator. This is the foundation for this book.

Ecological Contexts

Factors I can influence:	I can respond by:
Classroom physical environment	Rearranging environment
Curriculum	Individualizing & redesigning
Teacher language	Self-monitoring my language and developing scripts to increase effectiveness for reducing challenging behaviors and encouraging prosocial behavior
Schedule/routine	Analyzing and developing predictable and responsive routines
Center-wide support	Planning for crisis, familiarizing myself with community resources, and asking for help

Factors I cannot change:	However, I can respond by:
Health issues and developmental history	Investigating specific health conditions and developmental history
Community violence	Suggesting ways in which the family can address their child's fears
Child-rearing practices and parental choices (substance abuse, child maltreatment)	Providing information about effective parenting and safe, responsive child care
Family characteristics (poverty, intellectual capacity, biases)	Obtain information, promote dialogue, seek out resources
Cultural differences	Embracing diversity by understanding differences, seeking out cultural anchors, and asking questions

Intrapersonal Contexts

Factors I can influence:

Habitual ways of responding to situations and people

Attitudes and beliefs about behavior in educational settings

Feelings of safety and belonging

I can respond by:

Scripting responses to behaviors, using classroom routines, setting limits

Fostering an understanding of the classroom culture

Communicating safety procedures, what adult roles and items are in place to assure safety, and demonstrating routines and classroom procedures

Factors I cannot change:

Temperament (e.g., impulse control, activity level, mood, sociability, etc.)

Cognitive and language ability

Child's memory of traumatic experiences

However, I can respond by:

Individualizing expectations of classroom interactions with supportive scaffolding strategies

Providing a developmentally and individually appropriate curriculum with accommodations

Understanding and responding to child's emotional communication in sensitive and nurturing ways

Transactional Contexts

Factors I can influence:

Teacher reactions to child's behavior

Peer culture

I can respond by:

Acknowledging and addressing my own feelings toward the child and the challenging situation

Engaging in proximity control, designing productive peer groupings, and empowering children with language or gestures to reduce victimization

Factors I cannot change:

Family's initial feelings and thoughts

Peers' instinctive reactions to child's behavior

However, I can respond by:

Reflectively listening to families, reframing perceptions of family's relationships and reactions to child's behavior, and supporting situational problem solving

Reframing an understanding of the situation by modeling effective responses to undesired behaviors

Principle Four: Real Change Takes Time and We Must Make the Investment

Responses to challenges in the classroom should be grounded in practice that has been demonstrated to be effective for reducing or addressing behavioral challenges and the social-emotional contexts underlying these behaviors. The Council for Exceptional Children's Division for Early Childhood (DEC, 2000) asserts that a range of strategies and support services are needed to address challenging behaviors within a three-tiered model of service delivery. It is also imperative that families be part of the decision-making team that creates and develops a plan of action to address these challenges.

Intrapersonal Contexts

It is critical that teachers respond in sensitive and caring ways to the unique needs of children in their classrooms. Planning for a developmentally appropriate classroom usually takes into account the chronological age and gender composition of the children enrolled in a specific academic year. Based on an understanding of typical milestones in child development, teachers make assumptions regarding child skills, abilities, and experiences when designing the classroom schedule, physical arrangement, routines, limits, and specific learning activities.

However, the actual children who make up any given classroom present teachers with values and beliefs regarding acceptable methods of interaction with peers and adults resulting from differences in a) temperament, b) skill levels, c) preferences, d) home experiences, and e) prior educational experiences. In turn, teachers come to the classroom with individual values, tolerances, and instructional practices. Teachers must allow time to acquaint themselves with the unique needs of these individual children, and further, to understand the complex and changing situations which evolve as these children interact in novel settings with unfamiliar peers and adults.

Most experienced preschool teachers would agree that the numbers of children presenting serious challenges are increasing. In fact, recent estimates put this number at around one third of children currently enrolled in preschool classrooms serving children with and without identified disabilities (Hemmeter, Ostrosky, & Fox, 2006). Challenging behaviors are unique to each individual case, but, in general, Strain and Hemmeter (1997) describe them as involving "any behavior that is disturbing to you and that you wish to be stopped" (p. 2).

The chapters in Section I examine ways in which children challenge the classroom environment because of their preexisting temperamental characteristics, array of skills and preferences, and/or learned expectancies for adult–child and child–child interactions from home, community, and previous educational settings. Sometimes, teachers react to these challenging behaviors by responding that a child does not belong in a specific classroom because he or she is "immature." The implication is that the child will "grow out" of these temperamental characteristics or will learn the required skills or acquire traditional educational expectancies more readily in some other (more appropriate) educational environment. In our experience, this is the case in only the most extreme circumstances.

For most children it is the responsibility of the teacher to design a developmentally and individually appropriate classroom to meet the needs of all children enrolled in a given year. Teachers provide opportunities for children to learn to communicate preferences, negotiate play, and master skills within social contexts. Skilled teachers understand that effective instruction involves thoughtful environmental arrangements, consistent schedules and routines, and carefully planned and individualized suggestions, prompting, and modeling during child play. Such strategies foster independence and encourage skill development. These are all elements of that most basic of teacher strategies—scaffolding (Berk & Winsler, 1995). More specifically, *scaffolding* is the provision of informal teacher support to allow a child to perform a skill or accomplish a task with help that he or she might not be able to do independently. Chapters 1–3 provide examples of strategies that can be used as scaffolding for a number of specific child and family issues.

CHAPTER 1

Habitual Ways
of Responding to
Situations and People

Early education centers and the individual teachers in those centers often use varying approaches to get to know the children who will be enrolled in their classrooms each school year. This process begins as teachers review written information from their center's enrollment packet. Depending on the depth of information requested by the center, teachers typically gain some sense of the child's general health, developmental accomplishments (e.g., self-feeding abilities, toileting independence), preferences (e.g., play activities, food), typical schedule, previous educational or child care experiences, family makeup, and parental concerns. Some teachers prefer to meet the child for the first time in the family environment and, thus, make home visits. Other teachers schedule classroom visits, preferring to view the child in the structured environment of the center. The most important information for the teacher, however, is how the child's temperament, skills, expectations, and learned behaviors prepare him or her for success within the structure, limits, and continually changing demands of the group setting. Unfortunately, this information may be inaccessible until the child is observed interacting with peers and adults on a day-to-day basis in the classroom environment. The tools contained in this chapter are designed to be used during a center's admissions process as well as for classroom observation and planning once a child is enrolled at the center.

Child Temperament

Research in child development has identified "constitutionally based individual differences in reactivity and self-regulation" among children (Rothbart, 1989, p. 59). Indeed, beginning as early as infancy, parents and other caregivers often become aware of differences in temperamental tendencies between children. These differences are linked to overall reactivity of the central nervous system and consist of predispositions toward activity level and task persistence; adaptability to change; approach to novelty; general sociability; and the tone, expression, and regulation of emotion (Chess & Thomas, 1986; Kagan, 1994, 1997; Thomas & Chess, 1977). Keogh (2003) referred to temperament as the *how* of behavior—how the child interacts with peers, adults, materials, and activities. These temperamental predispositions seem to be relatively stable across time. Differences among children, obvious in early childhood classrooms, provide challenges for planning effective instructional environments (Presley & Martin, 1994).

Early research clustered these predispositions into three definitive temperament types: *easy, difficult,* and *slow to warm up* (Chess & Thomas, 1986; Thomas & Chess, 1977). Children with *easy* temperaments typically express positive emotions, approach novel situations with high levels of engagement and interest, and respond eagerly and cooperatively to changes in their environment. In the preschool setting, these children adjust easily, cooperate with teacher instruction, persist in play activities to a logical conclusion, and interact comfortably with their peers. *Slow-to-warm-up* children shy away from social situations, becoming anxious and tearful when encountering unfamiliar settings, adults, and children. Of most concern are children with *difficult* temperaments. These children are highly distractible, engage for only brief periods of time, and react aggressively and defiantly to changes in schedule and teacher direction. It is these children who are at greatest risk for social rejection and academic failure (Denham et al., 2001; Mendez, Fantuzzo, & Cicchetti, 2002; Walker, Berthelsen, & Irving, 2001; Webster-Stratton & Reid, 2004). Children with extreme temperamental variations can be disruptive and/or demand large amounts of a teacher's time. Teachers must learn to scaffold participation in classroom activities, designing appropriate levels of support for each situation according to a child's need.

In addition, although some research has not found significant gender differences in temperament (Presley & Martin, 1994), other studies have identified unique temperamental and interactional styles. Girls, on the whole, tend to be prosocial, task-persistent, and cooperative in classroom settings; and when they express aggression to peers, it tends to be relational in nature (i.e., exclusion from play, insulting another). Boys, compared with girls, typically are more noncompliant to teacher directions, engage in physical aggression more frequently, and are more intense, distractible, and active in play (Gleason et al., 2005; Russell, Hart, Robinson, & Olsen, 2003; Walker et al., 2001). Departures from these stereotypical expectations (e.g., high activity level and impulsivity in a girl) may result in increased levels of child conflict and rejection by peers (Gleason et al., 2005).

Temperamental Risk Factors

Several temperamental characteristics, long associated with the difficult temperament style, have become risk indicators for successful preschool adjustment and should be identified early and targeted for classroom intervention. This section will highlight five of those temperament risk factors: physical aggression, negative emotionality, high activity level, lower levels of task persistence as compared with same-age peers, and inflexibility and resistance in response to change.

Perhaps the characteristic that places a child at highest risk is frequent and escalating expressions of physical aggression, a characteristic that has been predictive for future school failure, delinquency, and substance abuse (Campbell, Shaw, & Gilliom, 2000; Sakimura et al., 2008; Stormont, 2002; Webster-Stratton, 2000). In their literature review of aggressive behavior in young children, Webster-Stratton and Reid (2004) estimated that 10% of young children exhibit aggressive behavior to an extent that it disrupts their school success. This figure approaches 25% among children of poverty.

Closely related to physical aggression is negative emotionality, which involves 1) frequent, intense, and prolonged angry outbursts (i.e., tantrums), 2) antisocial responses when observing signs of distress in others (i.e., laughing at another child's tears), and 3) poor emotional regulation (e.g., reacting with aggression and noncompliance when instructed to transition from free play). Children who display frequent and/or severe physical aggression typically have difficulty adjusting to preschool environments and experience repeated social rejection by peers (Denham et al., 2001; Presley & Martin, 1994; Webster-Stratton & Reid, 2004). In unstructured play situations, these children often are loud, overreact to frustration, and engage in high levels of conflict and fighting stemming from an insistence on having their own way (Presley & Martin, 1994). These children can be very difficult to distract from their negative moods and may have marked preferences in classroom activities and settings (Gleason et al., 2005).

In general, highly active and impulsive children are viewed by their parents and teachers as 1) less consistently engaged in classroom activities; 2) more disruptive during play; 3) more likely to be engaged in conflict situations; and, 4) over time, less liked by peers. There are some indications, however, that there are gender differences in regard to these characteristics, with higher activity levels being more easily tolerated within male friendship groups (Gleason et al., 2005; Mendez et al., 2002). Regardless of the impact on peer interactions, higher activity levels have been consistently associated with teacher identification of difficulties in classroom settings (e.g., fidgetiness, restlessness, poor task completion, unsafe running, climbing and jumping indoors) (Presley & Martin, 1994).

Hand-in-hand with higher activity levels is lower task persistence. Highly active children have difficulty listening to teacher directions and staying with an activity. They typically have substantial difficulty in large-group activities because they find it difficult to sit quietly and attentively for the time required. Often, they are finished with an activity long before the teacher has completed his or her lesson. Children with higher activity levels coupled with impulsivity and poor task persistence often violate classroom and center safety rules, coming up with unsafe variations for using play structures or materials (e.g., jumping from the top of play structures, building block towers well beyond a safe height, using manipulatives aggressively such as throwing counting blocks at another child) (Webster-Stratton & Reid, 2004). For safety reasons, children with these characteristics demand almost constant monitoring from their teachers.

Finally, children with difficult temperaments usually resist change and have low levels of adaptability. These children respond with resistance and negative emotionality when they are confronted with unfamiliar rules and limits, changes in caregivers, and/or alterations in schedule or routine. It is very difficult for teachers or parents to interrupt or distract them from a preferred activity, and they have difficulty waiting for any length of time (Presley & Martin, 1994).

The Child Temperament Assessment

The characteristics associated with a difficult temperament can result in significant challenges to the classroom routines and activities. The Child Temperament Assessment in Figure 1.1 is not meant to be used to screen out children for referral to other settings; rather, it can be used during a home or classroom visit to help the classroom teacher gain knowledge of risk factors that require modifications to schedule, activities, or routines prior to a child's entrance into the classroom. Specific strategies for teacher scaffolding are discussed in the section immediately following this assessment tool. Blank versions of all tools can be found on the CD-ROM that accompanies this book.

Purpose of This Tool	The purpose of the Child Temperament Assessment is to record specific child words and actions that will lead to a summary of the child's predispositions along six temperament predispositions that have been identified as important for classroom success.
When to Use This Tool	This assessment tool can be used by an individual teacher or in conjunction with other observers during the course of a home or classroom visit. This assessment also can be helpful as one of the decision-making tools to help determine optimal classroom place-

Child Temperament Assessment

Directions: In the first column, describe your impression of the child's general tendencies along six dimensions: emotional tone (e.g., What kind of a mood was the child in? Generally happy? Irritable? Fearful?), adaptability (i.e., Over the course of the observation, how did the child respond to interruptions or requests to stop an ongoing behavior?), approach to novelty (i.e., How comfortable was the child around unfamiliar adults and children? In the new classroom setting? When asked to complete a novel task?), overall activity level (i.e., How many activities did the child attempt during the visit? How fidgety or restless did the child seem? Was the child careless with classroom materials?), task persistence (i.e., How distractible was the child? Did the child finish a preferred task? A nonpreferred task as directed by the parent or teacher?), and aggression (i.e., What specific incidents of verbal, physical, and/or relational aggression were observed?). In the second column, record anecdotal notes of the child's words and actions as well as a narrative of the sequence of events that occurred. Number the events so that you can tell them apart. Use numerals to separate specific incidents used as supporting evidence for each temperament characteristic. You may refer to a specific incident as evidence for more than one characteristic (e.g., an observation such as "child hit the parent and screamed 'no' when asked to clean up" might be evidence for both poor adaptability and physical aggression).

Name of child: _Sean Fellerman_

Date, time, length, and setting of visit: _March 2, 2009; 90 minutes; classroom_

Name and role of observer: _Lisa Lambert, education coordinator_

Assessment of temperament characteristic	Evidence (use numerals to organize events)
● Variation/consistency of emotional tone and evidence for self-regulation: *Happy until routine change*	1) Laughed when playing with SH 2) Sang with teacher 3) Entered room greeting children and teachers—Greeted SH parent
● Response to frustration or change (adaptability): *Difficult time adapting to change in routine. Seemed or appeared frustrated and anxious.*	1) Called to teacher 5 times asking for help 2) Walked around the room—not engaged
● Approach to the unfamiliar: *Routine change—seemed uncomfortable—slow to respond to new directions* *Tentative—Cooking activity added to routine today*	1) Did not engage in cooking activity. 2) Scanned room frequently 3) Skirted periphery of classroom
● Activity level: *Very high*	1) Ran around edge of room 2) Crashed into shelves
● Task engagement and persistence/distractibility: *Briefly engaged—Moved around room briefly engaging or watching others—explored sensory materials*	1) Stopped in art area for 60 seconds—watched other children 2) Watched dramatic play, 45 seconds 3) Lifted items from science area 20 seconds See also #3 under Approach to the Unfamiliar
● Specific incidents of aggression (type): *Crashed into shelves and work—disrupted children*	1) Pushed FM when moving across room See also #2 under Activity Level

Figure 1.1. Child Temperament Assessment.

13

ment (i.e., choice of a.m. or p.m. class period, choice of teacher within center) and modifications.

How to Use This Tool

Complete the information at the top of the table to set your observation within time and place. The first column should be used to describe your impression of the child's general tendencies along six dimensions: emotional tone (e.g., What kind of a mood was the child in? Generally happy? Irritable? Fearful?), adaptability (i.e., Over the course of the observation, how did the child respond to interruptions or requests to stop an ongoing behavior?), approach to novelty (i.e., How comfortable was the child around unfamiliar adults and children? In the new classroom setting? When asked to complete a novel task?), overall activity level (i.e., How many activities did the child attempt during the visit? How fidgety or restless did the child seem? Was the child careless with classroom materials?), task persistence (i.e., How distractible was the child? Did the child finish a preferred task? A nonpreferred task as directed by the parent or teacher?), and aggression (i.e., What specific incidents of verbal, physical, and/or relational aggression were observed?). The second column allows space to record anecdotal notes of the child's words and actions as well as a narrative of the sequence of events that occurred. Numerals can be used to separate observations from anecdotal notes into discrete instances of supporting evidence for each temperamental characteristic.

Suggestions for Recording and Summarizing Information

1. Information from the child observation should be recorded with as much specificity as possible (e.g., *used angry words, spent less than 2 minutes on any activity*). Vague statements (e.g., *bad mood*) give little information for future planning.

2. Information written in the *Evidence* column should record the actual people and materials involved in each event (e.g., *Playing in playhouse with sister, took all the dolls away from sister and threw them out of the playhouse window; laughed when sister began to cry and ask for her dolls to be returned; hit sister and called her a baby before leaving the play area*). The recorded evidence provides useful information for similar classroom settings (e.g., necessity to monitor interactions with younger, more vulnerable classmates; need for close supervision during unstructured free play).

3. Anecdotal notes written in the *Evidence* column may overlap several temperament characteristics. The observer might indicate this by numbering the notes and recording this overlap (e.g., in the example given , *see also* #3 under Approach to the Unfamiliar could be recorded in addition to the evidence for Task Engagement and Persistence/Distractiblity).

4. There may be no opportunity to assess one or more of the temperamental characteristics during the home or classroom visit. This can be flagged as incomplete, with information to be gathered later.

5. Darken the circles before temperamental characteristics that appear negative in tone or at high probability of requiring planning for classroom support.

Scaffolding Individual Temperamental Characteristics

It is important that teachers view a child's temperament tendencies as long-standing and fundamental aspects of the child's physiological makeup. When teachers instead regard displays of temperament tendencies (e.g., resistance to change) as merely child choices, they view resulting behaviors as entirely defiant, noncompliant, and intentionally disruptive and respond with frustration and anger instead of problem solving for change (Keogh, 2003). An increased awareness of child temperament factors and problem solving for support will result in an optimal child adjustment to the classroom setting (Sakimura et al., 2008). This section discusses strategies for responding to the difficult temperament characteristics highlighted in Figure 1.1. Many of the strategies discussed can help prevent or interrupt expressions of physical and verbal aggression as well. Scaffolding low levels of task persistence, however, is treated later in this chapter under the skill of academic engagement.

Children who experience frustration and disappointment but can modulate their expression of these emotions are more apt to be chosen as friends than children who cannot. Children with poor self-regulation of emotional responses may experience peer rejection without the proximity and scaffolding of adults (Gleason et al., 2005). Scaffolding efforts should target alternative behaviors that allow the child to vent his or her negative feelings in an acceptable manner, negotiate the conflict, and/or solicit adult support. This might include such strategies as 1) creating a safe space within the classroom, a "calm-down" area where the child can get emotions under control, 2) encouraging the child to incorporate tangible reminders to "stop and think" before acting out frustration in an unsafe manner (e.g., strategically placed "stop" signs), 3) providing the child with a visual or verbal signal that will solicit adult support immediately upon its display (e.g., shouting "no" or holding up a colored card), and 4) direct instruction of problem-solving strategies for specific classroom situations.

Children who have difficulty adjusting to alterations in routine and/or who respond with anxiety and resistance to novel activities or situations typically will benefit from a slower pace and a highly predictable schedule. However, changes in daily schedule are inevitable, and novelty is an essential part of the learning process. To maximize the probability of successful adjustment for children with this temperament challenge, the teacher can incorporate a system of warnings and graduated prompts to introduce a change (Sakimura et al., 2008). The teacher may scaffold this situation by 1) instituting a prewarning at the beginning of the day (or several times during the week before) using a picture schedule to introduce the novel person, activity, or anticipated change in routine; 2) intentionally moving closer to the child just before the required participation and greeting the child by name; 3) providing the child with a specific warning of the impending change or a specific direction to attempt the unfamiliar activity; 4) including preferred peers to model the requested and unfamiliar actions; and 5) scaffolding the child's response with a graduated series of verbal, gestural, and physical prompts. These prompts may include talking about the novel activity or change in routine and the expected compliance, demonstrating (or peer modeling of) specific requested behaviors, and touching the child's elbow or shoulder to assist initiation of the activity.

Teachers may have to assess the physical arrangement of the classroom with an eye toward identifying "risky situations" that entice children with high activity levels and impulsive behaviors (Keogh, 2003). Open spaces or low barriers that encourage running, climbing, or jumping should be modified. In addition, children who are highly active may require more frequent changes in activities, shortened group time participation, and breaks for structured activities during long periods of free play (Sakimura et al., 2008). They also may require intentional teacher encouragement to participate in quiet activities such as puzzles, art projects, or construction tasks (Presley & Martin, 1994).

The Strategies for Support (Temperament) Tool

This tool may be completed independently or in collaboration with classroom staff and/or parents. It is important to use this tool to highlight the child's temperament strengths while prioritizing weaknesses for support.

Purpose of This Tool	The Strategies for Support (Temperament) Tool in Figure 1.2 guides strategy development to modify the classroom schedule, physical arrangement, peer groupings, teacher monitoring/proximity, and play activities to scaffold temperamental characteristics and increase the probability of classroom success.
When to Use This Tool	This tool can be used for strategy development and problem solving. It also can be used as a decision-making tool to help determine when modifications to the length of the child's day or additional resources are needed.
How to Use This Tool	The Strategies for Support (Temperament) Tool should be used in conjunction with the Child Temperament Assessment. The teacher should highlight temperament characteristics identified during the home or classroom visit and prioritize them in the first column. The teacher, along with parents and other classroom staff, then can brainstorm strategies for support in the specified areas.
Suggestions for Prioritizing and Implementing Teacher Strategies to Scaffold Temperament	1. In prioritizing the temperament characteristics and related strategies, keep in mind the importance of balancing the need for alleviating the personal distress experienced by the child with the importance of minimizing anticipated disruptions to the classroom schedule and activities. The most important factor is whether the child will have increased success (i.e., will enjoy his or her time in the classroom and benefit from it). This tool also could be used to suggest strategies for multiple children, as necessary.

Strategies for Support (Temperament) Tool

Directions: Use this form in conjunction with the Child Temperament Assessment. Highlight temperament characteristics identified during the home or classroom visit and prioritize them in the first column. Then, along with parents and other classroom staff, brainstorm strategies for support in the specified areas.

Name of child: _Sean Fellerman_

Date of meeting: _3/5/09_

Participants: _Lisa Lambert, education coordinator_ _Ruth Hicks, teacher_
Bettye Fellerman, mother
Bill Fellerman, father

Temperamental challenge	Change(s) in physical arrangement of classroom, Goal	Modifications in sequence or duration of scheduled activities, Goal	Use of selected peers or child grouping, Goal	Modifications of teacher proximity and/or strategies, Goal	Changes in child materials and/or activities, Goal
1. Distractibility	Review materials for streamlining. Minimize classroom displays. Sean will spend increased time engaged in appropriate classroom activities.	Free play—provide more explicit transitions within time frame. Suggest choices so that free play is not one long part of routine. Sean will transition smoothly between activities.	Sara Hammond helpful in conflicts over toys. Sean will be more engaged with fewer peer conflicts when grouped with Sara.	Have Sean near teacher during transitions. Extra warnings for changes. Sean will transition smoothly with at least one pre-warning and with close teacher proximity.	Develop transportation content—Use trucks and other vehicles. Sean will spend more time in the activity center when transportation content is included.
2. High activity, low engagement	Develop focal areas of interest to increase engagement. Sean will spend increased time engaged in appropriate classroom activities.	See above strategies and goal.	Provide positive feedback describing engagement at regular intervals—5 min. Help with choices when disengaged. See above goal.	Write stories about trucks with Sean. Find computer games with trucks. See above goal.	

Figure 1.2. Strategies for Support (Temperament) Tool.

2. Address each temperament challenge by suggesting changes that might be helpful in one or more of the identified areas: physical arrangement, sequence/length of activities, use of peers, teacher strategies, and changes in materials or activities.

3. Link each strategy to an expected goal for the child. For example, *creating a quiet place for calming down through the use of a fabric tunnel and teepee filled with soft pillows and toys in the book area* should be linked with *increased use of the calm-down area during times of frustration* and *decreased time spent yelling* or *having emotional outbursts in other areas.*

4. Select the top two to three temperament challenges and implement strategies that seem 1) most feasible given the resources of time, materials, and personnel; 2) least disruptive to the other children; and 3) most likely to directly support the child's success in the classroom.

5. Set a time to reconvene the participants to 1) review the effectiveness of the selected strategies in achieving child goals, 2) reprioritize challenges as necessary, 3) select additional strategies, and/or 4) discuss any other changes.

Developmental Skill Profiles

Along with temperament predispositions, children also vary in their progress within and across such developmental domains as cognitive, language, motor, and social skills. Some children seem to virtually leap over milestones, mastering each new skill right before our eyes. Others move at a snail's pace, each accomplishment accompanied by a huge investment of teacher and child effort. In addition, children approach the classroom environment with differences in mastery of so-called "readiness" skills (e.g., attention, emotional regulation, persistence). Complicating factors for classroom planning include involvement of children with 1) identified skill delays (e.g., language, motor), 2) atypical development (e.g., visual impairment, autism spectrum disorders), or 3) home situations in which English is the second language and is not spoken fluently. Classrooms follow curricular guidelines and teachers develop classroom activities based on expectations of typical child development (Bell & Barnett, 1999). Encountering numbers of children who depart from the norm in one or more areas can strain the teacher's planning ability.

Social Competence and Learned Behaviors

Socially and emotionally competent children appear mature for their developmental age, exhibiting prosocial behavior (i.e., helping others, readily sharing toys and materials, voluntarily taking turns with peers), positive emotional tone (i.e., appearing happy, relaxed, and interested), and controlled expression of such negative emotions as frustration and disappointment (Hemmeter et al., 2006; Logue, 2007).

Forging positive relationships with peers is apparently effortless. These children respond easily to teacher reasoning and limit setting and are flexible when interrupted in play (Mendez et al., 2002). They cooperate with peers, readily negotiating rules and tasks (Logue, 2007). They also appear to be more receptive to academic activities (Bierman, Torres, Domitrovich, Welsh, & Gest, 2009). These skills lead to overall success in the preschool classroom as well as in future academic settings.

Perhaps the most important foundation skill for social competence is age-appropriate language and communication skills (Hemmeter et al., 2006; Stormont, 2002). Higher levels of verbal skills are characteristic of children who are much more successful in peer and adult interactions (Mendez et al., 2002). These skills are essential for understanding and following group routines, compliance with teacher requests, and mastery of learning goals. Language delays and difficulties are frequently associated with challenging behaviors (Carr et al., 1994). Significant delays in receptive and expressive language necessitate increased planning on the part of the teachers and the consultation and intervention of outside professionals.

The ability to engage in constructive and effective social problem solving with appropriate emotional regulation is another critical skill for classroom success (Hemmeter et al., 2006). Effective problem solving during play involves attention to classroom limits, effective communication of needs and desires, listening, perspective taking, sharing of materials, and cooperation toward common goals (Walker, Stiller, & Golly, 1998).

A final skill, critical for learning, is academic engagement with appropriate levels of positive approach to unfamiliar activities (Mendez et al., 2002), attention to teacher instruction, and task persistence. The child who is actively engaged displays broad (i.e., samples many activities) and deep (i.e., sustains interest in activities until their completion) participation in classroom routines (Bierman et al., 2009; Logue, 2007). Task engagement requires an understanding and compliance with teacher expectations with regard to schedule, peer groupings, and planned activities (Hemmeter et al., 2006). As the child matures, expectations for sustained and independent work completion will increase. The child must ascertain the task directions, ask for help when needed, locate materials, understand when the task is completed, and perform all of these activities within the allocated time and without bothering others who are engaged nearby in similar tasks (Rous & Hallam, 1998). Analyzing any classroom activity into these separate components provides opportunities for intervention.

Many appropriate assessment tools exist to identify domain-specific skill delays and disorders (e.g., speech production and articulation issues; difficulties in visual memory or perception). These instruments may be used in a diagnostic fashion by relevant related professionals. This section, instead, provides a tool for teachers to use in assessing individual proficiency in the "readiness skills" identified in the preceding paragraphs.

The Child Skill Assessment

Experienced teachers are quite familiar with the skills that are necessary for classroom success (e.g., sharing, turn-taking). This tool assists the teacher in a comparison of the targeted child's performance on these critical skills with those of typical peers of the same age and gender.

| Purpose of This Tool | The purpose of the Child Skill Assessment in Figure 1.3 is to suggest parent interview questions and observation strategies that will provide valuable information about the child's array of developmentally expected skills and abilities. Children "stand out" when their skills and abilities differ widely from those of their peers. For this reason, the use of a typical comparison peer of the same age and gender is suggested. |

| When to Use This Tool | These questions and suggestions for observation can be used during the admissions process or as problems emerge in the classroom setting. |

| How to Use This Tool | The Child Skill Assessment lists questions to consider for the specific "readiness" skill areas. To assist in the process of goal and strategy development, the teacher is asked to compare the child's performance with that of a typical peer of the same age and gender. Each skill is listed followed by a number of guiding questions to describe the child's competence in that area. Rate each skill in the course of a parent interview or during observation in the home or classroom setting. Determine whether the child typically displays the skill. If so, indicate mastery by circling the words "Usually displays skill" in the appropriate box. If not, describe the difficulties the child encounters with the skill. Follow this with a description of the typical expectations for a child of comparable age and gender. This can be determined based on the teacher's previous experience or through actual observation of a comparison peer. |

| Suggestions for Interpreting the Information from the Child Skill Assessment | 1. The Child Skill Assessment provides an opportunity to assess the child's level of proficiency in the discrete skills composing social and communicative competence, conflict negotiation, and academic engagement. By carefully completing this assessment tool, the teacher (and others) should have a more accurate perception of challenges that the child will face in the classroom environment. |

2. Describing typical peer performance will provide a realistic picture of the skills expected for the average child enrolled in the classroom. This also will provide opportunities for goal setting and strategy development.

3. The Child Skill Assessment takes a strengths and goals perspective. In other words, through completion of the assessment, a number of skills will be identified that are strengths for the child. These can provide the foundation for future learning, and performance of these previously mastered skills can provide opportunities for affirmation.

4. Skills that are incompletely or inconsistently mastered can be prioritized for instruction and strategy development.

Child Skill Assessment

Directions: Rate each skill in the course of a parent interview or during observation in the home or classroom setting. Determine whether the child typically displays the skill. If so, indicate mastery by circling the words "Usually displays skill" in the appropriate box. If not, describe the difficulties the child encounters with the skill. Follow this with a description of the typical expectations for a child of this age and gender. This can be determined based on your previous experience or through actual observation of a comparison peer.

Name of child: *Xavier Katz*

Date and time of assessment: *11/7/09*

Name and role of person completing assessment: *Sharon Haders, Teacher*

Readiness skill	Selected child (circle "Usually displays skill" or describe the child's performance in this area)	Typical peer (same age, gender; describe peer's performance in this skill area)
Social competence		
1. Does the child readily *share toys and materials?* If not, describe specific situations and/or child actions that occur when sharing is expected.	Usually displays skill *Xavier does this with assistance.*	*A typical peer shares non-preferred toys and materials without adult assistance. Occasionally needs reminders to share preferred toys.*
2. Can the child *wait for a short time before taking a turn* in a preferred activity and/or with desired materials? If not, describe specific child actions that result in turn-taking situations.	(Usually displays skill)	*A typical peer can usually wait for a short time without adult assistance.*
3. Does the child *listen to others, taking into account their preferences, and cooperate in play?* If not, describe specific examples when this poses problems with peers.	Usually displays skill *Needs prompting from adults.*	*A typical peer almost always listens to other children and exhibits cooperation in group play.*
4. Does the child *express disappointment and frustration in appropriate, classroom-sanctioned ways?* If not, describe the child's usual expression of these emotions.	Usually displays skill *Xavier takes materials from other children. Creates conflict.*	*A typical peer rarely expresses disappointment and frustration using physical or verbal aggression.*
5. Does the child *express positive emotions* during greetings, interaction with peers, and approach to play activities? If not, describe the child's usual mood.	(Usually displays skill)	*A typical peer expresses positive emotions towards peers and adults on a daily basis.*

(continued)

Figure 1.3. Child Skill Assessment.

Figure 1.3. *(continued)*

	Child Skill Assessment *(continued)*	
Readiness skill	Selected child (circle "Usually displays skill" or describe the child's performance in this area)	Typical peer (same age, gender; describe peer's performance in this skill area)
Language		
1. Does the child *use age-appropriate verbal and non-verbal communication* to meet his or her needs within the classroom? If not, describe the child's typical manner of communication and the problems, if any, that this presents for peers and adults.	Usually displays skill *Uses physical communication rather than language—Speaks in one or two word sentences in conflict situations*	*A typical peer uses appropriate verbal and non-verbal communication in the classroom.*
2. Does the child *follow predictable daily routines and engage in familiar play activities* with ease? If not, describe some of the problems observed in this area.	(Usually displays skill)	*A typical peer follows daily routines and is readily engaged in a variety of classroom activities.*
3. Does the child typically *follow teacher requests and directions?* If not, describe some of the problems the child has with compliance with classroom expectations.	(Usually displays skill)	*A typical peer follows teacher requests and directions with occasional verbal reminders.*
Social problem solving		
1. Is the child able *to state classroom limits and follow them as appropriate?* If not, describe the difficulties that the child has with compliance with classroom limits.	Usually displays skill *Can state but when having conflict uses language only about his wants/needs*	*A typical peer is able to state classroom limits and follow them with occasional reminders.*
2. Is the child able to *perspective-take with peers, understanding their emotions and points of view?* If not, describe the difficulties that the child has with these skills.	Usually displays skill *Rarely reflects perceptions and emotions of peers*	*When a typical peer has conflicts with other children (e.g. turn-taking), he or she requires adult assistance to understand his or her peer's point of view.*
3. Is the child able to *generate alternatives during conflict situations and weigh the consequences of each before choosing a response?* If not, describe typical conflicts.	Usually displays skill *Rarely*	*A typical peer requires adult assistance to generate alternatives.*
4. Does the child *solicit adult assistance to resolve conflict situations?* If not, please describe the usual resolution of conflict situations.	Usually displays skill *Typically uses physical means, which summons adult assistance*	*A typical peer regularly solicits adult assistance.*

	Child Skill Assessment *(continued)*	
Readiness skill	Selected child (circle "Usually displays skill" or describe the child's performance in this area)	Typical peer (same age, gender; describe peer's performance in this skill area)
Academic engagement		
1. Does the child cooperate by *participating in appropriate activities as indicated by the daily schedule?* If not, describe the way in which the child has difficulty understanding and following the daily schedule.	(Usually displays skill)	*A typical peer participates in appropriate activities with minimal adult reminders and support.*
2. Does the child *participate in a variety of classroom activities?* If not, describe preferred and non-preferred classroom activities.	(Usually displays skill)	*A typical peer participates with minimal reminders.*
3. Does the child *follow teacher directions for initiation and completion of activities and safe handling of materials?* If not, describe activities that are particularly difficult for the child and typical behaviors in these settings.	Usually displays skill *Most of the time*	*A typical peer follows teacher's safety instructions with minimal reminders.*
4. Is the child able to *locate materials and complete age-appropriate activities independently, asking for teacher help as required?*	(Usually displays skill)	*A typical peer requires limited adult support.*
5. Does the child *participate in preferred activities for an age-appropriate length of time, completing tasks as appropriate without interfering with nearby peers?* If not, describe the child's typical number of activity changes or disruptions during free choice in the classroom.	(Usually displays skill)	*A typical peer completes activities in an age-appropriate manner without disrupting others.*

Teacher Strategies for Scaffolding Development of Child Skills

Teachers provide support for skill development in a number of ways: 1) arranging the physical environment to meet the needs of a unique group of children; 2) developing stable routines; 3) designing a predictable daily schedule; 4) selecting developmentally appropriate and interesting materials and activities; 5) giving clear directions; 6) planning and prompting transitions; 7) varying activities with regard to type, activity level, and size; 8) monitoring and prompting child engagement in specific activities; and 9) effectively communicating limits and safety rules (Hemmeter et al., 2006).

When children exhibit challenges within the classroom setting, teachers implement strategies to teach needed skills. Strategies might include direct instruction (e.g., teaching a child strategies for entering a play group), modeling and role playing (e.g., using songs, stories, or puppets to demonstrate effective problem solving), incidental teaching and/or prompting (e.g., reminding children of limits, making rules when specific violations occur), supporting communication attempts (e.g., expanding the child's nonverbal or one-word response to facilitate communication with a peer), and providing constructive feedback, praise, and acknowledgement of effort (e.g., "Wow, I know that you don't typically choose to go to the art table, but look at all of the hard work you did on this picture for mom.")

Scaffolding Social and Communicative Competence

Rules and limits allow children to feel safe and to negotiate classroom activities successfully and enjoyably. Rules should be few in number and clearly and positively stated in developmentally appropriate language; in addition, both compliance and noncompliance should be followed by natural or logical consequences (Hemmeter et al., 2006).

Direct instruction in social skills and problem solving also can be beneficial. Teachers may illustrate these skills with puppets, stories, or videotaped examples and then give children the opportunity to practice such skills as 1) rule following, 2) listening, 3) anticipating and comparing consequences of chosen behavior, 4) awareness and appropriate expression of emotions, 5) anger management strategies, and 6) friendship skills (e.g., prosocial behaviors such as helping, offering a turn, sharing, and play-initiation skills) (Webster-Stratton & Reid, 2004).

Peer-mediated interventions pair socially skilled children with children with lesser skills. It is usually most effective to use children of the same gender and age and to choose children who are comfortable with each other. The most successful scenario occurs when children of varying abilities naturally gravitate to the same friends and play areas—the intervention with the highest likelihood of success is one in which the natural flow of play is augmented with additional suggestions and instructions. Opportunities for these children to interact can be increased by assigning seats at snack, lunch, or group activities; placing the children in the same small groups for structured or unstructured activities; and calling the children to transition at the same time (e.g., to group, snack, or outside play). Peers can be prompted to give appropriate greetings; demonstrate strategies for joining an ongoing play group; suggest play actions to sustain interest; or model sharing, turn taking, and other aspects of conflict negotiation.

Scaffolding Academic Engagement and Task Persistence

Careful attention to the physical layout of the classroom can significantly reduce distractibility during planned activities. Furniture such as bookcases and shelves can be used to create visual boundaries between activities. Materials such as trays or aprons can limit the number of children participating in a given area, preventing overcrowding. The daily schedule also can be used to increase engagement. By 1) balancing activities that involve large and small groups, are independent and teacher-directed, and occur outside and inside; 2) choosing developmentally appropriate activities; and 3) attending carefully to the amount of time allocated to each activity, teachers can gradually increase a child's active participation throughout the day (Hemmeter et al., 2006). Visual schedules using photographs or line drawings can highlight the flow of activities for children who need this added degree of structure.

In addition, group time areas can be placed away from distraction, blocking the view of shelves of inviting toys or books, and directing the child visually toward the teacher with colorful posters and other theme-related materials. The length of group time should be adjusted to the attention span of the most active child; when this is unreasonable, careful attention should be given to shortening group time for individual children. Group time should contain a mixture of active and quiet participation as well as involve tangible objects and materials that are related to the teacher's lesson or activity (Lawry, Danko, & Strain, 2000).

The next step in getting the child to become engaged in timely and appropriate classroom activities is to increase compliance to teacher requests or directions. For maximum effect, these directions should be 1) given in close physical proximity, beginning with the use of the child's first name and ending in short sentences composed of simple, developmentally appropriate language, 2) stated clearly as a request for completion of one specific response that is well within the child's ability to understand and perform, 3) accompanied by the amount of teacher assistance necessary to complete the task in a timely manner, and 4) followed by constructive feedback and encouragement. One behavioral strategy that has had some success in improving direction following is behavioral momentum (Nevin, 1996). In this strategy, the teacher usually gives three requests in quick succession, beginning with easier, high-probability requests, and moving to more difficult, low-probability requests. Each episode of child compliance is followed by praise or a specific, tangible reward. The hope is that the child's compliance with the two, easier tasks will result in a boost of momentum to carry him or her logically through to the next more difficult or non-preferred task (Santos, 2001).

Teachers use proximity and prompting to support children's task persistence and engagement in academic tasks. Play partnering involves one-to-one engagement with the child, suggesting play activities, facilitating entry into ongoing play with peers, commenting on child actions, and mediating for the resolution of conflicts. This strategy can be time- and resource intensive. Direct teacher prompting can be diminished by providing toys at the appropriate developmental skill level for the varying abilities of children, rotating toys so that interest remains high, and using peer models to demonstrate play activities.

Casey and McWilliam (2007) have presented a method for obtaining quick estimates of child engagement during ongoing play. Their tool, Scale for Teachers' Assessment of Routines Engagement (STARE), gives a quick snapshot of the content and complexity of engagement (e.g., with whom the child is playing; with what materials; the appropriateness of play given classroom limits, schedule, the intent of the activity). Engagement ratings range from nonengagement (i.e., wandering the room, acting aggressively, crying, staring) to active (i.e., appropriate activity choice, following directions, completing the task independently) and describe the sophistication level of the child's play (i.e., the amount of communication and social interaction displayed or the level of cooperation or pretense involved).

The Strategies for Support (Skill Development) Tool

Teachers use interviews or home/school observations to prioritize safety and foundation skills using this tool. Care should be taken to have realistic skill expectations, comparing the child's skills to those of typical peers in the same classroom.

Purpose of This Tool	The purpose of the Strategies for Support (Skill Development) Tool in Figure 1.4 is to suggest classroom strategies to facilitate development of individual child skills.
When to Use This Tool	The strategies in this tool may be implemented concurrently or sequentially, prioritizing individual skills. This can be used by the individual teacher or in concert with other center staff. The tool also can be used as a decision-making device to help prioritize changes to existing schedule, activities, child groupings, or teacher support and to determine the degree of outside resources that may be necessary for the child to be successful in the classroom.
How to Use This Tool	This tool lists suggestions for strategies linked with specific areas of skill development. To assist in plan development, the teacher is asked to identify skills that are critical to the child's success. Skills are listed in prioritized order (i.e., #1 is most important). The teacher,

Strategies for Support (Skill Development) Tool

Directions: To assist in plan development, the teacher is asked to identify skills that are critical to the child's success. Skills are listed in prioritized order (i.e., #1 is most important). The teacher, independently or in collaboration with classroom staff and/or parents, identifies modifications to put into place to directly teach or indirectly support skill development. The same form can be used in future meetings to review successful strategies, record progress toward skill mastery, and identify areas where there is need for further skill prioritization or strategy generation.

Name of child: *Samantha Newell*

Date of meeting: *12/1/08*

Participants: *Kim Schoenig, Teacher; Susan Tani, Administrator; Carrie Newell, Mother*

Prioritized skill	Modifications					
	Physical arrangement of classroom	Schedule, activities, or materials	Limits or teacher directions	Direct skill instruction	Child grouping or peer mediation	Incidental teaching or play partnering
1. Remaining in classroom	Bell on door Move dramatic play away from door Stop sign on door	None	Teachers open the door	Video posted on computer of child walking to door and stopping. Teacher states limit.	Facilitate play-partner with Lisa, preferred peer who is highly compliant with this rule	Safety discussion—Teachers keep children safe Children stay with teachers
2.						
3.						

Figure 1.4. Strategies for Support (Skill Development) Tool.

27

independently or in collaboration with classroom staff and/or parents, identifies modifications to put into place to directly teach or indirectly support skill development. The same form can be used in future meetings to review successful strategies, record progress toward skill mastery, and identify areas where there is need for further skill prioritization or strategy generation. Dates can be used to denote separate entries.

Suggestions for Prioritizing and Implementing Specific Strategies

1. In prioritizing the developmental skill areas and related strategies, it is important to take into consideration the educational philosophy and common practices of the early childhood center and the comfort level of the classroom teacher. The most important factor is whether the teacher actually can implement the suggested strategies, given the constraints of the individual classroom (i.e., staffing, needs of other children).

2. Address each problem skill area with a description of specific changes that might be instituted in physical arrangement, sequence and/or length of activities, limits or teacher directions, direct skill instruction, use of peers, or specific teacher strategies such as peer partnering and incidental teaching.

3. Link each strategy to an expected goal for individual skill development; for example, the strategies of play partnering and incidental teaching of play actions with non-preferred toys and materials are linked to the goal of increasing the child's time spent in infrequently chosen activities.

4. Select the top two to three skills and implement strategies that seem 1) most feasible given the resources of time, materials, and personnel; 2) least disruptive to the other children; and 3) most likely to directly support the child's success in the classroom.

5. Set a time to reconvene the participants to 1) review the effectiveness of the selected strategies in improving child skills, 2) reprioritize challenges as necessary, 3) select additional strategies, and/or 4) discuss any other changes.

Individual Child Preferences

One way to increase engagement is to conduct a focused observation of the activities in which a child spends most of his or her free time, identify what he or she chooses first during free play, and pay attention to what activities and objects the child resists sharing, taking turns with, and leaving. In addition, parents can provide information about interests not readily apparent in the classroom.

The Child Preference Observation Tool

The teacher is asked to spend time directly observing the child's behavior during a variety of daily activities. This tool allows the teacher to describe thoroughly the child's behavior during activities (indoors and outdoors) throughout the classroom day. The inference is that the child will spend more time (with less conflict) when engaged in preferred activities or with preferred materials and peers. By capturing details (e.g., specific peers, type of play, time spent in play) of preferred and non-preferred areas, strategies can be developed to increase the quality and variety of the child's engagement throughout the day.

Purpose of This Tool

The purpose of the Child Preference Observation Tool in Figure 1.5 is to structure observation in the classroom environment in order to identify the child's preferences for activities, materials, and peers.

When to Use This Tool

This tool facilitates assessment of the child's preferences using focused observation during unstructured indoor and outdoor play and structured activities conducted individually with the child.

How to Use This Tool

This observational tool is designed for use within the classroom environment during unstructured free play and structured, teacher-directed activities. For unstructured play, the recorder should note the activities selected, the materials and peers involved in each activity, and the time spent in each activity. For particularly active children, additional sheets may be necessary. The same information should be recorded for teacher-directed activities, along with notations of any noncompliant or disruptive behaviors.

Suggestions for Assessing the Relative Consistency and Strength of Preferences

1. Using the summary section at the bottom of the tool, highlight the unstructured activity area or areas with the longest sustained participation. Describe the preferred materials and peers.

2. Review the same information with an eye toward classroom activities not selected. Does the child spend the entire time during free play in one or two areas? With one or two peers? Does the child resist teacher or peer invitations to play in other areas? Are there peers whom the child consistently avoids? With whom there are frequent conflicts?

3. Review the child's participation in teacher-directed activities. What activities hold the least interest for the child? What emotional expressions or disruptive behaviors occur as the child expresses resistance to participation in these activities?

4. How can preferred activities or peers be incorporated into non-preferred areas or activities?

Child Preference Observation Tool

Directions: Use this tool inside the classroom environment during unstructured free play and structured, teacher-directed activities. For unstructured play, record the activities selected, the materials and peers involved in each activity, and the time spent on the activities. For particularly active children, additional sheets may be necessary. The same information should be recorded for teacher-directed activities, along with any noncompliant or disruptive behaviors.

Child: _Adam Black_

Date: _12/4/09_

Person observing and role: _Lerrien Short, teacher_

Unstructured free play (inside)

Activity (use additional sheets as necessary)	Area	Materials	Specific peers/type of play (solitary, parallel, associative, cooperative)	Time spent actively engaged
Dumping sand, playing with dinosaurs	Sensory table	Sand, small dinosaurs, cups, spoons	Alone for 10 minutes Parallel with Sam for 7 minutes Pushed sand with Sam for 3 minutes	20 minutes
Reading book	Book area	A Hunting We Will Go	Teacher reads and sings	10 minutes

Unstructured free play (outside)

Activity (use additional sheets as necessary)	Area	Materials	Specific peers/type of play (solitary, parallel, associative, cooperative)	Time spent actively engaged
Playing Robot	Open space on playground	None	Trey Humphries, Collin Murphy—Chasing children, talking like robots	10 minutes—redirected because some children afraid
Digging holes	Sandbox	Shovel, sand	Trey—Digging in same hole. Threw sand at wall	10 minutes

Structured teacher-directed activities

Group(s) (use additional sheets as necessary)	Content	Materials	Specific peers/type of play (solitary, parallel, associative, cooperative)	Time spent actively engaged
Morning meeting	Book—The Worm Book Discuss worm habitat Point out materials on shelves	Book Pictures of worms and habitat Worm farm	Parallel listening. Tried to engage Collin by rolling and rocking	12 minutes
Mealtime(s) (use additional sheets as necessary)	Area	Materials	Specific peers/type of play (solitary, parallel, associative, cooperative)	Time spent actively engaged
Breakfast	Table in the art area	Cup, teaspoon, bowl	Sydney, Andrew, David, parallel	7 minutes
Small-group instruction (use additional sheets as necessary)	Area	Materials	Specific peers/type of play (solitary, parallel, associative, cooperative)	Time spent actively engaged

Activity areas with longest sustained participation:	Activity areas with lowest sustained participation:
Summary: Playing with sand	Summary: Did not engage with art, manipulatives, or dramatic play
Preferred materials: Sand, shovels	Non-preferred materials: Quickly finished breakfast. Seemed to avoid fine motor activities. Did not engage in dramatic play materials (doctor office)
Preferred peers: Trey and Collin	Non-supportive peers (evidence of conflict/off-task behavior): N/A

Figure 1.5. Child Preference Observation Tool.

Child Preference Parent Interview Tool

Parent interviews provide critical insights into child behaviors. In concert with the Child Preference Observation Tool, completion of the Child Preference Parent Interview Tool provides useful information on the behaviors that the child displays during preferred and nonpreferred activities in the home and/or alternative child care setting. In most situations, this information will confirm observations in the classroom setting. In others, however, information gained from the parent interview may suggest alternative activities, materials, and strategies for engaging the child. In either case, recording the parents' perspective is beneficial.

Purpose of This Tool	The purpose of the Child Preference Parent Interview Tool in Figure 1.6 is to identify topics of interest and activity preferences that may be incorporated into nonpreferred areas and activities of the classroom day in order to increase sustained and active participation.
When to Use This Tool	This tool should be used whenever the teacher identifies activities or materials frequently resisted by the child. Assessment is indicated when resistance interferes with mastery of important skills (e.g., the child never participates in fine motor activities of any kind, including drawing, manipulatives, or sensory activities). When used with the Child Preference Observation Tool, the interview tool can provide important information about the individual preferences of the child.
How to Use This Tool	The interview tool lists questions to assess child interests and preferences. Parents are invaluable resources, and parent–teacher collaboration can result in a complete picture of the child's thematic interests and preferred activities. This can be completed, over the phone or in person, during parent conferences or classroom visits, or during a scheduled home visit. At times, it may be helpful to get information from each of the child's parents as well as from extended family members (e.g., grandparents), other child care providers, or consultants (e.g., speech therapist, occupational therapist, physical therapist, home intervention specialist).

Suggestions for Assessing the Relative Consistency and Strength of Preferences

1. Begin the interview by explaining the reason for the assessment. Emphasize the importance of the child's active participation across the classroom day and its link to skill development. If you have completed the Child Preference Observation Tool prior to the interview, share the classroom findings with the parent(s) and/or other interviewees.

2. Examine consistencies across the classroom and home settings—this may indicate the strongest child preferences.

3. Another indication of pronounced preference is when child choices are consistent across play activities and media (e.g., likes Sesame Street decorations, books, television programs, and video games).

Child Preference Parent Interview Tool

Directions: Use this interview tool over the phone or in person, during parent conferences or classroom visits, or during a scheduled home visit. At times, it may be helpful to get information from each of the child's parents as well as from extended family members (e.g., grandparents), other child care providers, or consultants (e.g., speech therapist, occupational therapist, physical therapist, home intervention specialist).

Name of child: *Adam Black*

Date: *11/29/09*

Respondent's name: *Jim Black/Rachel Black*

Setting: *Home visit*

Relationship to child: *Parents*

Interviewer: *Lerrien Short, teacher*

1. Does your child have any preferred characters or themes? For example, are there media characters or other figures that he or she prefers to have as themes for his or her toys, bedding, or media play?

   Loves to play robots. Does not really know what that is. Talks like a robot and loves Thomas the Train.

2. When you read to your child, what books does he or she prefer?

   Does not like to read.

3. When your child has free time, what toys does he or she typically select? Have difficulty sharing?

   Likes to play with airplanes, trucks. Does not want brother playing with his trucks.

4. During what type of activity does your child actively resist interruption? What does he or she typically do? Say?

   Playing with trucks. Playing robot. Cries, refuses. Goes back to the activity.

5. If you were going to give your child a reward for "good behavior," what type of activity or toy would you select?

   Thomas the Train.

6. Are there neighborhood friends whom your child particularly enjoys playing with? Are they boys or girls? Older or younger?

   Mostly younger brother

7. Is there anything else that you can tell me about the types of activities that your child consistently enjoys at home?

   Loves to run around outside. Rough sometimes with younger brother.

Figure 1.6. Child Preference Parent Interview Tool.

4. Take care to separate child preferences from activities that the parents prefer for him or her to pursue (e.g., the parent may prefer that the child read books, but the child may actually spend much more time watching movies and broadcast television and playing computer games).

Incorporating Child Preferences into the Daily Schedule and Activities

Child preferences can be incorporated for a variety of purposes. First, preferences can increase quality and length of engagement in both preferred and nonpreferred activity centers. Second, preferences can be used as rewards for complying with teacher directions during other activities. Finally, preferences can be used as vehicles for skills instruction.

In this author's experience, most children have marked preferences for activities that can be incorporated into classroom routines in a developmentally appropriate manner. For example, one child with autism spectrum disorder spent most of his free time reading about or watching videos about marine animals. The teacher was able to broaden the child's interest in infrequently visited classroom areas by rotating materials involving ocean life themes through the different classroom activities week by week (e.g., cutting playdough with dolphin shapes, stamping fish shapes on blue paper at the art table, turning the housekeeping area into a beach theme). She easily was able to keep to her plans for the rest of the classroom by incorporating his preferences into existing themes (e.g., using ocean-themed stationery for letter writing, substituting plates and cups shaped like fish into the housekeeping area, keeping books with illustrations of marine animals in the reading area).

Once you have identified areas and activities that are particularly attractive to the child, these same activities/materials can be used to prompt appropriate, cooperative performance of nonpreferred activities or learning tasks. That is, the teacher may restrict access to the preferred activity until the child has successfully participated in a nonpreferred task or activity. For example, a child who never works at the writing center might be prompted to complete tasks increasing in difficulty and duration in order to earn time at a preferred activity such as a computer game.

Finally, preferred themes and activities can form the context for learning activities. For the child who resists premath activities but loves playing with cars and trucks in the block area, counting and graphing activities can be incorporated into the preferred area. For example, the child might count the number of small cars that can fit on top of different sized blocks, and the teacher and child might construct a graph for the numbers associated with large, medium, and small blocks. Ownership of the activity could be expanded by having the child share the graph during group time.

Another aspect of preferences is choice making. There are many ways in which choices can be introduced into the classroom setting. Children can make reasonable and logical (if limited) choices during snack, free play, large- and small-motor activities, and group time. Choices can be communicated verbally or using print, pictures, or objects. The child should be offered the choice close in time to accessing the activity, and any limits should be explained using developmentally appropriate language (McCormick, Jolivette, & Ridgley, 2003).

Conclusion

The beginning of each classroom year brings children with different combinations of temperamental tendencies, skills, and preferences. This chapter has provided methods for assessing these variations using interviews and observations. In addition, many teacher strategies have been suggested to address child temperamental challenges and skill impairments.

CHAPTER 2

Attitudes and Beliefs about Behavior in Educational Settings

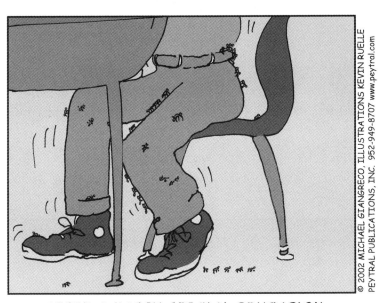

© 2002 MICHAEL GIANGRECO, ILLUSTRATIONS KEVIN RUELLE
PEYTRAL PUBLICATIONS, INC. 952-949-8707 www.peytral.com

AFTER A HASTY SPECIAL EDUCATION
PLACEMENT FOR BEHAVIOR PROBLEMS,
SCHOOL OFFICIALS WERE EMBARRASSED
TO LEARN THAT MARTY REALLY DID HAVE
ANTS IN HIS PANTS.

Many children come to early childhood classrooms with beliefs and experiences that lead to instant success. They come from home and community environments where the expectations are virtually a perfect match with those of the classroom. These children seem to quickly understand the culture of the classroom, adopting teacher language and learning rules and limits with ease. They display prosocial behavior (*see* Chapter 1) that is valued by teachers and peers and use social problem-solving skills that they have practiced from infancy.

Other children bring attitudes and habitual ways of interacting that are at odds with the classroom climate. These children have difficulty negotiating this apparent disconnect between their two realities. Often, the school provides a new and slightly unsettling world view, one that is not supported at home. These children become confused, testing the limits in each setting in order to discover effective ways to meet their needs. It is important that the teacher establish trusting relationships with these children, acknowledging and responding to their confusion and scaffolding children's efforts to adopt new ways of interacting with other children and adults. This chapter addresses assessment of primary characteristics of the home environment, including 1) sources of family stress and support, 2) parenting styles, and 3) sibling relationships and conflicts. It also provides suggestions for conferencing with parents and collaborating with professionals in other settings.

Home Experiences and Expectations

All children must learn to adapt when confronted with differences in adult expectations and styles of interaction. Children must negotiate inconsistencies between teacher and parent communication patterns, maturation expectations, and disciplinary practices. For example, at home, the child may be used to a more unpredictable family-centered schedule. At school, the child may be faced with the need to wait his or her turn for resources that are immediately available at home. Within the family setting, the child may experience undivided adult attention, and limits for unacceptable behavior may be permissive. In the classroom, relaxed rules and unlimited attention may be unsafe and impractical because of the higher ratio of children to adults.

Children from families with limited resources face even greater challenges when negotiating the contrasting expectations of school and home. They often enter a vastly different world when stepping from the bus into the early child care center. At school, resources are plentiful, and the children each get ample servings of food during lunch or snack. Broken toys are replaced, and there are always enough materials and activities for each child.

In some cases, children may be used to making choices and asserting independence far beyond that which is developmentally appropriate. These children often come from single-parent homes with multiple siblings—isolated families that do not have the support of relatives or adult friends. The children may be quite used to caring for themselves while the primary caregiver prioritizes work, social interests, or substance abuse over child care. It is important to add that many single-parent homes do *not* fit this pattern, and it is critical that teachers and administrators avoid jumping to this conclusion in every case.

Children may enter school with a perception of the world as a chaotic and unpredictable place. Family instability may be exacerbated by multiple moves, caregivers who come and go unpredictably, financial misfortunes (e.g., loss of job; child support), and substance abuse. Children may not be prepared for the emphasis on stability, predictability, and limits that is present in the classroom setting (Hemmeter et al., 1996).

Families' educational backgrounds and attitudes toward school may be vastly different from those of the preschool teachers and staff. This is complicated further by families with cultural and linguistic differences and parents who may value different competencies than those expected in the educational environment (Mendez et al., 2002).

It has been determined that the family emotional climate (e.g., degree/type of emotional expressiveness in the family, exposure to interparental and sibling conflict, parental consensus on child-rearing philosophy and methods) is extremely important in determining the school success of young children (Modry-Mandell, Gamble, & Taylor, 2007). Whether one or both parents have mental health issues such as depression or substance abuse also plays a role in determining school success (Hemmeter et al., 1996; Sakimura et al., 2008).

Family Eco-map Tool

One tool for visually depicting the complex issues and relationships in any family environment is the family eco-map (Hartman, 1995; McCormick, Stricklin, Nowak, & Rous, 2008), shown in Figure 2.1. With this tool, significant individuals, relationships, and settings can be displayed visually. This strategy further allows the teacher to build rapport while assessing family areas of conflict and sources of informal (e.g., friends, neighbors) and formal (e.g., social services, counselors, medical resources) support. Convention requires that circles represent females, squares identify males, and line quality between the various shapes be used to identify qualitative aspects of relationships (Hodge, 2005).

Purpose of This Tool	The purpose of the Family Eco-map Tool is to gather information about areas of existing and potential conflict and stress as well as sources of formal and informal support while establishing a collaborative relationship with the parent.
When to Use This Tool	The Family Eco-map Tool can be used by the individual teacher or administrator, alone or as part of a team. The tool could be used prior to admission. It also is likely to be helpful when the stress in the family environment is suspected of playing a contributing role to difficulties the child is experiencing in the classroom.
How to Use This Tool	1. The symbol for the child should be placed in the center of the paper, using a circle for a girl, a square for a boy. By convention, the child's age is placed in the middle of the shape. 2. Additional shapes are drawn around the child, illustrating the important caregivers and institutions with which the child has contact.

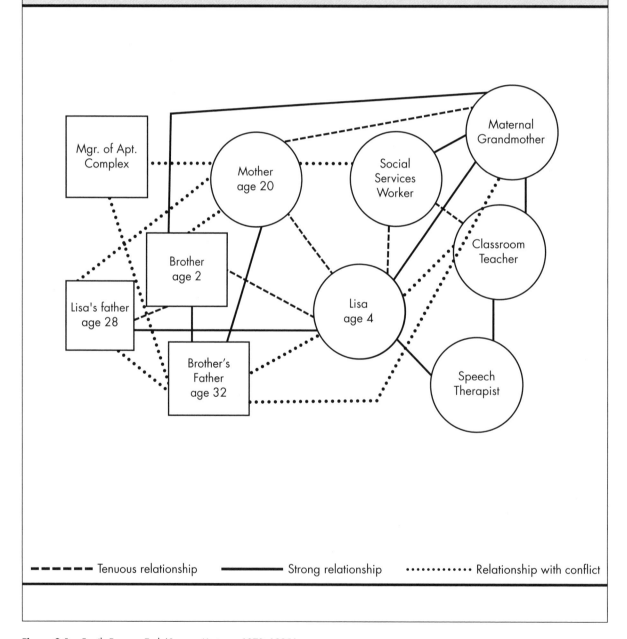

Family Eco-map Tool

Directions:

1. Place the symbol for the child in the center of the paper, using a circle for a girl, a square for a boy. By convention, the child's age is placed in the middle of the shape.
2. Draw additional shapes around the child, illustrating the important caregivers and institutions with which the child has contact.
3. Moving outward from the child, use other shapes to illustrate representatives of community agencies and settings with whom the parents have contact and who exert indirect influence on the life of the child.
4. Draw lines to illustrate the strength and emotional tone of the relationships, with lightly drawn or dashed lines indicating weak relationships, solid lines indicating strong associations, and dotted lines denoting conflict.

- - - - - Tenuous relationship   ——— Strong relationship   ········· Relationship with conflict

Figure 2.1. Family Eco-map Tool. (*Sources:* Hartman, 1978, 1995.)

3. Moving outward from the child, still other shapes can be used to illustrate representatives of community agencies and settings with whom the parents have contact and who exert indirect influence on the life of the child.

4. Lines are drawn to illustrate the strength and emotional tone of the relationships, with lightly drawn or dashed lines indicating weak relationships, solid lines indicating strong associations, and dotted lines denoting conflict.

Suggestions for Interpreting the Family Eco-map

1. Once you have mapped the important people in the child's life, you can begin to interpret the relationships among them. As you can see from this example (Figure 2.1), Lisa only has strong, supportive relationships with her speech therapist, her grandmother, and her father. She has weak and unstable relationships with her mother and the social worker. The relationships of most concern, however, are Lisa's conflicts with her brother, brother's father, and the teacher. These are individuals with whom she experiences direct and daily friction, and this will pose an ongoing problem for Lisa. Relationships among important people in Lisa's life also can be examined.

2. The total number of conflict-ridden relationships that are depicted in this family eco-map could give the teacher insight into some of the difficulties that Lisa is experiencing in the classroom. Strengthening the relationship with Lisa's mother and partnering with her to get help (e.g., family counseling, financial help) with these issues could reduce the overall stress in Lisa's home life.

3. The family eco-map can be used to identify sources of support as well. Lisa's grandmother and the speech therapist may be important resources for developing plans to address Lisa's challenging behaviors in the classroom.

Attachment

Parent–child relationships differ widely in emotional tone, reciprocity, and responsiveness. *Attachment* is the stable affectionate bond that caregivers share with their child (Ainsworth, 1989). Parents have varying levels of experience, confidence, and competence. Some parents take great joy and pride in their children's accomplishments and enjoy giving affection and receiving affection from their children. Others see parenting as a much lower priority, overwhelmed with the problems of daily living (e.g., mental health issues, substance abuse, financial worries, conflict with other family members). A secure attachment, in which the parent and child are sensitive to each other's moods and needs, has been linked with social competence and higher self-esteem in young children (Urban, Carlson, Egeland, & Sroufe, 1991).

Kochanska, Aksan, Prisco, and Adams (2008) described a "mutually responsive orientation [that] is a positive, mutually binding, and mutually cooperative relationship that evolves in some parent–child dyads" (p. 30). In this type of relationship, both child and parent are exquisitely sensitive and responsive to cues from the other, enjoy being with each other, and successfully cooperate to establish daily routines. As in the attachment literature, this reciprocity predicts child social competence with other caregivers and peers.

Parenting Styles

The earliest typology of parenting styles was developed by Diana Baumrind (1966, 1996). Three parenting styles were defined: *authoritarian, permissive,* and *authoritative.* These early studies consistently linked disciplinary styles to positive (or problematic) child outcomes in academic and social arenas.

Authoritative parents are portrayed as responsive to their children's communicated needs; these parents use reasoning to achieve compliance. Their ultimate goals are child self-control and social competence. Parents using this disciplinary style are warm and affectionate, consistently following through with consequences, whether they be rewards or punishments (Jewell, Krohn, Scott, Carlton, & Meinz, 2008; Letiecq, 2007).

Authoritarian parents interact with their children in a rigid, punitive, and demanding manner, emphasizing the importance of control; child obedience is the most highly valued outcome of any parent–child interaction. This harsh parenting style, particularly when it involves verbal and physical aggression, may lead to future child behavior problems (Hemmeter et al., 1996). Paradoxically, however, it has been shown that children of authoritarian fathers, in particular, exhibit higher levels of physical aggression (Russell et al., 2003).

Permissive parents make few demands on their children, instead expecting the child to make his or her own (often developmentally inappropriate) decisions. The permissive parent values the child's approval and contentment above all. Even when limits are established, there is little follow-through with discipline.

A fourth style of parenting, suggested by Maccoby and Martin (1983), is the most problematic of all. The *uninvolved neglecting* style is typical of parents who do not provide the supervision, support, or affection that their children require for provision of their basic needs.

Researchers emphasize the importance of parental consistency in disciplinary strategies across settings and problem behaviors. The situation becomes particularly difficult when parents disagree on their child-rearing and parenting styles. In these situations, negative and disruptive child behaviors escalate (Modry-Mandell et al., 2007). One particularly lethal mismatch of parenting styles is when the mother has an authoritarian disciplinary style (e.g., rigid developmental expectations and rules coupled with little warmth) and the father is permissive and emotionally disengaged from the parenting process (Jewell et al., 2008). Children from families with this particular mismatch are more likely to act out with aggression, defiance, and noncompliance in home and school settings.

The most positive outcomes (at least for Caucasian, middle class families) have come from parents who use an authoritative parenting style—a balanced, consistent, and rational approach to child rearing and discipline (Jewell et al., 2008). As mentioned previously, parents who share a mutually responsive orientation with their children (characteristics that compose the authoritative style) are less likely to use power-assertive (i.e., spanking, reprimanding) disciplinary methods and have children who demonstrate higher levels of compliance and emotional self-regulation (Kochanska et al., 2008). This authoritative orientation is consistent with the disciplinary approach used in early childhood classrooms and forms the basis of most parent management training.

Brief Parenting Style Assessment Tool

Teachers and other professionals can use this device (Figure 2.2, The Brief Parenting Style Assessment Tool) to assess the parenting beliefs and practices in the home environment. This brief questionnaire examines the extent to which the parent endorses the importance of daily interaction with the child, setting rules/limits, and granting age-appropriate autonomy to the child. This is but one of many methods that the early childhood professional may use to learn more about the child's home environment, and should never be used to make decisions about such important issues as neglect or abuse. Instead, the tool is intended to be used as a discussion-starter for parent conferences.

Purpose of This Tool	The purpose of this tool is to assess the parenting style used most frequently in the child's home. The Brief Parenting Style Assessment Tool is not intended as an exhaustive assessment of parenting beliefs and practices. As mentioned previously, parents may conflict in their beliefs and practices around child rearing. In this case, it might be helpful to have each parent complete the tool independently.
When to Use This Tool	This tool can be used by teachers and other early childhood staff to assess the types of disciplinary methods that are used in the home environment. It also can be used to communicate differences in child management philosophies between home and school. It is best to have the parent complete the tool at home before meeting with the teacher. This allows the time for carefully considered responses and may generate parent reflection on desired changes prior to the scheduled conference.
How to Use This Tool	The Brief Parenting Style Assessment Tool lists a series of statements that highlight parenting beliefs and practices reflective of three dimensions that underlie parenting styles: responsiveness, demandingness, and support for child autonomy (Baumrind, 1991; Darling & Steinberg, 1993; Grolnick & Ryan, 1989; Maccoby & Martin, 1983). Values are summed to identify the preferred parenting style: authoritarian, permissive, or authoritative.

Brief Parenting Style Assessment Tool

Directions: Ask the caregiver to complete the Brief Parenting Style Assessment Tool, filling in his/her name, the child's name, and the caregiver's relationship to the child. Explain that different caregivers come to the parenting situation with unique personalities and life experiences, and those are reflected in the caregiver's individual parenting style. In addition, the characteristics of individual children demand unique ways of responding—resulting in different parenting syles for children within the same family. With this in mind, have the caregiver read each statement, indicating yes or no, as to whether the statement adequately reflects the caregiver's parenting behaviors with this specific child. Directions for scoring follow the questionnaire.

Name of child: *Jacob K.*   Date: *4-4-2010*

Name of person completing assessment: *Julie B.*

Relationship to child: *guardian*   Dominant parenting style: *authoritative*

Circle Y (true for me) or N (not true for me) to the following statements:

1. My child and I talk daily about things that happen at school. (R)	⒴ N
2. I have strict rules that I think are in the best interests of my child, and I expect my child to follow them to the letter. (D)	⒴ N
3. I plan little celebrations to reward my child when he or she has accomplished something special at home or school. (R)	⒴ N
4. Sometimes I let it slide when my child disobeys my rules. (–D)	Y Ⓝ
5. I listen to my child's point of view when we disagree. (A)	⒴ N
6. I am so busy that it is rare that I can just sit down and listen to my child's problems. (–R)	Y Ⓝ
7. I think it is important to punish a child every time he or she breaks a rule, regardless of the situation. (D)	Y Ⓝ
8. With all the demands in my life, I do not watch out for my child the way I should. (–A)	Y Ⓝ
9. I usually give my child choices in what he or she eats, wears, and plays. (A)	⒴ N

Figure 2.2. Brief Parenting Style Assessment Tool.

Suggestions for Scoring the Brief Parenting Style Assessment Tool

Each of the questions is followed by a letter in parentheses. Questions followed by *R* assess the degree of *responsiveness*—the degree of interest and involvement the parent expresses in the child's life. Questions followed by *–R* indicate that an answer of *No* is scored in the direction of higher responsiveness. Questions followed by *D* indicate the degree of *demandingness*—the degree of strictness and rigidity the parent displays toward obedience and rule breaking. Questions followed by *–D* indicate that an answer of *No* is scored in the direction of higher demandingness. Questions followed by *A* assess the degree of support for child *autonomy*—the degree of independence or maturation expectations that the parent has. Questions followed by *–A* indicate than an answer of *No* is scored in the direction of higher support for age-appropriate child autonomy.

1. Give one point for agreement on each of the following items:

    1. *Responsiveness* score: 1 (*Y*), 3 (*Y*), and 6 (*N*)

        TOTAL *R* ___3___

    2. *Demandingness* score: 2 (*Y*), 4 (*N*), and 7 (*Y*)

        TOTAL *D* ___3___

    3. Support for *Child Autonomy* score: 5 (*Y*), 8 (*N*), and 9 (*Y*)

        TOTAL *A* ___3___

2. Determine which attributes are high (2–3) or low (0–1). Select the most appropriate parenting style based on the following criteria:

    1. Authoritative parents have high scores in *responsiveness, demandingness,* and support for *child autonomy.*

    2. Authoritarian parents have high scores in *demandingness* but low scores in *responsiveness* and support for *child autonomy.*

    3. Permissive parents have high scores in *responsiveness* and support for *child autonomy* but low scores in *demandingness.*

    4. Uninvolved parents have high scores in support for *child autonomy* but low scores in *responsiveness* and *demandingness.*

Sibling Relationships and Conflict

As discussed previously, interparental conflict and high numbers of stressful family life events can have devastating effects on young children. Exposure to negatively charged emotional exchanges between parents, along with disagreements about child rearing and discipline, can lead to increasing rates of sibling conflicts as well as child behavior problems at home and in other settings (Modry-Mandell et al., 2007).

Sibling conflict is natural and expected and typically involves arguments over toys (i.e., Who owns it? Who had it first?), space (i.e., Who gets to sit where? How close is too close?), and plans for the content and sequence of play activities (Howe, Rinaldi, Jennings, & Petrakos, 2002). As siblings are typically 1 or more years apart in age, complicating factors include power, size, and language competence, with parents often intervening in favor of the younger, more vulnerable sibling (Perlman, Garfinkel, & Turrell, 2007). This may be due, in part, to the fact that older siblings use physical and verbal aggression to dominate if unchecked by an adult, whereas younger siblings frequently use physical aggression to compensate for less mature verbal skills.

Conversely, even when child temperament and family characteristics are taken into account, a warm, responsive, and affectionate relationship with a sibling can facilitate social competence (Modry-Mandell et al., 2007). Sibling relationships have been characterized as natural opportunities for learning conflict resolution (Stormshak, Bellanti, & Bierman, 1996). Children can learn skills in negotiation, reasoning, perspective taking, social problem solving, and compromise (Perlman et al., 2007). However, distinctions can be made between destructive and constructive styles of sibling conflicts (Howe et al., 2002). Destructive conflict is riddled with emotional intensity, name calling, high levels of coercion and physicality, and issue shifting (i.e., the content of the argument spreads beyond the current time and setting), whereas constructive conflict is characterized by low levels of emotion and high levels of collaboration and negotiation. Although destructive conflict harms the sibling relationship, constructive conflict enhances and strengthens it.

Parents play a role in fostering constructive rather than destructive conflict. Parents who respond to sibling conflicts with self-oriented comments (e.g., "Stop yelling. I can't hear the television.") or opposition (i.e., "Stop fighting right this minute you two!") do not teach their children appropriate, alternative methods for resolving their conflicts. In both of these situations, the conflict is more likely to become destructive, escalating into physical confrontation. Similarly, parents who just step in to physically punish one or both children—removing toys, hitting or threatening each sibling without verbal justification—increase the likelihood of future, more serious conflicts. These children do not learn to make independent decisions (Perlman et al., 2007).

More constructively, parents who justify their intervention (e.g., "It's not safe to throw the toys. You'll each have to choose another activity." "Lisa had it first and it's her toy. She can have a turn and then it would be nice if she would share with you, because you are so interested in trying it.") model verbal explanations and prosocial behaviors (Perlman et al., 2007).

Much can be learned about children's conflict negotiation styles from interviewing parents about typical sibling interactions when disagreements arise over play materials (i.e., possession, use), themes, or use of space. It is important to determine the frequency and typical progression and outcomes of sibling conflicts and the methods parents use to intervene.

Parent Interview—Sibling Rivalry Tool

This tool can be used by teachers to gain insight into parent support for negotiations between siblings during conflict situations. The interview guide depicted in Figure 2.3, the Parent Interview—Sibling Rivalry Tool, asks the parent to describe typical

Parent Interview—Sibling Rivalry Tool

Directions: Ask the parent the following questions regarding sibling rivalry.

Name of child: *Jake Davis*   Date: *9/15/09*

Respondent's name: *Leah Welch*   Setting: *Home Visit*

Relationship to child: *Mother*   Interviewer: *Cheryl Reed*

1. What ages are your children? How well do they get along at home?

   Jake, 4
   Lily, 3
   Cameron, 6 mo.

2. Most children have disagreements at some time or another. When _____*Jake*_____ (child listed above) disagrees with his or her sibling(s), what do they usually argue about?

   Toys—Jake does not want his sister and brother to play with his things.

3. How does _____*Jake*_____ (name of child listed above) usually express his or her emotions? Does he or she use words or actions? Give me some examples.

   He screams and hits. He takes his toys back.

4. What does _____*Jake*_____ (name of child listed above) do to get his or her way? What is successful for him or her?

   He is bigger. He hits his sister and she cries. I have to make them stop.

5. If _____*Jake*_____'s (name of child listed above) sibling is older, how does he or she typically try to get his or her way?

   NA. His sister calls mom.

6. Describe a time (if any) when the argument between your children really got out of hand. What happened?

   They just scream and cry. He hits his sister and sometimes hurts her.

7. If you have to step in to handle the situation, what do you usually say and do? What would you NEVER say and do? Who do you generally side with? Why?

   He gets punished. He has to put his toys away. Sometimes he has to put them away for a long time. I would never hurt him.

Figure 2.3. Parent Interview—Sibling Rivalry Tool.

conflicts between children in their home. Questions address the triggers for conflict, the actions and expressed emotions of each of the children involved, and the typical ways in which the parent intervenes to resolve the conflict.

Purpose of This Tool	The purpose of the Parent Interview—Sibling Rivalry Tool is to identify the frequency, content, and nature (destructive or constructive) of typical sibling conflicts and parent mediations.
When to Use This Tool	This tool can be used by teachers during problem-solving meetings precipitated by peer conflicts within the classroom. This can provide important contextual information about the child's conflict negotiation history as well as offer an opportunity for consultation on parenting disciplinary strategies.
How to Use This Tool	Figure 2.3 lists open-ended interview questions to which parents may respond. Follow-up questions allow specificity.
Suggestions for Interpreting Information from the Parent Interview—Sibling Rivalry Tool	1. The open-ended questions allow the parent a lot of latitude in the information they provide. However, you should be able to identify themes in child and parent behaviors. 2. Look for evidence of similar patterns in the classroom and home conflicts. Does the parent see the arguments as frequent and serious? Does the parent indicate that they ever escalate to an unsafe level? Use this as an opportunity to collaborate with parents to devise plans that can be implemented consistently at home and at school. 3. Look for inconsistencies between parental disciplinary techniques and strategies that would be acceptable in the early childhood setting. Use this as an opportunity for suggesting alternative strategies for use in the home.

Collaborating with Parents

Although most parents are interested in their child's progress, it can become demoralizing when every contact with the school is over challenges rather than successes. As each day seems to end with a recounting of all the child has done wrong, parents may become numb and disengaged; the attitude may become, "You deal with it— it's happening at school, and it's not my problem." For this reason, it is important to provide as balanced a report as possible. Attending to the communication from parents is key—acknowledging their frustration and disappointment (even when unspoken) over their child's lack of success goes a long way to engaging them in solving the problem.

When parent collaboration on behavioral challenges becomes necessary, teachers should initiate contact with the parents, clearly stating the reason for a phone call or meeting in simple, precise language (Spinelli, 1999). Open-ended questions will allow the parent to set the initial pace and tone of the discussion. It may be important to spend more time than usual at the beginning of this type of conference, allowing the parent to talk about their personal challenges before redirecting the conversation to the individual child's performance in school. Some parents will spend a significant amount of time discussing other siblings, financial worries, or marital problems. This is important contextual information.

The parent also may convey information that makes the teacher wonder if the parent is describing the child who is in his or her classroom. The child's behavior at home and at school may be radically different; for example, the parent may report that the child displays a level of independence or compliance in the home environment rarely seen in the classroom. The teacher's first reaction may be to doubt this information. In fact, it is irrelevant whether the child actually displays these behaviors at home; what is important is that the parent thinks (or wants the teacher to accept) that he or she does. That is important information. The goal becomes to help the child display the successful behaviors in the classroom environment; in this way, teacher and parent have begun to collaborate—team members with a common goal.

Each parent conference should end with a period of clarification and summary, a discussion of next steps and plans. In some cases, the parents may insist on goals and priorities that are only tangentially related to the child's classroom success (e.g., housing concerns). This is an opportunity to suggest resources that the parent might pursue.

Parent Conference Documentation Tool

This tool can be used by teachers to collaborate with parents around child-related problems that emerge in the classroom setting. The conference interview guide depicted in Figure 2.4, the Parent Conference Documentation Tool, encourages teachers and parents to specify child-related concerns and goals for change and to identify strategies to be implemented in the school and/or home settings.

Purpose of This Tool	The purpose of the Parent Conference Documentation Tool is to funnel discussion from broad to specific issues, specifying future plans, goals, and strategies for identified child problems.
When to Use This Tool	The Parent Conference Documentation Tool can be used whenever the teacher feels the need to conference with the parent in order to communicate information about 1) child challenges, 2) goal setting, 3) individualized strategies, 4) progress, and 5) needs for additional resources.
How to Use This Tool	The Parent Conference Documentation Tool divides the interview into four stages: opening concerns, goal development and strategizing, progress to date, and next steps. When communicating the initial concern, be specific, generating classroom examples of child behaviors when describing the problem situation. Record the parent's response to this concern. Indicate whether this is similar to or

Parent Conference Documentation Tool

Directions: When communicating the initial concern, be specific, generating classroom examples of child behaviors when describing the problem situation. Record the parent's response to this concern. Indicate whether this is similar to or different from behaviors observed in the home. Record any recent home-related changes or other concerns that might have affected the child. State the desired change in general terms before identifying specific goals and strategies for school and home. End with any progress updates or requests for additional resources, and schedule the next parent conference.

Name of child: *Maria Santos*   Date of conference: *10/1/09*

Participant(s) and roles: *Cheryl Reed, teacher*   Setting: *Teacher office*

Marlena Santos, mother

Specific classroom-related concern(s):

Maria is very shy. She tends to play alone. Does not engage with other children. Engages with materials for long periods, but does not play with other children.

Parent concerns and/or response:

Want Maria to do well at school. Want her to fit in. Want her to have friends.

Desired change:

Would like Maria to play with more children. Would like her to feel comfortable speaking up in group. Would like her to communicate needs.

Specific classroom goals:	Specific home-related goals:
Maria will engage in associative play for extended time.	*Maria will talk about friends at school.*
Maria will communicate classroom needs to teacher (bathroom, help with activity, food choices).	

Teacher responsibilities:	Parent responsibilities:
Maria loves the art area. I will set up cooperative activities and invite Sydney to work with Maria. I will pair Sydney and Maria in dramatic play.	*I will read the book the teacher sends home each night.*
I will make a book for Maria about the classroom in which she and Sydney work together and ask each other for materials.	*I will ask about Sydney.*

Classroom progress since last conference:	Home progress since last conference:

Need for additional classroom resources:	Need for additional resources at home:

Date of next conference: *10/15/09*

Figure 2.4. Parent Conference Documentation Tool.

different from behaviors observed in the home. Record any recent home-related changes or other concerns that might have affected the child. State the desired change in general terms before identifying specific goals and strategies for school and home. End with any progress updates or requests for additional resources, and schedule the next parent conference.

Suggestions for Interpreting Information from the Parent Conference Documentation Tool

1. Highlight any inconsistencies between parent and teacher impressions of the area of concern or desired behavior. Address these inconsistencies before developing goals and strategies.

2. Assess the feasibility of selected strategies before agreeing to implement them.

3. End the meeting by reviewing the agreed-on goals and strategies.

4. Provide the parent with a copy of the completed documentation tool at the end of the meeting.

Communicating with Parents Between Conferences

Frequent contact with parents may be necessary when a problem is severe and/or when it occurs in multiple settings (e.g., with multiple caregivers, at home and at school, at school and in after-school care). It also may be important to communicate about the child's performance in the classroom when contingencies (i.e., rewards or punishments) are provided at home. Kelley (1990) describes the use of this strategy for a variety of purposes (e.g., conveying classroom information, monitoring progress toward child goals) in her book, *School-Home Notes: Promoting Children's Classroom Success.*

Parent Communication Note

This tool can be used by teachers to communicate with parents around child-related issues. The Parent Communication Note can be structured to provide information about general classroom performance (e.g., "Ricky listened to his teachers all day" or "Monique played safely with her friends in ALL the centers today") or address more specific information about a skill or challenge (as illustrated in Figure 2.5). In return, parents can communicate with teachers about the child's performance in the home.

Purpose of This Tool

The purpose of this tool is to provide specific information about an aspect of the child's behavior targeted for change. The note may include information about the specific strategies discussed previously and the child's response to those strategies.

Parent Communication Note

Subject: _Lily Wears Her Glasses All Day!!_

Date: _10/1/09_

Goal: _____Lily_____ (name of child) will _wear her glasses at least 55 minutes of each_ _hour of the classroom day, except during naptime._

Strategies:

o _Lily will be reminded to put on her glasses if she is observed to remove them during play._

o _If Lily is not compliant with this reminder, she will be offered a 5-minute break and told to put them_ _in her cubby._

o _At the end of 5 minutes, Lily will be told to put on her glasses. If she resists again, she will be told_ _"Your glasses help you see. You need to wear them. Remember, you are going to celebrate with Mom if_ _you can wear them all day." Upon further resistance, the glasses will be placed in the cubby for safety_ _till the end of the day._

o _____

Circle all that apply:

o _Lily wore her glasses_ all (most) some none of the day

o _____Lily_____ (name of child) took ___2___ 5 minute breaks today

o _____Lily_____ (name of child) gets to celebrate!

o _____Lily_____ (name of child) needs to try again tomorrow!

Comments:

_____

_____

_____

_____

_____

_____

_____

_____

Figure 2.5. Parent Communication Note.

When to Use This Tool

The Parent Communication Note can be used by teachers, parents, and other classroom personnel. Anyone who has the responsibility of observing the child's behavior, implementing strategies, and recording progress may communicate using this note. Copies of the notes can be retained and used to monitor the child's progress.

How to Use This Tool

The Parent Communication Note provided in Figure 2.5 illustrates the following important elements: Date, goal, level of support and performance, and opportunity for reward.

Suggestions for Interpreting the Parent Communication Note

1. This note provides opportunities to record 1) the implementation of the plan, 2) the effectiveness of the identified strategies, and 3) the need for replanning.

2. Both teacher and parent have daily feedback as to the success of the plan.

3. Copies of the dated Parent Communication Notes can be used for data collection, and the child's progress can be graphed. For this example, the teacher might choose to visually portray each day in terms of the level of teacher assistance required (e.g., number of breaks used) or the level of success (e.g., amount of the day she wore her glasses—all, most, some, or none). For ease of graphing, the variables could be assigned numbers (e.g., all = 3, most = 2, some = 1).

Educational Experiences and Expectations

Most children come to the early childhood center having spent time in multiple settings (e.g., child's home, child care, homes of extended family or friends, community child care, church). Caregivers in each of these settings vary widely in terms of 1) training and experience; 2) knowledge of child development; 3) number of children for whom they are expected to provide care; 4) expectations for child independence, social competence, and compliance; and 5) child management strategies (Hemmeter et al., 2006). The child may be confused about conflicting expectations, and the issue of whether he or she has been "good" on a particular day becomes ever more complicated for both the parent and the child.

Tool for Communicating across Child Care Settings

This tool can be used by caregivers in various child care settings to communicate around child-related issues. The Tool for Communicating across Settings (as illustrated in Figure 2.6) can identify challenges unique to each setting or common across several settings. Care providers can suggest strategies (i.e., common caregiver techniques, words) that can be implemented to improve consistency in responding.

Tool for Communicating across Child Care Settings

Directions: During telephone calls or visits to other child care settings, use this tool to collect information about the child's behavior. Collaborative problem solving across settings may be a direct result of this exchange of information.

Name of child: _Cameron Rhoda_

Caregiver(s) and roles: _Shelly Richards,_
Kindergarten Teacher, Megan Phillips, After School
Teacher

Name/role of recorder: _Katherine Rippe,_
Administrator

Date: _9/3/09_

Specific classroom-related concern(s):
Cameron is slow to warm up in the classroom. He has trouble with transitions in routines.

Alternate setting concerns/response:
Cameron resists rules during after school program. Cries easily. Seems to need adult presence regularly.

Information about alternate setting (length of time child spends in setting, location, adult/child ratio, typical disciplinary strategies, other factors):
Cameron arrives on the van at 2:30. He is picked up by his father at 6:00. Cameron is one of the youngest in the group. The after school program is in the gym at Peabody Elementary. He is one of 35 children with 2 teachers.

Consistencies between settings:	Conflicts between settings:
Adults present, some materials the same. Two children from his class in after school program.	More children, less structure, age difference

Need for further contact/collaboration:	Need for additional information:
Need to share strategies as year progresses. Need to share materials and routines. Work at pairing children in classroom for after school.	

Suggestions for change:
Include more kindergarten specific equipment in after school program. Provide quiet space for kindergarten children to rest.

Figure 2.6. Tool for Communicating across Child Care Settings.

Purpose of This Tool	The purpose of this tool is to document contacts with other caregivers about common problems experienced across settings.
When to Use This Tool	This tool can be used by the teacher in collaboration with the parents and other caregivers. It is used most effectively when there is an identified area of concern that occurs in two or more settings.
How to Use This Tool	The Tool for Communicating across Child Care Settings can be used during the course of (or following) telephone calls or visits to other child care settings. Collaborative problem solving across settings may be a direct result of this exchange of information.
Suggestions for Using the Tool for Communicating Across Child Care Settings	1. Information can be used to identify inconsistencies in adult expectations and strategies across settings that may be contributing to the challenge in the early childhood classroom. 2. The information collected with this tool may provide a springboard for future sharing of information and resources across settings.

Conclusion

Children may be exposed to conflicting standards for acceptable behavior. Parents and other caregivers may differ in their understanding of developmentally appropriate expectations for young children. They may use disciplinary strategies that are in direct conflict with the philosophy of the early childhood setting. Sibling conflicts may provide poor models for conflict negotiation with classroom peers. This chapter discussed methods for assessing and problem solving around these issues in order to increase consistency across settings.

CHAPTER 3

Feelings of Safety and Belonging

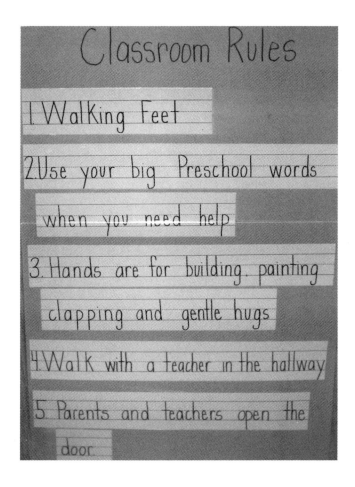

Teachers and administrators take seriously the mandate that the early childhood center should be a safe environment for learning. Entryways are monitored, and strangers are required to have officially sanctioned reasons to be in the building.

Unsafe Communities as a Cause for Concern

For child care centers that enroll children from poor, urban neighborhoods, violence may be a complicating factor. Community buildings may be virtually abandoned, empty and shuttered, providing havens for gangs and drug dealers. Drive-by shootings and robberies may be common. Playgrounds may be unfit and unsafe for child use, littered with used condoms, drug paraphernalia, and empty beer bottles. Simply transporting the child safely to and from school may pose extreme challenges for parents and teachers (Letiecq, 2007; Wallach, 1995).

Daily exposure to crime-ridden and violent communities may change the way in which parents interact with their children. Letiecq (2007) found that African American fathers in violent neighborhoods reported 1) increased monitoring of the child's independent play, 2) direct instruction in neighborhood safety rules, 3) restrictions on viewing of media violence, 4) injunctions to fight back when threatened in order to be protected from harm, and 5) increased levels of participation in neighborhood advocacy and community action organizations. Children from these neighborhoods may be traumatized by exposure to community violence and may be excessively dependent on adult guidance, afraid to make independent decisions and checking in for permission for each activity. This section provides tools for teachers to use in identifying emotional concerns and responding with specific strategies.

A Safe, Warm, and Welcoming Space

Upon arrival at the classroom door, children should feel that the space is their own (Poland, Pitcher, & Lazarus, 2005). The room's furnishings and materials should be designed with each child's safety in mind, and teachers should closely supervise all activities. Teachers should work hard to establish individual relationships with each child and family, encouraging a sense of identification with the school (i.e., "This is our (my child's) classroom") (Hemmeter et al., 2006).

These safeguards, however, may fail to reassure some children. These children, whether due to temperament or a history of traumatic experience, feel anxious and emotionally overwhelmed. Teachers are challenged to respond to the emotional communication of children in sensitive and nurturing ways, especially when these problems continue far beyond the first few weeks of school. Children need to feel safe and connected to the classroom. It must become a haven for learning, an environment where they are valued and to which they belong. The teachers should be warm and inviting, greeting the children by name and welcoming them into the classroom. The physical arrangement of the classroom, including furniture and decorations, should exude comfort and engage the child immediately (Xu, 2006).

The National Association of School Psychologists provides clear safety guidelines for school personnel to follow (NASP, 2006) to manage crisis situations. These guidelines fall into four basic categories: 1) preparedness policies, 2) building design and security, 3) communication strategies (e.g., with parents, local emergency responders, and community leaders), and 4) direct instruction of children. Each school should have written crisis policies, identifying procedures to follow for specific emergencies and key roles for individual personnel. Issues to be covered in a comprehensive crisis policy range from communication with parents and the media to the contents of the classroom emergency supply box (Poland et al., 2005). This policy should be reviewed and updated as new issues emerge (e.g., evacuations for accidents involving toxic chemicals should the center be located near manufacturing facilities or transportation routes). Administrators should require staff familiarity with these policies and include safety content in training for new and current staff.

The school building itself should be clean and in good repair, well-lighted during day and nighttime use (Poland et al., 2005). Entry to the area used for child care should be physically separate from parts of the building used for other purposes. There should be a single point of entry into the child care center, and access through this area should be monitored at all times. Teachers should implement a sign-in system to record the name of the visitors and the purpose/location of the visit. Use of visitor badges allows other staff to identify and report unfamiliar adults in the building. Administrators, teachers, and other staff (e.g., bus drivers) should fully apprise the door monitors of any potentially dangerous or disruptive visitors (e.g., provide names and/or photos of individuals banned from picking up particular students). Some situations necessitate the involvement of emergency responders to safely remove such individuals (e.g., in situations of parental substance abuse or custody disputes). Security systems (e.g., locked doors with restricted entry, metal detectors, remote video cameras) may be indicated in high-crime neighborhoods.

Administrators and staff should communicate safety guidelines clearly. Parents should understand the rationale for each restriction and should be given opportunities to participate in policy development and revision. Files should contain updated parent contact information, and plans for communication during a crisis should specify a preplanned reunion spot (Poland et al., 2005). Community neighbors can serve as external eyes and ears, assisting the staff by notifying them when unfamiliar adults are seen in the vicinity of the walkways, parking lots, or playgrounds.

Children should be involved in safety procedures in a developmentally appropriate manner. Teachers should greet children with calm reassurance, welcoming them into "their school." Disaster drills should be practiced regularly (i.e., earthquake, fire, tornado, intruder) to familiarize children with the alert signal, the evacuation or sheltering procedures, and the safe place for each scenario (Poland et al., 2005). It is important that information about the reasons for these drills be given in a measured and developmentally appropriate manner. Children need to learn how to protect themselves from danger, but lengthy, detailed information can confuse and frighten them.

Center Safety Plan

This tool guides teachers and administrators through the planning process for crisis preparedness. The Center Safety Plan, outlined in Figure 3.1, identifies key personnel, materials, and procedures for a wide variety of emergency situations.

Purpose of This Tool

The purpose of the Center Safety Plan is to assist administrators or teachers in assessing safety issues related to unplanned emergencies. This tool can be used to determine when new policies should be developed and/or when policies or instructional strategies should be modified.

When to Use This Tool

The Center Safety Plan can be used by administrators and other members of a facility crisis team to assess classroom and building safety. The most effective use of this tool may be as a planning device for crisis preparedness and/or intervention teams. The tool is meant to be used as part of a dynamic assessment process, one that is continually revisited and in which crisis plans are modified as conditions warrant.

How to Use This Tool

Convene a representative group of administrators, teachers, and parents as an assessment team. Identify specific strategies in each category, and assign responsibilities for every element of the crisis plan. Develop plans for assembling necessary equipment, materials, and information. Assign roles to specific team members and write crisis scripts to be followed for specific disaster scenarios. These scripts will outline staff member responsibilities in sequential order. Figure 3.1 lists categories of crisis planning, roles for key players, and sample strategies for addressing each goal.

Suggestions for Writing a Center Safety Plan

1. The Center Safety Plan should be thought of as a work in progress. Staff members leave employment, and assigned roles change. The director should specify an annual review date to allow reconsideration of assigned roles, building security measures, and specific disaster and/or emergency action scripts.

2. Drills provide opportunities for identifying weak links or holes in the process. Coordinators should provide opportunities for feedback from teachers and staff. This will increase plan efficiency.

3. Parents and professionals in the community change names, locations, and phone numbers. Keeping this information updated can be a challenge, but every minute is well spent if it facilitates communication during a crisis.

Center Safety Plan

Directions: Convene a representative group of administrators, teachers, and parents as an assessment team. Identify specific strategies in each category, and assign responsibilities for every element of the crisis plan. Develop plans for assembling necessary equipment, materials, and information. Assign roles to specific team members and write crisis scripts to be followed for specific disaster scenarios. These scripts will outline staff member responsibilities in sequential order.

Safety category	Plan Steps (assembling a center safety planning team) (Identify administrator, teacher, parent, and community representatives)

Preparedness

Preparedness Steps

- Plan and provide training for safety-related issues.

1. Create a list of specific trainings to be scheduled.
2. Determine the most cost-effective way to provide this training.
   a. Who can provide the training?
   b. Who should be trained?
   c. Who can fund the training?

- Select teachers and staff members for specific roles.

Roles to be filled:

1. *Record monitor*: Ensures that emergency contacts are complete and current
   Name and contact information: _Maggie Dawson_
2. *Materials and equipment coordinator*: Ensures that the classroom crisis box is filled with emergency supplies (e.g., flashlights, radios, tools, emergency cell phone, parent contact information) and that all equipment has fresh batteries and is in working order
   Name and contact information: _Jean Marie Dill, teacher_
3. *Parent contact*: Notifies parents via web site announcement, text message, email, and/or phone call in the event of a crisis; provides details and further instructions; develops a sample parent letter for debriefing after the immediate crisis is over
   Name and contact information: _Jill Ambrose_
4. *Teacher or staff contact*: Generates an emergency signal to notify teachers and staff via text message, email, and/or phone call in the event of a crisis; provides details and further instructions; coordinates teacher reports of child safety
   Name and contact information: _Jean Marie Dill, teacher_
5. *Media contact*: Supplies all administratively vetted information to print, radio, and television media; coordinates media requests for interviews; trains staff in rules regarding communication with the media and protection of children and families from exploitation
   Name and contact information: _Patrice Lopez, principal_
6. *Medical coordinator*: Organizes first aid efforts and contacts emergency personnel as needed; plans for special health needs of children and staff during the crisis
   Name and contact information: _Robin Jenkins, school nurse_
7. *Building safety and security coordinator*: Monitors security measures and requests any necessary repairs or additions; plans emergency drills and evaluates their effectiveness; plans and posts evacuation routes and procedures for specific disaster or emergency situations; trains teachers and staff to recognize security alert signals; assesses reports of security threats and contacts emergency responders; directs emergency responders upon their arrival
   Name and contact information: _Patrice Lopez, principal_
8. *Counseling and bereavement coordinator*: Contacts community resources for counseling teachers, other staff, parents, and children after an event; arranges privacy for these contacts; plans support and remembrance activities for future anniversaries of the event
   Name and contact information: _Janice Nobel, school guidance counselor_

Figure 3.1. Center Safety Plan.

(continued)

Figure 3.1. *(continued)*

Center Safety Plan *(continued)*

• Identify community resources.	1. Medical: *Count General Medical Center*
	2. Counseling: *Ms. Nobel has list of names*
	3. Social services: *Ms. Nobel has list of names*
	4. Substitute teachers/staff: *Ms. Lopez has the current list*

Building safety

Building Safety Steps

• Plan and provide training for building safety.

1. Familiarize all teachers, staff, and parents with the center safety equipment and guidelines for its use.
2. Train teachers and staff to follow specific action scripts for different disaster scenarios.
3. Train administrators, teachers, and staff concerning the use of materials in the classroom emergency box. Inform all staff about the location of emergency utility shut-offs.

• Contract for installation of security measures, and develop policies.

1. Develop a system for monitored entry, check-in, and identification of visitors to the center.
2. Lock all other doors to the building.
3. Make sure that the hallways, classroom exits, and other public areas are well-lighted and free of obstructions.

• Identify evacuation procedures and safe shelter areas; write action scripts (specify steps for individual teachers and team roles).

1. Fire
2. Tornado
3. Hurricane/flood
4. Earthquake
5. Toxic chemical release
6. Accident/explosion
7. Armed/dangerous intruder

Communication

Communication Steps

• Develop guidelines and templates for parent contacts.

1. Communicate in an accurate and timely manner during and immediately after the event.
2. Develop templates for informational letters and agendas for parent debriefing conferences prior to a need for their use.
3. Direct parents to community resources for lingering physical and emotional problems.

• Contact and secure necessary community resources.

1. Invite selected community responders to tour the child care center prior to an emergency situation.
2. Allow community responders, as appropriate, to introduce themselves to the children and explain their roles.

• Develop guidelines for discussing situations with the media.

1. Store media guidelines in an easily accessible place.
2. Make arrangements for another media person to fill in when the person filling the role of Media Contact is unavailable.

Direct child instruction

Child Instruction Steps

• Develop and conduct disaster and/or emergency drills.

1. Conduct disaster and/or emergency drills frequently, and give instructions in developmentally appropriate language.
2. Create action scripts that contain teacher language that is calming and reassuring to the children while encouraging unquestioning compliance with teacher directions that will keep the children safe.

Separation Anxiety

Children differ markedly in their reactions to daily, temporary separations from their primary caregivers. Some children's social interactions are marked by shyness, hesitancy to enter ongoing play, and difficulty adjusting to new and unfamiliar settings. These children may have significant difficulty overcoming their fears of interacting with strange adults, visiting in the homes of friends, or entering new classroom environments; and they may take a long time to become comfortable separating from their caregivers (Presley & Martin, 1994). In fact, many of these consistently fearful children may experience extreme physiological responses to such seemingly low-threat situations, reacting with rapid heart rates and high levels of stress hormones (Talge, Donzella, & Gunnar, 2008).

Many fearful children literally freeze, and it may be difficult to read their emotional reactions to classroom situations (Presley & Martin, 1994). Their reactions to novel play activities or social overtures from children and adults may be painfully slow and tentative, and they may rarely express enthusiasm or interest.

Xu (2006) categorized toddler reactions to parental separation as *active, aggressive,* or *quiet.* In this study, *active* children had parents who stayed in the classroom for a brief period of time after drop-off. They talked and played with their children and exchanged a few words with the teacher before separating. Their children, in turn, became more quickly engaged with peers, running around the room, laughing, and talking with their peers. *Quiet* children, on the other hand, had parents who were less socially interactive. These parents left quickly without speaking with teachers or other parents. These children withdrew socially after their caregivers left, sitting or walking around the room and watching their peers at play. *Aggressive* children reacted to the separation with emotional outbursts.

Separation Anxiety Assessment

This tool helps teachers document specific parent, teacher, and child words and actions during the separation process. The Separation Anxiety Assessment, Figure 3.2, asks teachers to record detailed information in an effort to identify areas for strategy development. In this example, we capture a snapshot of the teacher, parent, and child interactions that define Kamiea's difficulties with separation. Strategies might be developed to target either the parent's or teacher's words or actions in order to prevent or respond more effectively to Kamiea's ensuing emotional outburst.

Purpose of This Tool	The purpose of the Separation Anxiety Assessment is to identify child and parent behaviors that exacerbate separation anxiety. Teachers next prioritize these behaviors by frequency, duration, and severity; and specific parent and child behaviors become important intervention targets.
When to Use This Tool	This tool can be used by teachers and administrators to problem-solve situations when separation anxiety continues to disrupt child play and learning for far longer than would be anticipated

Separation Anxiety Assessment

Directions: Describe the child's, parent's, and your behaviors during the process of dropping the child off at the facility. Use numerals to separate and organize discrete classroom events.

Name of child: _Kamiea Nelson_

Name and role of observer: _Matt Brown,_
Assistant Teacher

Date, time, and length of observation:
_10/1/09_

Assessment of separation anxiety	Evidence (use numerals to organize events)
• Description of parent's behaviors during morning drop-off routine (e.g., sequence of events, duration of parent visit, specific words and/or actions, expressed interest and/or involvement in center materials or play activities, emotional display)	1. Walks with Kamiea into classroom. 2. Helps K. to hang coat. 3. Around room talking about materials on shelf. 4. Hesitates when K. begins to cry. 5. Sits in chair beside K. 6. Gets up and walks toward door. 7. Looks toward teacher with apologetic expression as K. begins to protest. 8. Quickly leaves classroom and building.
• Greeting behavior (e.g., teacher to child, teacher to parent)	1. Says to parent, "Good morning." Watches from side of room. 2. Says, "Kamiea, Brianna is here."
• Child's behavior upon arrival (e.g., greeting to teacher or peer, participation in scheduled activities and/or routines, emotional display)	1. Walks slowly, holding mom's hand. 2. Pulls back toward the door. 3. Looks at teacher. Looks at B.
• Child's response to parental leave-taking (e.g., protest [verbal and/or motor] behaviors, interactions with teachers and/or staff, interactions with peers, entry into play activities) as well as reported differences when dropped off by other caregivers	1. Cries loudly. 2. Pulls mom's hand. Lies on floor. 3. Says, "Mama, Mama."
• Specific incidents of aggression (e.g., type, frequency, severity, victim)	1. Hits own head. 2. Bites own hand.
• Scheduled activities during drop-off; elapsed time until child was fully engaged	Breakfast beginning. No specific activities. Fifteen minutes until engagement with teacher
• Preferred activities: classroom activities that sustain child interest and participation	Book reading, dramatic play.
• Other potentially contributing factors	1. Mom brought K. very early today 2. K. seems tired, has runny nose

Figure 3.2. Separation Anxiety Assessment.

by 1) the child's chronological age, and 2) the amount of time spent in the classroom setting.

How to Use This Tool

The Separation Anxiety Assessment provides opportunities for an observer to specify the details of the problematic separation. Prompts guide the teacher or outside observer to describe both the parent's and child's words and actions upon entry and during separation. Observers are asked to record the teacher's greeting and the scheduled activity. There is also a place to record the child's preferences and typical play behaviors when engaged in this activity. The tool can be used to assess variability that may occur during separation from different caregivers.

Suggestions for Interpreting Information from the Separation Anxiety Assessment

The observer should record, in as specific detail as possible, the words and actions of the parent, teacher, and child. The observer can assess whether the planned classroom activities are interesting and accessible for the child. Triggers for specific separation behaviors can be examined (e.g., the identity of caregiver dropping off the child, the number and identity of peers already in the room, the consistency of drop-off times, and the predictability of the daily schedule). Home-related factors (e.g., insufficient sleep, sickness, move, new baby, family member with an illness) also can be examined and noted as potential contributing factors.

Scaffolding Children with Separation Anxiety

Children with separation anxiety may need close teacher proximity throughout the classroom day, necessitating an investment of increased amounts of individual teacher time. They will not become quickly engaged in novel or unfamiliar activities and will need patient teacher encouragement to become engaged in play (Presley & Martin, 1994).

The following list includes strategies for intervening with children with separation anxiety:

1. Specific parent behaviors (words/actions) can ease or disrupt the child's transition to the classroom. Particularly when a child senses that his or her caregiver is anxious or sad about the time that the child spends away from him or her, the child may react in a similar manner. Parents should be encouraged to speak positively about the interest level and variety of play activities that the child may select and scaffold the child's play entry. Words such as, "It looks like you're having a really good time with your friend in the sensory table; I'll see you when you go to the playground this afternoon" help make the separation a predictable and comfortable part of the child's day.

2. Parents who are ill or working long hours may have unpredictable schedules, spending less total time alone with the child. This inconsistency may aggravate fears of abandonment during the child's time at school.

3. Teacher behaviors also can impact the ease with which the child separates from the caregiver. If the teacher spends enjoyable time with the child during other parts of the day, the child may learn to trust and value time with the teacher. As the child perceives school as an environment filled with loving and attentive adults, the separation anxiety may ease.

4. Scheduled activities and materials can be carefully selected to incorporate the child's preferences. This may entice the child to become engaged more quickly than when nonpreferred or neutral activities begin the day.

Naptime Concerns

Naptime is often a difficult time of the daily schedule for children who experience problems with emotional self-regulation. These children have a tough time self-soothing during the transition toward sleep. This is the most important time of the day to incorporate consistent, familiar routines. Teachers can interview parents to identify conditions that are effective in easing the child into sleep.

Children vary widely in their reactions to caregiver strategies such as 1) transition music or stories, 2) on-the-cot quiet activities such as play with books or stuffed toys, 3) cot arrangement, 4) room lighting, 5) security objects from home, and 6) caregiver backrubs or singing (Phillips, Hensler, Diesel, & Cefalo, 2004). Some children slip into the routine with ease, falling asleep within minutes regardless of the noise and activity around them. Others require structured naptime routines that are rigid and unvarying. These children react with sleeplessness when a staff person is absent or other children demand teacher attention. These same children may benefit from the longest naps and, consequently, react with irritability and tears when they cannot get to sleep.

The most effective approach to problem-solving naptime behaviors may be to use a direct observational tool known as an *A-B-C event recording* (as described in Knoster & McCurdy, 2005). The *A* stands for *antecedent* variables, or trigger events that precede the behavior(s) of interest and may be related to its occurrence. The *B* stands for the *behavior(s)* exhibited by the child in this problem situation, and the *C* stands for the *consequences* in the immediate context that may be maintaining the behavior(s).

Trigger events for disruptive and noncompliant naptime behaviors (e.g., getting off cot; bothering other children; talking loudly; crying, kicking, or trying to hit caregiver) may logically include such factors as 1) stimulating activities prior to naptime (e.g., outside play, active free play), 2) disruptive behaviors of other peers, 3) inability to dim the room, 4) overcrowding of cots, 5) absence of usual caregiver, or 6) failure to bring naptime security object. All or none of these factors may predispose the child toward disruptive naptime behaviors.

Conversely, the consequences that the child is exposed to *after* he or she begins to act out during naptime may be maintaining the challenging behaviors. Possible consequences include 1) peer attention, 2) 1:1 teacher attention, and 3) escape to a room with activities for older nonsleepers. By identifying antecedents and consequences that promote and/or reward compliance with the naptime routines, these children may successfully nap.

Naptime Behaviors Assessment

Directions: This assessment lists suggestions for specific behaviors, triggers, and consequences that have been connected with preschool behavior. Circle all that apply and specify others as indicated.

Antecedent or trigger events (circle all that apply)	Specific naptime behaviors with frequency of occurrence (2 = all of the time, 1 = some of the time, 0 = none of the time)	Consequences or maintaining events (circle all that apply)
Parent reported change in home routine (specify) (circled) *Father out of town; mother arrives late in the morning*	Crying on cot 2 1 (0)	Parents are called to pick up the child
Parent and/or teacher observed difference in child's demeanor and/or health (specify) *Tired, easily frustrated*	Talking loudly (2) 1 0	(circled) Caregiver comforts the child until he or she falls asleep
Change in classroom schedule or planned activities (specify) *None*	Noncompliant to routine (specify) (2) 1 0 *Refuses to lie down for nap*	Caregiver provides verbal reprimand
Activity preceding nap was stimulating (specify) *No*	Restless 2 (1) 0	Peers provide attention to child
Preferred naptime caregiver is absent	Playing loudly on cot (2) 1 0	(circled) Caregivers provide a succession of toys or quiet activities to the child on his or her cot
Preferred peer is absent	Leaving cot (2) 1 0	Caregivers allow child to roam around the room during naptime
Room is brightly lit, crowded, or noisy	Bothering other children (specify) (2) 1 0 *Kicks shelf*	Caregiver places child in time out in another room
Temperature of room has changed (specify)	Whining 2 (1) 0	Caregiver ignores noncompliant behaviors if quiet
Security object is missing (specify)	Engaging in tantrum behaviors (specify) (2) 1 0	Caregiver changes placement of child's cot
		Caregiver allows child to stay up, playing in another room
		Other (specify) _____

Figure 3.3. Naptime Behaviors Assessment.

Naptime Behaviors Assessment

The Naptime Behaviors Assessment (Figure 3.3) can be used by teachers, individually or in collaboration with other caregivers, to identify specific behaviors that occur during the naptime routine. The teacher should describe the naptime problem in terms of trigger events (antecedents) for the child's noncompliance and consequences (maintaining events) provided by peers or caregivers. There are prompts to identify changes that may have occurred in the classroom or home environments and may be contributing to the problem.

Purpose of This Tool	The purpose of this tool is to assess the factors that trigger disruptive and noncompliant behaviors during the naptime period.
When to Use This Tool	The Naptime Behaviors Assessment can be used by teachers or other staff to problem-solve an effective plan for intervention. Individual team members should use this assessment tool to hypothesize triggers and/or maintaining variables and verify these with subsequent observations.
How to Use This Tool	This tool can be used to 1) specify the problem behaviors associated with naptime, 2) identify risk factors, 3) address short- and long-term goals, and 4) plan intervention strategies. The tool can be completed alone or in collaboration with teachers or parents. This tool lists suggestions for specific behaviors, triggers, and consequences that have been connected with preschool behavior.

Strategies for Supporting Naptime Behaviors Tool

This tool can be used by teachers to plan changes in the naptime routine based on information from the Naptime Behaviors Assessment (Figure 3.3). The Strategies for Supporting Naptime Behaviors Tool (Figure 3.4) asks caregivers to prioritize specific antecedents and consequences for strategy development. As is illustrated in Figure 3.4, changes may be requested in the home environment as well.

Purpose of This Tool	The purpose of this tool is to translate the results of the Naptime Behaviors Assessment into a specific plan to reduce disruptive behaviors during naptime.
When to Use This Tool	The Strategies for Supporting Naptime Behaviors Tool can be used by teachers or other staff members to structure an effective plan for intervention. Individual team members should complete this tool after completing the Naptime Behaviors Assessment. Prior to de-

Strategies for Supporting Naptime Behaviors Tool

Directions: This tool can be used to 1) identify changes in antecedents and/or responses to antecedents (e.g., changes in the physical arrangement of the nap room or activities immediately preceding the transition), 2) prioritize problem behaviors for intervention (e.g., leaving the cot), 3) specify acceptable alternative behaviors (e.g., quietly remaining on the cot for 15 minutes), and 4) identify changes in consequences/responses to consequences (e.g., allowing the child to play with tabletop activities after resting for the specified time). The tool can be completed alone or in collaboration with teachers or parents.

Antecedent or trigger events			Specific naptime behaviors		Consequences or maintaining events		
Specific antecedent	Strategy	Person responsible	Problem behavior	Alternative behavior	Specific consequence	Strategy	Person responsible
1. Arrives late in the morning	Bring before 10:00 A.M.	Karen (mother) Fred (father)	Runs around room to be chased Talks to S.F. Kicks shelf	Lies on cot	No attention	Give positive attention for going near cot	Carolyn
2.							
3.							
4.							
5.							
Comments:							

Figure 3.4. Strategies for Supporting Naptime Behaviors Tool.

velopment of the plan, the teacher should conduct observations to further specify the hypothesized antecedents, behaviors, and consequences.

How to Use This Tool

This tool can be used to 1) identify changes in antecedents and/or responses to antecedents (e.g., changes in the physical arrangement of the nap room or activities immediately preceding the transition), 2) prioritize problem behaviors for intervention (e.g., leaving the cot), 3) specify acceptable alternative behaviors (e.g., quietly remaining on the cot for 15 minutes), and 4) identify changes in consequences/responses to consequences (e.g., allowing the child to play with tabletop activities after resting for the specified time). The tool can be completed alone or in collaboration with other caregivers or parents.

Suggestions for Interpreting Information from the Naptime Assessment and Intervention Tools

1. These tools can be used to identify important antecedents and consequences that may be triggering and maintaining the disruptive naptime behaviors.

2. It is important for team members to come to a consensus on acceptable alternative behaviors and intervention strategies (i.e., changes in antecedents and consequences). Implementation of any changes should be consistent across caregivers.

3. Careful data collection is key to the success of any intervention plan. Figure 3.4 identifies individuals responsible for implementing the specific strategies and provides a comments section for implementation suggestions. Strategies for data collection and progress monitoring are discussed in Chapter 11.

Conclusion

Child care centers may be located in neighborhoods that present safety challenges. These challenges can be addressed with specific plans to ensure that the early childhood center is a safe haven for the child. Children respond to these uncertainties with anxiety and fear. Entry into the classroom and naptime are two specific routines during which these anxieties may emerge. This chapter discussed methods for assessing separation anxiety and naptime concerns and suggested intervention strategies for individual children.

Environmental Contexts

Classrooms for young children contain a confluence of interrelated systems and processes. Some of these systems and processes are designed with great care and effort. Others seem to spontaneously develop without much thought or planning. Whether these systems are planned or unplanned, they influence the behavior of children and teachers.

Most children adapt to classrooms with little or no difficulty; however, some children require more supports to understand and respond appropriately to the environment and expectations. For these children, the teacher must fully understand the impact of the environment on individual children and make modifications to support the children.

As stated in the introduction of this book, classrooms function much like natural ecologies. A change in one element of the classroom can mean changes in another. A change in behavior for one child can lead to changes for another child. Think of a situation in which teachers design a transition activity for children as they move from clean-up inside to outside play. Perhaps teachers decide to provide opportunities for children to read books while they wait for other children and adults. This may precipitate a change in the layout of the classroom (larger book area) and a change in the number and types of books.

The elements of classroom environments have been categorized into two types—*fixed* and *dynamic* (Barnett, Bell, & Carey, 1999). *Fixed* classroom factors refer to elements of the classroom that are relatively stable and under the control of the teacher. They include the room arrangement, classroom rules, materials on the shelves, and routines. *Dynamic* classroom factors are made up of teacher behaviors that interact with those of children. These factors include the type and level of learning experiences provided, methods for management of transitions, and the strategies for grouping children. Behavior is influenced by both of these types of classroom factors.

Section II provides guidance for teachers in planning and developing both fixed and dynamic classroom elements. Chapter 4 provides guidance for evaluating room arrangement, space, and materials. Chapter 5 presents ways to think about the curriculum for the group and for the individual. Chapter 6 details strategies to evaluate and plan schedules, routines, and transitions. Each chapter provides tools for observing and altering elements of the classroom ecology to support the group and the individual.

Designing the
Physical Classroom Space

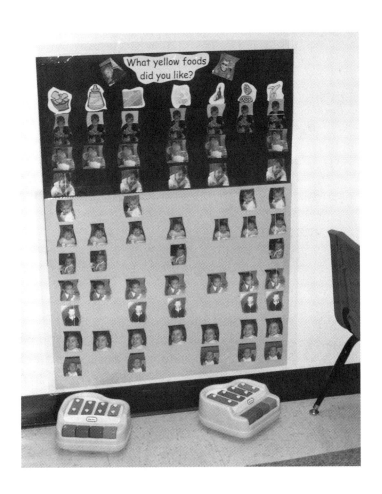

Early education environments are made up of interdependent elements. The design of these elements has a direct impact on the behavior of children. Often, teachers do not notice the ways that children use the classroom and materials until something goes wrong. However, the tempo of the movement of children, the use of materials and space, and the ways children engage with planned experiences are to a large degree a direct result of the work teachers do to understand the individual needs of children in the classroom.

Teachers can influence the quality of behavior in classrooms through careful planning and design of the environment. To do this, teachers need information to make decisions. This chapter provides guidance for classroom design and tools for collecting information about the impact of the classroom environment on children.

Basic Guidelines

Young children are active learners. They should be expected to use their bodies to explore materials. They run, roll, taste, shake, smell, and talk to learn about the world around them. Because of this, the equipment, materials, and layout of the room must be carefully planned to guide the intended use and expected behavior in the classroom. Planning an environment that allows children to use their bodies and natural social inclinations can prevent many problems.

All children need guidance for appropriate behavior at some time. But, sometimes a lack of planning and implementation can exacerbate challenges that children experience. For example, when materials are placed haphazardly on shelves, children may not be able to infer a use for the materials. Or, they may not perceive a pattern that guides cleanup. This could result in materials being used differently than intended and challenges with cleanup.

Small changes in the furniture and materials in the classroom can make huge differences in the behavior of children. Teachers must be careful observers to know which elements of the environment may add to a child's difficulties. Teachers must use knowledge of early learning and the individual children in their classrooms to design environments that prevent problems. The tools that follow in this chapter are designed to be used whenever a change in the environment is anticipated.

Classroom Setup

Setting up the right classroom environment can support the role of teachers by supporting appropriate behavior of children. Clear ground rules and limits can be reinforced by the layout of materials and equipment. When the classroom is set up to meet the needs of the children in the room, teachers can move from group to group supporting learning rather than policing the classroom to set limits.

The surveys, time samples, and checklists in this section are designed to guide teachers in the design and setup of their classrooms. Each tool uses a different method for collecting information for teachers to analyze. These observation and discussion tools can be used to prevent some typical, inappropriate behavior in the classroom. In addition, they can be used to diagnose whether the classroom design contributes to challenges.

General Survey of Classroom Elements

It is sometimes helpful to step back to observe and reflect upon the basic elements of the classroom environment. This is especially true when challenging situations arise. Evaluating the basics of your classroom design, using the General Survey of Classroom Elements tool (Figure 4.1) can help to prevent frustrating experiences.

Purpose of This Tool	The purpose of this questionnaire is to stimulate thought about elements of the classroom known to affect behavior. This tool can be used as a discussion starter for teaching teams, as a tool when observing other classrooms to gain insight.
When to Use This Tool	This tool can be completed whether children are present or absent at the time of observation.
How to Use This Tool	Figure 4.1 lists questions to guide thinking regarding room design and setup. Answer each of the questions in the space provided. Use information obtained from actual observation for your answers. Use the column on the right to write down any comments you may have about your observations.
Suggestions for Framing Your Analysis	

1. *How big, in square feet, is the largest space in the classroom?* There is no right or wrong answer to this question. Understanding the size of the space helps to think about the intended use for the space. Is this too big for the learning intended? Is it too small? Would children be inclined to wrestle or chase one another? It may be helpful to compare the size with other classrooms.

2. *What is the largest number of children who play in one area?* In general, the larger the number of children who play together in one space, the more social skills needed to maintain play. In addition, the less time teachers spend setting limits about the number of children in a space, the more time they can spend on teaching social skills. Deciding the number of children allowed in an area depends on the children in the group. Think about the children's strengths and learning needs to establish goals, then design experiences. The established limits should be determined by the individual skills of children, the goals, and the intended experiences.

3. *How do children know the limits of the classroom?* All teaching teams should establish ground rules. They should be brief, few in number, and consistently enforced. Deciding how limits will be communicated depends on the children in the group. Some

General Survey of Classroom Elements

Directions: The following is a list of questions to guide thinking regarding room design and setup. Answer each of the questions in the space provided. Use information obtained from actual observation for your answers. Use the column on the right to write down any comments you may have about your observations.

Classroom name: *Eagles*

Name and role: *Sharon Winters, classroom teacher*

Questions for reflection	Response	Comments/analysis
1. How big is the largest space in the classroom (square feet)?	*30 sq. ft*	*Seems small for group; need more space*
2. What is the largest number of children who play in one area?	*4*	
3. How do children know the limits of the classroom?	*I tell children*	*Need a way to remind them*
4. Are there many spaces for children to play in small groups? Is there at least one space for children to play alone?	*6, yes*	*When everyone is here, it seems crowded*
5. How do children know where materials belong?	*Labels—written and pictures*	
6. Are there low, moderate, or high levels of visual stimulation? Auditory stimulation?	*High*	*Very noisy from 10:00–11:00*
7. Which children need the proximity of an adult or supportive peer to be successful socially?	*Jason Caren Sophie*	*Difficult with only two teachers*
8. Are quiet and active areas clearly defined and separated?	*Block building becomes noisy; near books*	
9. Is it easy to see where children are expected to walk when moving from one area to another?	*Some areas*	*Children bump into block construction. Need more thinking about traffic here.*
10. Are chairs, tables, and shelves child-sized so that children can access materials independently?	*Yes*	

Figure 4.1. General Survey of Classroom Elements.

children need concrete reminders such as bracelets or numbers of chairs for sitting around a table. Think about the individual children in the room and design both the ground rules and communication around their needs for support.

4. *Are there many spaces for children to play in small groups? Is there at least one space for children to play alone?* Children learn many social skills by playing in small groups. Teachers can take advantage of opportunities for scaffolding learning by designing the space to accommodate positive social experiences. When conflicts arise, they often can be traced back to a mismatch between the design of the space and amount and types of uses children find for the space. Providing many opportunities for working in small groups allows children to better match play with the environment. In addition, teachers are better able to move from group to group while scaffolding experiences. Teachers can call attention to peers who model positive social interaction and can help children extend play by verbalizing feelings when children do not. It is also helpful for teachers to model problem-solving skills.

5. *How do children know where materials belong?* Cleanup time often results in conflicts between teachers and children. When cleanup seems overwhelming to children, they may resist. Classrooms with materials underfoot can create a chaotic feel and increase the tempo and stimulation level. When materials are placed on shelves in an orderly way, children learn respect for them. Providing concrete indicators (e.g., pictures on shelves) of where things belong helps make the task less difficult.

6. *Are there low, moderate, or high levels of visual or auditory stimulation?* Children have differing abilities for tolerating sensory stimulation. Some children have a low threshold for differences in intensity or patterns of things they see, touch, smell, or hear. Children may react when they try to get increased or decreased levels of sensory stimulation. Understanding the child's behavior is aided by an understanding of the sensory levels in the classroom.

7. *Which children need the proximity of an adult or supportive peer to be successful socially?* Sometimes, all it takes to support positive social interactions is for a teacher to move closer to a student. Teachers facilitate positive interactions by working with team members to move near children who may need them. Providing just enough support for children to develop skills of their own is essential. In addition, teachers can facilitate learning by grouping children with peers who naturally support their prosocial learning.

8. *Are quiet and active areas clearly defined and separated?* Children are more likely to behave in intended ways if they can see concrete area delineations. Children can then monitor their

own tempos by moving to areas that meet their needs. For example, children who need less stimulation can move to a book area. Children who need more stimulation can move to a block building area.

9. *Is it easy to see where children are expected to walk when moving from one area to another?* Well planned and established traffic patterns in the classroom can cut down on chaotic movement around the classroom. When children begin to move in ways that disrupt learning, teachers can support calm movement by analyzing traffic patterns. For example, long spaces can encourage running. Low shelves at the end of a pathway can encourage jumping. Observe traffic patterns and make adjustments as needed.

10. *Are chairs, tables, and shelves child sized so that children can gain access to materials independently?* When children enter classrooms, they become members of a learning community. Many expectations are new to them. Children may need support for learning the expectations; however, once learned, the classroom runs more smoothly. Teachers do not need to be the intermediary between children and classroom materials and equipment. When classrooms are organized well, teachers can function in their primary role—facilitating experiences that extend learning.

Child Groupings

The arrangement of the classroom and the guidelines for use of space can determine how children play and work together. As children move through the environment, they will gravitate toward particular groups based on their interests, their history with materials, and the friendships that they have developed. Disputes over property, space, and attention from peers and adults can arise when the use of space is not considered. For this reason, it is important to plan for the size and types of groupings that children will form.

Teachers may wish to encourage certain types and sizes of groupings of children. This is especially true when designing learning experiences or behavioral supports. Children use different social skills when working alone, working in a small group, or working in a large group. Skills such as turn taking, sharing, and waiting are developed in groups. Depending on their level of skill development, some children find working in large groups more challenging than working in smaller groups. It is important for teachers to understand the skills of children in their classroom and plan supports so that they can adapt to the changing nature of this important classroom element.

Once teachers know the types and pattern of the groups forming in their classrooms, they can plan supports for children. Teachers do this by thinking about the current use of the environment, the skills of children in the group, and the adaptations that can be made. Children can be grouped to interact with helpful peers. Spaces where large groups congregate or engage in unacceptable behavior can be rearranged. Symbols can be placed in learning spaces to communicate the limit for the number of children in the space.

Time Sample of Types of Groups in the Classroom

This tool (Figure 4.2) assists teachers in gathering data on the types of groupings that exist in the classroom. Once teachers collect this data, they can use the information to support positive learning.

Purpose of This Tool	The purpose of the time sample is to provide information about the time children spend in various types of groups. This tool also may help teachers gauge the number of children engaging in different types of activities.
When to Use This Tool	This tool is helpful for understanding one element of the social context of the behavior of children in groups. The types of groups in which children participate influence the amount of social learning. Use this tool to gauge the proportion of time children spend in different types of groups.
How to Use This Tool	Count the number of children engaged in each type of experience during the time indicated. Record the number in the appropriate box.

Suggestions for Reflecting on Your Observations

1. *Whole group*: Whole-group experiences can be difficult for some children. It is important to have clear goals when these experiences are designed. The types of social skills children learn in whole groups are limited. They may learn turn taking and joint attention. However, some children need extra supports to be successful in whole groups. Whole-group experiences should be a small portion of the overall types of activities in the classroom. They should be timed to the skills and needs of the children in the group. Extra supports such as teacher proximity and delineated spaces for sitting must be provided for children who need them. If whole groups are planned, the space must be designed so that children can sit comfortably and attend.

2. *Small group*: Designing experiences for groups of three to four children provides teachers with many opportunities for individualizing learning. Teachers should intentionally plan the experiences around goals for individual children. When small-group experiences are designed well, children can support each other's learning. In addition, small-group formats allow teachers more focused time to observe and support children's

Time Sample of Types of Groups in the Classroom

Directions: Count the number of children engaged in each type of experience during the time indicated. Record the number in the appropriate box.

Classroom name: _K-2_

Completed by: _Tyler A._   Date: _4/14/10_

Time	Whole group	Small group (adult facilitated)	Small group (child facilitated)	Solo play
9:00		2	9	1
9:15		2	8	2
9:30		0	13	4
9:45		0	13	4
10:00	16			1
10:15	16			1
10:30	16			1
10:45		1	14	2
11:00		2	10	5
11:15		2	10	5
11:30		1	14	2
11:45		2	12	3
12:00		17 (lunch)		
12:15		17		
12:30		17		
12:45		10		7

Figure 4.2.   Time Sample of Types of Groups in the Classroom.

development of skills and knowledge. Teachers should design many areas in the classroom to encourage small-group play.

3. *Free play*: Free play should be a major part of the young child's classroom experiences. Children develop many skills when they are provided ample time to move to areas of interest in small, self-selected groups. Teachers then must work as a team to provide the supports children need. These supports may vary from staying in close proximity to one child, to helping another child verbalize feelings, to providing a third child with prompts to help him or her solve problems with peers. Teachers must be accessible by moving about and working with one another in the classroom. Teachers should provide opportunities for children to select materials independently and move to areas that interest them.

4. *Routine tasks*: Caring for young children requires the implementation of many routine tasks. Just like at home, children eat, brush their teeth, and need help with toileting. Sometimes, teachers get caught up in implementing the task and forget the opportunities that exist for learning. To minimize the role of the teacher in the management of routine tasks, the environment should be designed so that children can work to independently meet their needs.

5. *Transitions*: Transitions in the classroom have been identified as a particularly significant time for children to exhibit challenging behavior. Chapter 5 addresses transitions in depth. When thinking about transitions, however, it is important to plan the space where transitions will take place. If children are required to wait during a transition, finding a space where children can easily be occupied is helpful. For example, asking children to meet in the book area for a transition would provide opportunities for book reading while children wait.

Ground Rules

Children need to understand the rules of the classroom in order to follow them. Teachers may have expectations for behavior that seem clear to them but may not seem clear to others in the room. Further, teachers within the same classroom may differ in their expectations. It is very important that teachers communicate clearly and often with each other and the children.

One way that teachers can make the rules of the classroom clear is to set ground rules. In this case, ground rules represent the rules that everyone in the classroom, teachers and children alike, are expected to follow. They should 1) be few in number, 2) represent those behaviors that are generally agreed on by all adults in the classroom, 3) be positively stated, and 4) be explicit. Examples include the following:

- Children and teachers walk in the classroom.
- Teachers and parents open the doors.
- Children walk with a teacher in the hall.
- Children use words when they need help.

Every child and teacher in the classroom should know and be able to talk about the ground rules. Some teachers may ask the students to help them compose the ground rules and create charts as visual cues. It is extremely important that all teachers follow through when ground rules are ignored. The tool below will help teachers in discussing ground rules.

Ground Rule Discussion Tool

This tool (Figure 4.3) is helpful in discussing the effectiveness of ground rules.

Purpose of This Tool	The purpose of the Ground Rule Discussion Tool is to help teachers organize their thoughts and reach agreement about the classroom's ground rules.
When to Use This Tool	This tool should be used whenever a new child or adult comes into the group.
How to Use This Tool	Discuss the ground rules with the teaching team. Write each of the ground rules in the space provided. Discuss what you will do so that the rule is clearly communicated. Document these prompts and cues in the middle column on Figure 4.3. Describe the ground rule in detail so that everyone understands it.

Interest and Engagement of Children

The more engaged children are in classroom experiences, the less likely they will exhibit challenging behavior. Teachers design interest areas that they think children will enjoy. Sometimes, however, children do not choose to participate in an activity as intended. When this happens, teachers must analyze what they know about the children and the classroom design. They must observe the environment to determine what the children are doing and use professional judgment to make changes so that children may benefit.

Challenges in the classroom may arise when children do not find particular spaces, furniture arrangements, or materials interesting. When their interest wanes, children may wander aimlessly in the classroom, use materials inappropriately, or create their own variety of interesting activities by chasing one another or wrestling. Each of these types of activities can create concerns for teachers.

Ground Rule Discussion Tool		

Directions: Discuss the ground rules with the teaching team. Write each of the ground rules in the space provided. Discuss what you will do so that the rule is clearly communicated. Document these prompts and cues in the column below. Describe the ground rule in detail so that everyone understands it.

Ground rule stated positively	How do children know? (words, picture clues, group time, incidentally)	Detailed explanation of rule
1. *Children walk in the classroom*	*Pictures of children walking on chart*	*Children do not run in the classroom. Children walk from area to area.*
2. *Adults open the door*	*Picture of adult opening the door on chart*	*Parents can open doors. Teachers do not ask children to open doors. Teachers can open doors.*
3. *Quiet voices in the classroom*	*Picture of child covering ears on chart*	*Children can talk enthusiastically but do not yell. Teachers do not yell across the classroom.*
4. *Take care of people and toys*	*Pictures on chart of child hugging another child and child placing toy on shelf*	*Children touch people and materials gently. Toys are placed on the shelf when finished.*
5.		

Figure 4.3. Ground Rule Discussion Tool.

Children come to classrooms with diverse interests and learning histories. Their understanding of how to use materials and equipment may differ. Children need to be taught how to use classroom materials and expectations for behavior in the classroom. Research has shown that when children are oriented to materials, rules, and expectations early in the year, they are better able to manage their own behavior later (Cameron, Connor, & Morrison, 2005). Once it is clear that children know and understand the rules, teachers also may need to use prompts so that children use materials appropriately. Picture cues and teacher presence may be helpful when children need reminders.

The discussion and observation tools that follow assist teachers in developing environments that are appealing and interesting to children. The tools can be used to set up an environment or to modify an environment that is not working.

Interest-Focused Parent Discussion Tool

This tool (Figure 4.4) contains discussion prompts to help teachers obtain information about the interests of children in their classrooms. Topics of the discussion prompts include family members, favorite activities, friends, and distracters.

Purpose of This Tool	The purpose of this tool is to provide teachers with information about events and topics that are meaningful to the children in their classrooms. Information gathered provides a beginning point for planning engaging environments. This tool also can be used as one source of information for planning curriculum experiences.
When to Use This Tool	Teachers can use this tool when new children come into the room or to gain information when children seem to be wandering or avoiding areas of the classroom.
How to Use This Tool	Use this tool as a discussion starter. The tool should not be read word for word. The discussion can be held in person or on the telephone. Tell the parent that you want to get to know all of the children in your classroom so that you can plan engaging experiences. Use each of the prompts listed to gain information. Questions should be adapted to address specific situations and needs.
Suggestions for Framing Your Analysis	1. Often conflicts develop when children are guided to participate in activities in which they are not interested. They may try to avoid the activity by refusing or by using other inappropriate methods. Understanding children's interests can provide a bridge to make a nonpreferred activity more accepted.
	2. When children resist certain activities, teachers can sometimes avoid offering those activities. However, if the activity is important to the child's development and learning, this avoidance may lead to a downward spiral. Teachers may avoid the activity, and, therefore, children do not develop the skill. In

Interest-Focused Parent Discussion Tool

Directions: Use this tool as a discussion starter. The tool should not be read word for word. The discussion can be held in person or on the telephone. Tell the parent that you want to get to know all of the children in the classroom so that you can plan engaging experiences. Use each of the prompts listed to gain information. Questions should be adapted to address specific situations and needs.

Name of child: *Ian Callaghan*   Name of parent: *Amy Callaghan*

Classroom: *Toddler I*   Date: *5/9/09*

Does your child play with any friends or family members? What are their names? Who does he or she enjoy playing with the most? Tell me a little about the types of things they play.

Ian plays with older sister and cousins. He loves his older cousin Rob. He plays outside once a week.

When your child is alone, what are the types of activities or games he or she plays?

Ian plays with his toys such as cars and trucks in his bedroom. He climbs outside on backyard equipment.

Does he or she have a favorite toy? How does he or she play with that toy? How long does he or she typically play with that toy?

Ian will play with trains for hours. Sometimes it is very difficult to redirect Ian to other activities such as playing with friends.

Tell me about your family. What would you say are your child's favorite things to do with family members?

He really likes to play with Rob. He sees his extended family every Sunday. Ian likes to play outside with his cousins, aunts, and uncles.

Are there any topics in which your child seems particularly interested?

Ian really likes trains. He sometimes seems too interested in them. He also loves his pets—his dog and his cat. Ian likes fish too.

Some children can focus on one or two toys or activities and not use others. Are there any topics or toys that your child uses too much or that make it hard for him or her to focus on other things?

Trains.

Are there any activities that your child particularly dislikes? What do you do when that happens?

Ian does not like to sit for long periods of time. Ian does not like books. I let him run after long periods of sitting.

Is there anything else I should know about your child that will help me plan things that interest him or her?

He is very active. He loves to run and climb. Ian has a difficult time sitting unless he is playing with trains.

Figure 4.4. Interest-Focused Parent Discussion Tool.

turn, children may then continue to avoid the activity because they do not have the skills to feel comfortable participating. Teachers must understand the interests of children in order to have more ideas for designing space, materials, and curriculum that are meaningful.

3. Sometimes children can be so interested in an activity, space, or content area that they have a hard time disengaging. This can result in splintered learning because children do not take full advantage of the designed environment. The design of the environment can help teachers redirect children to spaces and materials that will extend learning.

Time Sample of Classroom Areas Used

Teachers can be proactive in planning supports for social and academic learning by gathering information about how children use the classroom. Figure 4.5, Time Sample of Classroom Areas Used, is a useful tool for collecting such information. Once patterns are identified, teachers can use the environment as a means for scaffolding skills.

Purpose of This Tool	The purpose of this time sample is to give teachers a broad picture of the numbers of children who choose to use areas designed for learning in the classroom.
When to Use This Tool	This observation tool should be used when children seem to engage in conflict as a result of crowding or poor traffic flow. It may also be helpful to understand conflict over materials or inappropriate use of materials.
How to Use This Tool	Write the number of children located in each of the learning areas at each 15-minute point. For example, at 8:30, record the number of children in each of the areas. Count and record the numbers of children again at 8:45. Continue until the information covers the times of day needed.
Suggestions for Reflecting on Your Observations	1. The areas listed in this time sample are examples of areas typically found in early childhood education classrooms. However, classrooms differ in the types of areas included. For example, some classrooms may integrate science, math, literacy, and manipulatives into one area. In order for teachers to understand how children move around the room, the columns on this table should be revised so that they match the areas of the classroom being observed. 2. It is important for teachers to make areas of the classroom inviting. When children move to only one or two areas, they

Time Sample of Classroom Areas Used

Directions: Write the number of children located in each of the learning areas at each 15-minute point. For example, at 8:30, record the number of children in each of the areas. Count and record the numbers of children again at 8:45. Continue until the information covers the times of day needed.

Name of classroom: *Eagles* Date: *9/27/09*

Completed by: *Janice K.*

Time	Art	Book	Sensory table	Dramatic play	Block	Manipu- lation	Writing	Math
8:30		4		3		3		
8:45		4		3		3	2	
9:00		3	3	4		5	1	1
9:15	2	3	2	4		6		
9:30	4		3	3		4	1	
9:45	4		3	4		6		
10:00	3		3	4		5		
10:15	3		3	4		5		2
10:30	3		2	4		5	1	
10:45								
11:00								
11:15								
11:30								
11:45								
12:00	Lunch	Lunch	Lunch	Lunch	Lunch	Lunch	Lunch	Lunch

Figure 4.5. Time Sample of Classroom Areas Used.

are not receiving the comprehensive learning experience intended. Teachers must think about the reasons children do not choose certain areas. They must analyze what they know about the children, the amount of time the experience has been available, and the type of introduction to the space the children have received. Decisions can then be made as to whether the lack of involvement in the area is a result of the amount of time the area has been available, the introduction children have had to the area, or the types of experiences designed within the area.

3. This time sample provides teachers with information regarding the rapidity at which children change from area to area in the classroom. When children move quickly, the traffic flow can create challenges. Teachers must then think about ways to engage children for longer periods of time so that the level of involvement can be deeper and more complex.

4. Because this tool is used to provide a rough gauge of how children use and move about the room, another observation tool may be needed to target specific learning areas and children. This tool can be modified to target one child to help teachers understand how that child uses the classroom as a whole.

Sensory Stimulation

All young children use their senses to learn about the world around them. As children age, they learn to integrate the sensory inputs so that they respond in a way that is congruent with their previous experiences. Children learn to process and integrate sensory stimulation at differing rates. For a variety of reasons, children exhibit differing levels of tolerance for sensory stimulation (Thompson & Rains, 2009).

Some children receive pleasure from a great amount or types of sensory stimulation, and some children try to avoid stimulation. It can be distressing for children to be placed in environments that do not match their tolerances for sensory stimulation. Children who seek high levels of sensory stimulation may react in unacceptable ways in an effort to *receive* more stimulation. And, children with low levels of tolerance for sensory stimulation may respond inappropriately in order to *avoid* sensory stimulation (Miller, Robinson, & Moulton, 2004).

Early childhood classrooms present many different levels and types of sensory stimulation. It is important for teachers to be aware of the sound, light, textures, and smells in the classrooms they design (Dunn, 2001). When teachers design environments with spaces that vary in levels of sensory stimulation, they provide children options for acceptable ways to seek the types and levels they prefer. For example, classrooms should be designed with quiet *and* active spaces. There should be areas with different lighting. There should be opportunities for children to play in large groups or alone. The tools below provide teachers with information about the stimulation levels of their classrooms and information about the preferences of children.

Levels of Sensory Stimulation Scale

In order to understand the impact of sensory stimulation on specific children in the classroom, teachers must look closely. Children may demonstrate difficulties subtly. The Levels of Sensory Stimulation Scale (Figure 4.6) is a useful tool for assessing the level of sensory stimulation in the classroom. In order to understand linkages between behavior and sensory stimulation, teachers should observe, make adjustments to the stimulation level, and observe again.

Purpose of This Tool	This scale has been designed as a tool to make judgments about the level of sensory stimulation in the classroom.
When to Use This Tool	This scale is used when teachers want to understand the levels of sensory stimulation in the classroom. It is the first step to matching the environment with the needs of children.
How to Use This Tool	Use this tool in conjunction with observations of children and the environment. It can be used to rate specific areas of the classroom or overall levels of sensory stimulation.

Suggestions for Framing Your Analysis

1. Judgments about the sensory levels in the environment are colored by teachers' own tolerance for sensory stimulation. It is very important to watch children to understand how they are processing the stimuli. Watch for over- or under-reactions to stimuli, such as avoidance, aggression, spinning, rocking, or emotional distress.

2. Children process sensory stimulation differently, and tolerance for stimulation may change from day to day or even routine to routine. For example, some children may become more distressed with sensory stimulation when they are tired. Knowing individual tolerances helps teachers to plan.

3. Communication with parents provides important information for putting behavior in context. This is true for all knowledge and skill development. Parents have much to share regarding the types of environmental stimulation that occur and coping strategies they use at home.

4. Sometimes children require teachers to scale down the environment. When children are distressed by too much sensory stimulation, it may be helpful for teachers to analyze areas of the room that seem problematic. Decreasing the numbers of materials and modifying visual displays may help children struggling to integrate sensory stimulation.

5. Remember that gross motor play is an important support for children in integrating sensory stimulation. Swinging, sliding, rolling, and running can help. Some children with sensory integration issues may avoid these types of activities. Providing

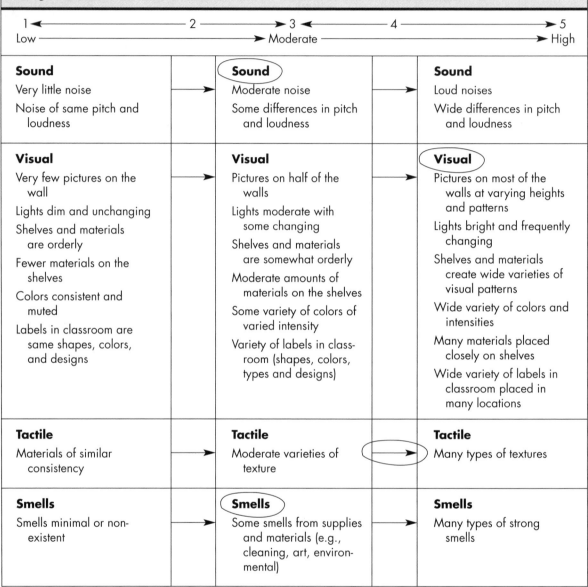

Levels of Sensory Stimulation Scale

Directions: Use this tool in conjunction with observations of children and the environment. It can be used as a rubric to rate specific areas or overall levels of the classroom. Circle items as they apply to the classroom being evaluated.

1 ⟵———————— 2 ———⟶ 3 ⟵———— 4 ————⟶ 5
Low ————————————————⟶ Moderate ————————————————⟶ High

Sound Very little noise Noise of same pitch and loudness	**(Sound)** Moderate noise Some differences in pitch and loudness	**Sound** Loud noises Wide differences in pitch and loudness
Visual Very few pictures on the wall Lights dim and unchanging Shelves and materials are orderly Fewer materials on the shelves Colors consistent and muted Labels in classroom are same shapes, colors, and designs	**Visual** Pictures on half of the walls Lights moderate with some changing Shelves and materials are somewhat orderly Moderate amounts of materials on the shelves Some variety of colors of varied intensity Variety of labels in class-room (shapes, colors, types and designs)	**(Visual)** Pictures on most of the walls at varying heights and patterns Lights bright and frequently changing Shelves and materials create wide varieties of visual patterns Wide variety of colors and intensities Many materials placed closely on shelves Wide variety of labels in classroom placed in many locations
Tactile Materials of similar consistency	**Tactile** Moderate varieties of texture	**Tactile** Many types of textures
Smells Smells minimal or non-existent	**(Smells)** Some smells from supplies and materials (e.g., cleaning, art, environ-mental)	**Smells** Many types of strong smells

Figure 4.6. Levels of Sensory Stimulation Scale.

equipment and materials that allow children to ease into activities may help them.

Brief Event Sample with Stimulation Levels

Evaluating classroom stimulation levels is somewhat subjective. To minimize subjectivity, use the Brief Event Sample with Stimulation Levels (Figure 4.7) while observing focal children.

Purpose of This Tool	This tool has been developed to provide teachers with information about the stimulation levels present during specific challenging events. Teachers can observe individual children to understand the extent to which environmental stimulation is related to the child's behavior.
When to Use This Tool	Use this tool when you suspect that a child may be sensitive to sensory stimulation. The rating scale helps teachers understand whether the challenging events are associated with high or low levels of sensory stimulation.
How to Use This Tool	This tool can be used throughout the day. Write the child's name and the date of the observation on the top. Complete the information each time the child engages in a behavior or a series of behaviors that are challenging to teachers and/or the child's peers. First, note the time of day and the routine of the day (e.g., free play, lunch). Second, record the names of the children near the child. Third, rate the level of stimulation in the area in which the event occurred using the Levels of Sensory Stimulation Scale in Figure 4.6. Finally, describe the incident, including any comments you have about the situation, in the last column.
Suggestions to Frame Your Analysis	1. It may be hard to determine the cause for challenging behavior when many things are going on. It is helpful to sort elements of the circumstances surrounding the behavior. Often all we know is that things tend to happen in certain circumstances. The time, the children nearby, and the stimulation level can be analyzed to determine whether any of these elements tend to occur with the behavior in question. 2. Decisions about interventions should not be made based on one observation. Observing on different days across a couple of weeks provides a more complete picture. 3. Once a picture of elements associated with incidents begins to emerge, teachers can modify one of the elements to see whether the behavior changes. For example, if a picture emerges of an increase in negative behavior during transitions when many

Brief Event Sample with Stimulation Levels

Directions: This tool can be used throughout the day. Write the child's name and the date of the observation on the top. Complete the information each time the child engages in a behavior or a series of behaviors that are challenging to teachers and/or the child's peers. First, note the time of day and the routine of the day (e.g., free play, lunch). Second, record the names of the children near the child. Third, rate the level of stimulation in the area in which the event occurred using the Levels of Sensory Stimulation Scale in Figure 4.6. Finally, describe the incident, including any comments you have about the situation, in the last column.

Child's name: _Molly Sierra_   Date: _1/13/10_

Completed by: _Ms. Kelly_

Time of day and routine	Children near the child	Stimulation level 1–5	Incident
10:02—free play (dramatic play)	Lui Jacob	Visual 4 Sound 5	Molly screams for toy.
10:07—free play (dramatic play)	Lui Jacob	Visual 4 Sound 5	Molly screams for more space.
10:20—free play (dramatic play)	Fiona Macy	Visual 5 Sound 3	Molly screams—takes pencil from Macy.
10:24—free play (art)	Fiona Macy	Visual 5 Sound 3	Molly screams for paper.
10:27—clean up	Jacob Kaylee	Visual 5 Sound 5	Molly pushes Jacob and runs around room.
10:30—clean up	Molly alone	Visual 5 Sound 5	Molly runs around room.
10:35—large group (book reading)	Molly alone	Visual 3 Sound 3	Molly cries and does not want to come to group.

Figure 4.7. Brief Event Sample with Stimulation Levels.

children are around and the sensory stimulation is high, modifying the level of sound, noise, and visual stimulation at that time will provide more complete information about the elements contributing to the behavior.

Conclusion

Children enter early education classrooms with different temperaments, learning approaches, and histories. Their understandings of the expectations in the classroom vary dramatically. How teachers design the classroom can guide children in ways to use the space and materials to further their learning and development. Haphazardly designed environments can add to difficulties children experience as they move about the room and interact. Teachers know the children in the room and should design the environment based on that knowledge. Systematic observation and discussions with families provide the foundation for understanding the needs of children in the class.

CHAPTER 5

Using Responsive Curriculum to Support Behavior

Children are born learning and are highly motivated to do so. They conduct experiments, test theories, observe, and duplicate successful experiences (Stipek, 2002). Because of this, educators should not be the *center* of the child's learning. Rather, they should partner with children and families to design experiences that intentionally provoke children to explore, explain, and play with ideas and content (Hyson, 2008; Stipek & Seal, 2001).

Left to their own devices, children's learning could take many paths. Some of those paths are not always for the best. For example, children in the classroom who are learning play skills may engage in aggressive behavior rather than using more sophisticated social strategies because it is the easiest way to interact. Because learning builds on learning, these early ways of interacting provide direction for later experiences. The longer teachers wait to guide appropriate play and learning strategies, the more possible it is for children to fall further and further behind. Teachers must be proactive in seeking information about children and supporting their interests and needs.

Context for Social and Academic Skills

It is up to teachers to provide the context for long-term success in learning social and academic content and skills. To do this, they must think carefully about the content presented to children and the strategies they use for developing meaningful experiences and relationships (Copple & Bredekamp, 2009). Children need adult guidance and supports to be sure that the learning path they take is helpful to them over the years to come.

Social and academic skills in the classroom are mutually dependent (Ladd, Herald, & Kochel, 2006; McClelland, Morrison, & Holmes, 2000). The experiences teachers design along with the relationships children develop play an essential role in shaping outcomes for children (Burchinal et al., 2008). Because of this, children need opportunities to learn academic and social skills in both the short and long term. Intentionally planned curricula can serve as both prevention and intervention for teaching appropriate responses in the classroom (Pianta & LaParo, 2003).

Classroom conflicts can result when the social or academic expectations for children are different from their skill levels (Lara-Cinisomo, Fuligni, Ritchie, Howes, & Karoly, 2008; Lin, Lawrence, & Gorrell, 2003). Some of the types of conflicts include the following:

- Children may act out in an effort to avoid activities that are too hard for them.

- Children may engage in inappropriate behavior when they are bored.

- Children may use threatening verbal or physical behavior when they lack social skills or language to solve problems.

- Children may have difficulty inhibiting impulses when opportunities to learn to do so are lacking.

The classroom curriculum provides a framework that describes and guides the goals and objectives of experience in the classroom, the processes through which children will learn, the activities caregivers provide, and the context in which experiences will take place. All children deserve the opportunity to learn to very high standards. Teachers as designers and facilitators play an essential role in assuring that what is planned and intended actually takes place.

Curriculum planning begins with core understandings of theories, research, content standards, and evidence-based practices of early development and learning. Often, teachers jump to curriculum planning without learning about the individual children in their classrooms. A better way to design the curriculum is to use planned mechanisms for gathering information about each child before designing experiences.

Using these core understandings, teachers begin the curriculum planning process by getting to know children through conversations with parents, observation, screening, and progress monitoring. Once caregivers have information about children, lesson plans and experiences can be developed that are developmentally and individually appropriate. Only then can the goals and objectives of the classroom be matched to specific understanding and skill levels of individual children and the group as a whole.

A curriculum should be both horizontal and vertical. That is, content for children should be planned to meet the general developmental needs of children across specific age groups. In addition, a curriculum must also meet the needs of individual children as they learn, develop, and grow (Tomlinson & Hyson, 2009). Teachers must ask themselves whether their expectations for the skills and behaviors of children in the classroom are based on what they know about each individual child or on the expectations for a generic age group. Teachers balance the needs of the whole group and needs of individual of children.

In addition to gathering information about individual children, it is important that teachers do not stop at the lesson planning and activity implementation stage. They must reflect on the progress children make to assure that intended experiences are meaningful to children (Hyson, 2008). Plans must be revised once teachers evaluate how children respond. This cycle is repeated as children gain more and more experience and are challenged to engage in higher levels of problem solving. The following tools can be used to gather information about how children respond to the classroom curriculum.

Anecdotal Observation of Activity Tool

Teachers need methods to observe how children use materials and engage socially to solve problems. Figure 5.1 provides a template for recording all information the teachers view as helpful in planning for children. This tool is open ended and can be used to track changes that ocur over time.

Purpose of This Tool	The anecdotal observation form is used to jot notes about observations of children in the classroom. Specific skills, interests, or dispositions can be recorded on the form. Information gathered through anecdotal observation provides a brief description of engagement of children throughout the program year. Progress can be tracked when anecdotes are regularly recorded.

Anecdotal Observation of Activity Tool

Directions:
1. Write the child's name and your name on the form. Be sure to add the date and time the incident occurred. Record the number of children present.
2. Check the location in the classroom where the incident occurred.
3. Check the appropriate focus or content area for the observed incident.
4. Briefly record the observation. Describe behaviors, materials, and children and/or adults involved. Information in this section should be objective and not infer motive or include opinions.
5. Describe your response and judgment about what you saw. Looking at previous recorded observations will provide perspective for this observation. Completing this section may need to be done sometime after the initial observation to allow time to reflect on the incident. Using what you know about the child and family, child development, program expectations, and current research, describe why the observed incident is important to the child.
6. Record your plans based on this observation. Are there curriculum modifications that need to be made? Will you talk with the child's parents? Will you involve the child's peers? Will you continue doing what you are doing?

Child's name: _Shelly Richards_   Date: _8/5/09_   Time: _10:10_

Number of children present: _15_   Observer: _Carol_

Location

_x_ Art	___ Book/reading area	___ Routine (snack, Morning Meeting, group, in line, etc.)
___ Dramatic play	___ Math	
___ Blocks	___ Writing	___ Special
___ Computer	___ Science	___ Music
___ Sensory	___ Gross motor—outside	Other: _____
___ Manipulative	___ Gross motor—inside	_____

Focus

___ Cognition	___ Language arts	Other: _____
_x_ Language	___ Mathematics	_____
___ Social-emotional	_x_ Social studies	
___ Motor/physical	___ Science	

Observation:

Shelly was working with watercolor. She painted brown and orange into a rectangle saying to Lily, "This is where my abuela lives in Mexico. She has a dog."

Observer reflection:

Lily did not understand at first. I prompted Lily to ask Shelly. She explained, "My mama's mama." We then began to talk about Mexico and the ways it was the same as Cincinnati—houses, food, pets. We also talked about differences—language, etc.

Plan:

I will bring in some books about Mexico. We will also talk about families. I will use the Spanish and Korean words for grandmother and grandfather.

Figure 5.1. Anecdotal Observation of Activity Tool.

When to Use This Tool

The anecdotal observation can be completed during the day—in real time—as children are observed. It also can be used after the fact as teachers remember what a child did during the day. Anecdotal records should be completed regularly so that progress can be monitored. One or more recorded anecdotal observations per week allows teachers to see changes in the interests, understandings, and skills of children in the class.

How to Use This Tool

For convenience, place blank copies of the Anecdotal Observation of Activity Tool on clipboards around the classroom. This will ensure that a form is always available when needed.

As children move about the classroom, look for interactions that represent meaningful engagement with peers, materials, ideas, and concepts. This could be new information or something the child has done before but that provides new insight into the child's growth. Complete the following steps:

1. Write the child's name and your name on the form. Be sure to add the date and time the incident occurred. Record the number of children present.

2. Check the location in the classroom where the incident occurred.

3. Check the appropriate focus or content area for the observed incident.

4. Briefly record the observation. Describe behaviors, materials, and children and/or adults involved. Information in this section should be objective and not infer motive or include opinions.

5. Describe your response and judgment about what you saw. Looking at previous recorded observations will provide perspective for this observation. Completing this section may need to be done sometime after the initial observation to allow time to reflect on the incident. Using what you know about the child and family, child development, program expectations, and current research, describe why the observed incident is important to the child.

6. Record your plans based on this observation. Are there curriculum modifications that need to be made? Will you talk with the child's parents? Will you involve the child's peers? Will you continue doing what you are doing?

Suggestions for Using This Tool

1. The amount and types of interactions children have in the classroom are important. Teachers may plan a comprehensive curriculum but if children do not engage in all of the experiences offered, they may get a scaled-down version of the curriculum intended. This could have long term implications for learning.

2. It is important to observe the intensity of engagement and the amount of time children spend in learning experiences. Teach-

ers must make judgments about when to continue learning experiences and when to make changes. Without knowing the level of the child's participation, it is impossible to know what and how much to change.

3. Anecdotal observations are collected over time. Information collected may be reviewed across days, weeks, and even months. It is easy to forget the details of any incident. For this reason, it is important to be as objective and descriptive as possible when recording the actual anecdote. Writing a comment such as *She is happy today* may not provide information for planning new experiences. Detailed information provides the context for understanding learning and development over time.

4. Teachers must use their knowledge and skills to make judgments about the progress children make. These judgments are kept separate from the observations. Judgments should be based on individual characteristics of children and families. In addition, teachers must base judgments on what they know about research and their past classroom experiences. Reflecting on the specifics of the observation helps teachers to summarize their thoughts about the importance of the information described.

5. It does no good to collect information if it is not used. Teachers should use the observation and their reflections to design experiences that will challenge the child to solve problems, learn skills, and develop closer relationships. It may not be possible to develop action steps for each anecdotal observation; however, teachers must always ask themselves why they are collecting this particular anecdote and whether this will help them plan in a way that will benefit the child.

It is important to look for patterns in the curriculum experiences in which children participate. If children avoid particular learning centers or engage in simple unchanging types of interactions with peers and materials, their growth could be limited. Pooling observation information at predetermined points of time aides the analysis of growth and provides a springboard for curriculum planning. The following tool is used to summarize information from anecdotal observations on a monthly basis.

Monthly Summary of Anecdotal Observations

To be sure that teachers reflect on change over time, it is helpful to collapse information about children into meaningful summaries. Figure 5.2 can be used for individual reflection or group reflection. Teachers can then provide support for continuing to provide similar curricular supports or to change the direction.

Monthly Summary of Anecdotal Observations

Directions:
1. After compiling anecdotal observations about a given child for one month, count the number of times an observation has been made in any particular area of the classroom. Record that number in the appropriate section.
2. Count the number of observations in that month for any given type of focus area. Record the number in the appropriate space.
3. Read the observation section of all of the anecdotes for the month. Summarize which learning standards are addressed in the observations. Standards may include program or district standards, state or federal standards, or standards set by accrediting bodies.
4. Read all of the teacher reflections and responses for the observations. Look for patterns of growth in skills, understanding, and dispositions related to learning. Summarize your thoughts in the space provided.
5. Record your action steps based on your reflections.

Child's name: _Shelly Richards_ Month: _August_ Year: _2009_

Completed by: _Carol_

Number of observations for each area of the classroom listed below:

_1_ Art	___ Book/reading area	___ Routine (snack, Morning
_3_ Dramatic play	___ Math	Meeting, group, in line, etc.)
___ Blocks	___ Writing	___ Special
___ Computer	___ Science	___ Music
_1_ Sensory	___ Gross motor—outside	Other: _____
___ Manipulative	_1_ Gross motor—inside	_____

Number of observations for each focus area listed below:

___ Cognition	_1_ Language arts	Other: _____
_3_ Language	_1_ Mathematics	_____
_3_ Social-emotional	_1_ Social studies	
___ Motor/physical	___ Science	

Observed engagement that is aligned with learning standards (please describe):

Talking about other countries—Mexico, Korea
Working independently
Wrote first letter of name, found name for group—found Mary's name
Matched apples for apple tree game—one to one.

Summary of monthly observed progress:

Seemed to have a system for matching—rather than random—started at left and worked to right

Future steps:

Extend culture learning by adding content
Continue matching with counting—maybe make a pet game? She loves dogs.

Figure 5.2. Monthly Summary of Anecdotal Observations.

Purpose of This Tool	The purpose of this tool is to provide an easily read and understood summary of the patterns of a child's involvement in the planned curriculum.
When to Use This Tool	This tool can be used at regular intervals to get a picture of the progress children make.

How to Use This Tool

1. After compiling anecdotal observations about a given child for one month, count the number of times an observation has been made in any particular area of the classroom. Record that number in the appropriate section.

2. Count the number of observations in that month for any given type of focus area. Record the number in the appropriate space.

3. Read the observation section of all of the anecdotes for the month. Summarize which learning standards are addressed in the observations. Standards may include program or district standards, state or federal standards, or standards set by accrediting bodies.

4. Read all of the teacher reflections and responses for the observations. Look for patterns of growth in skills, understanding, and dispositions related to learning. Summarize your thoughts in the space provided.

5. Record your action steps based on your reflections.

Suggestions for Using This Tool

1. Learning and development in early childhood can be sporadic. Children may exhibit skills on one day and not the next. Because of this, it is important to follow a child's progress over time. The monthly summary of anecdotes provides a general description of the opportunities a child has to experience the curriculum. Simple exposure to social situations, learning centers, and materials will provide some level of support. Without knowing what and how the child engaged over the month, teachers have no way of knowing whether the planned curriculum met learning goals.

2. As teachers and children interact, they may unknowingly create ways of approaching certain learning experiences and avoiding other experiences. For this reason, it is important to analyze any learning centers or focus areas that children engage in frequently or infrequently. Reasons for the differences may not be obvious. Once differences are found, it may be necessary to design observations that zero in on the underlying cause for low or high levels of engagement in learning areas (See Figure 1.5 in Chapter 1).

3. It is also important to look for changes in the frequency, duration, or intensity of time spent in specific learning areas. Changes

could take place for many reasons. Children could avoid areas if the content is too easy or too hard. They could be attracted to an area of focus because the teacher has found a theme or concept that is of particular interest. When teachers analyze the patterns of use, they can use what they know to increase the use of all elements of the curriculum, thereby providing a broader foundation for success.

4.   The most important step in the curriculum planning process is turning the information gathered into meaningful experiences for children. Lesson planning cannot become a routine task. Teachers should be able to see the connections between what they have observed about a child's understanding and the experiences planned. When teachers can see that connection, they are better able to help the child make that connection. It may be helpful for teachers to talk about observations with other teachers and supervisors to clarify the link between observations and planned experiences.

Creating Meaningful Experiences

Challenging behaviors can be prevented when children are engaged in meaningful learning experiences (Casey & McWilliam, 2007; McClelland et al., 2007). To become purposefully engaged in the experiences teachers plan, children must be interested in the content and have the skills to access the activities. Natural curiosity, motivation to learn, and interest provide the internal mechanisms for creating sustained attention and interaction (Fantuzzo, Perry, & McDermott, 2004). Skill levels provide the external mechanisms for engagement.

Teachers plan a curriculum and then must observe children using the materials, attending to the content, and interacting with children and adults to make judgments about effectiveness. To do this, teachers observe how children attend, the length of time they persist at an activity, and the types of cognitive and social strategies they use to interact (Hyson, 2008; McWilliam & Kruif, 1998). After observing, teachers must synthesize their observations to better understand the points of engagement for the child.

Levels of engagement are determined by many factors. As mentioned in Chapter 1 and earlier in this chapter, interest and preference play an important role. But, why do children prefer one learning experience over another? Skill levels, personal experiences, habit, and learning history all contribute to patterns of activities children select in the classroom. Teachers must gain a basic understanding of how the children use the curriculum experiences provided. The tool below provides a way for teachers to collect basic information about children's patterns of engagement with specific content areas.

Time Sample of Individual Participation in General Content Areas

Often teachers have a sense of what children do in the classroom, but lack specific information to validate their impressions. Figure 5.3 can be used as a part of a system of data collection so that decisions are made based on facts. Modification of the curriculum content is an important tool for supporting positive behavior.

Purpose of This Tool

The purpose of this tool is to provide teachers with information to analyze patterns of participation for individual children in general content areas. Information gathered can inform initial decisions about whether individual children are experiencing the classroom opportunities provided to them.

When to Use This Tool

This tool should be used on a regular basis when teachers have questions about the opportunities to learn for each child in the classroom. Use this tool at least monthly when concerns about particular children arise.

How to Use This Tool

Place this time sample on a clipboard and store it in a place that is easily reached during the day. Cover with a blank sheet of paper or store out of sight to keep the information recorded confidential. At each time interval, place an X indicating the content area in which the child is participating.

Suggestions for Using This Tool

1. The tool gives a picture of the overall time children spend with specific content areas in the classroom. Children need ample time with content to process the information and practice skills. To master skills and understand concepts, children may need repeated exposure.

2. In addition to providing a snapshot of the time children spend with content, this tool provides information about the patterns of experiences individual children receive. Children spend extended time in activities they prefer. They may avoid activities they do not prefer. Or, they may seek out experiences that allow them to use skills they have mastered. Once the patterns are noted, teachers must reflect on potential reasons for the differences. Questions include the following:

   • Does the child have differing skill abilities that make content more or less accessible?

   • Does the child feel safe in particular areas due to familiarity?

   • Are there cultural influences that make one content area more or less favored?

3. The tool gives no information about the quality of engagement with the content areas listed. Time is not the only factor in understanding a child's approach to a given content area. Teachers must also look for the types of sophistication in which

Time Sample of Individual Participation in General Content Areas

Directions: Place this time sample on a clipboard and store it in a place that is easily reached during the day. Cover with a blank sheet of paper or store out of sight to keep the information recorded confidential. At each time interval, place an X indicating the content area in which the child is participating.

Child's name: _Jonah C._   Date: _10/7/09_

Time	Art	Reading	Sensory (sand/water)	Role play	Block building	Fine motor manipulative	Writing	Math	Science	Gross motor
8:30						X				
8:45									X	
9:00								X		
9:15			X (5 min)		X (5 min)					
9:30			X							
9:45					X (5 min)	X (5 min)				
10:00			X							
10:15			X							
10:30						X				
11:00								X		
3:30			X		X					
3:45					X					
4:00						X				
4:15			X		X					
4:30			X							

Comments: _Jonah moved through areas quickly—sometimes only 5 minutes per area. He did not engage in dramatic play, book reading, or art. Dramatic play could help him engage. He spent longer periods in the water play area. I will plan for more engagement in dramatic play—use sensory activities to help develop relationships with peers._

Observer: _Matt M._

Figure 5.3. Time Sample of Individual Participation in General Content Areas.

the child engages. Are materials used appropriately? Do children use the opportunity for its intended purpose? Do children practice particular aspects of the content? Are the problem-solving strategies simple or complex? The time sample above will not answer these questions.

Impact of Culture

One very important contributing factor to the types and levels of engagement of children in the classroom curriculum is that of *culture*. Schools and early education programs are becoming more and more diverse. As schools become more diverse, learning histories, skill levels, and personal interaction patterns become diverse. It is becoming increasingly difficult to engage children using a one-size-fits-all curriculum. A curriculum must be responsive to the differences of the individuals in the classroom. Cultural, linguistic, ethnic, social, religious, and performance style differences create challenges for designing a relevant curriculum (Gay & Howard, 2001; Ladson-Billings, 1997).

To become culturally competent, teachers must understand and respond to cultural differences. The amount of independence expected of children; the ways children use eye gaze, smiling, and touching; and the space allotted between individuals when speaking are all examples of culturally based values and behavior (Gonzalez-Mena, 2008). Research also indicates that cultural differences exist with regard to degree of independence, self-control, and respectfulness (Okagaki & Kiamond, 2000). Emerging research on gains for differing ethnicities and cultures has begun to show that African American and Hispanic children tend to be more successful in communal or cooperative learning groups, whereas Caucasian children fare better with individualistic, competitive structures (Hurley & Allen, 2009; Mashburn, 2008). Because each individual is steeped in his or her own culture, it is necessary to actively seek information about the values and beliefs of each family served so that behavior is not misattributed.

It is often impossible to match the cultural backgrounds of teachers and children in the classroom. This fact has prompted many educators to look deeply at the structure of classrooms and the methods teachers use to engage children in learning experiences. Teachers must become competent at observing, respecting, and responding to a wide variety of culturally based experiences. They must ask themselves whether elements of the intended or enacted curriculum contribute to differences in the behavior of children in the class.

Palmer has stated, "We teach who we are" (1998). Teachers bring their own learning histories, personal interaction patterns, and linguistic styles to the classroom. Often, those patterns and styles do not match those of the children in the class (Howard, 2001). Both the types of experiences teachers design and the way teachers organize the classroom are based on their own experiences. Teachers must actively reflect on their own backgrounds to understand where disconnects with children may exist.

Because of background differences, it is very important for teachers to communicate the goals for instruction clearly to children. And, it is important for teachers to give children clear guidance on appropriate ways for children to engage in the experiences. Research has demonstrated that when teachers orient children to the classroom and also provide clarity around their instructional goals early in the year, children are better able to manage their own activities later (Bohn, Roehrig, & Pressley, 2004; Cameron et al., 2005; Lewis, 2001).

Teachers can react strongly when children behave in ways that are not congruent with their own culture. For example, some teachers react strongly when children speak to them in angry tones or call them names. This may seem to communicate disrespect. But, the idea of respect is socially constructed. The adult's idea of respect takes many years to develop. In these instances, it is very important for teachers to step back and think about the behavior from the child's perspective. Teachers should ask themselves whether the message they heard from the child is the message the child intended. Teachers must look for the miscommunication that could spark automatic behavior for the adult or the child.

Tolerance Levels Rating Scale

Mismatched tolerance levels can create a difficult situation for children and teachers. It can also be the source of difficulties among children. Figure 5.4 provides a template for analyzing similarities and differences in tolerance levels. Once tolerance levels are known, modifications can be made to minimize mismatches.

Purpose of This Tool	The purpose of the Tolerance Levels Rating Scale is to give teachers information for purposeful reflection on their tolerances for situations, which may be different than the tolerances of the children in the classroom.
When to Use This Tool	This tool should be considered every time a new individual enters the group or whenever teachers struggle with challenging behavior.
How to Use This Tool	Read each of the statements. Rate your tolerance level for the items described by marking an *X* on the continuum; a *1* denotes very low tolerance, and *5* denotes very high tolerance. Then, think about the children in the classroom. Think about a child or parent in your classroom for whom you work to feel connected. Do you think the child or parent would answer the questions the same way? Think about why or why not. What can you do to bridge the gaps in tolerance levels? How does the curriculum in the classroom reflect your tolerance levels? What can you do to be more accepting? How can you design a broader range of experiences?
Suggestions for Using This Tool	1. Teachers' judgments about how children use materials and equipment are seen through the lens of culture. The first step in designing a culturally respectful and responsive curriculum is to understand how our own values, practices, and beliefs may be reflected in the curriculum we design. It is very important to be honest; only then can teachers build bridges to differing sets of values, practices, and beliefs.

Tolerance Levels Rating Scale

Directions: Read each of the statements. Rate your tolerance level for the items described by marking an *X* on the continuum; a *1* denotes very low tolerance, and *5* denotes very high tolerance. Then, think about the children in the classroom. Think about a child or parent in your classroom for whom you work to feel connected. Do you think the child or parent would answer the questions the same way? Think about why or why not. What can you do to bridge the gaps in tolerance levels? How does the curriculum in the classroom reflect your tolerance levels? What can you do to be more accepting? How can you design a broader range of experiences?

My tolerance for children who need repeated amounts of help to complete work

1	2 X	3	4	5
none		moderate		very high

My tolerance for large amounts of physical activity

1	2	X 3	4	5
none		moderate		very high

My tolerance for the rights of the individual *over* the rights of the whole class

1	2	3	X 4	5
none		moderate		very high

My tolerance for using modalities other than oral language to understand problems and communicate

1	2	X 3	4	5
none		moderate		very high

My tolerance for breaking rules

1	2 X	3	4	5
none		moderate		very high

My tolerance for bossiness

1	2	3	X 4	5
none		moderate		very high

My tolerance for confrontation

1	2 X	3	4	5
none		moderate		very high

My tolerance for challenging authority

1	2 X	3	4	5
none		moderate		very high

My tolerance for children using materials in unplanned ways

1	2	3 X	4	5
none		moderate		very high

My tolerance for people who speak directly regardless of emotion

1	2	3 X	4	5
none		moderate		very high

My tolerance for people who touch regularly

1	2	3	4 X	5
none		moderate		very high

My tolerance for gazing directly into the other person's eyes when I speak

1	2	3	4 X	5
none		moderate		very high

Figure 5.4. Tolerance Levels Rating Scale.

2. Relationships in the classroom are important parts of the curriculum. Children learn social skills to reach higher and higher levels of problem solving, communication, and enjoyment. In addition, children feel more able to seek help and support from the teacher when they share a warm, positive relationship (Ladd et al., 2006; Pianta, 1999). Sometimes our cultural differences can impede building those relationships. In those cases, teachers must actively plan ways to be more accepting and communicate positively.

3. Think about a child for whom you have concerns. Do you think your beliefs and tolerances are matched with those of this child? For example, do you think your tolerance for activity levels are the same? Is your tolerance for aggression the same? If not, what are some action steps you can take to communicate about your differences?

Engagement

Teachers can support engagement through direct interactions with children. They also can support engagement by designing learning centers and schedules that match the needs for children in the classroom. Once teachers know the tolerances, understanding, and skill levels of children in the classroom, they can work to extend the time and intensity at which children are involved in the content.

Teachers have to start somewhere in their planning. Beginning with understanding the current classroom elements, teachers can reflect on the steps they will take to gradually increase the skills and interests of children. The tool below provides questions for reflection.

Checklist for Guiding Engagement

Sometimes a teacher's planned curriculum does not take place. It is important to watch the children to determine whether they are actually engaging in the intended curriculum. Figure 5.5 provides information so that teachers can find ways to enact the intended curriculum if children are not engaging as the teacher originally intended.

Purpose of This Tool	The purpose of this tool is to give teachers a basic awareness of the elements necessary for engagement for evaluation of the intended and actual curriculum.
When to Use This Tool	This tool should be used quarterly as an ongoing self-evaluation or as needed. Teachers will find it helpful to use this tool when the curriculum is changed or as issues arise with engagement for particular children.

Checklist for Guiding Engagement

Directions: The first step in using this tool is to analyze how a curriculum is planned. Think about the information used to develop themes, projects, and experiences. Think about how decisions are made to select materials and about the expectations for use of those materials. Then, look for evidence that the conditions described in the tool are met or not met. If they are met, check *Yes.* If not, check *No.* Write the evidence or example of how the condition is met in the appropriate column.

Observer: _Janet Johnson, principal_

Conditions	Yes	No	N/A	Evidence
Learning centers allow children to use more than one way to gain knowledge (e.g., language, visual, kinesthetic, aural, tactile)	✓			*Science center offers multiple learning experiences.*
Learning centers provide opportunities for cooperative learning groups		✓		
Topics and themes used to frame the curriculum have personal meaning or importance to children in the group	✓			*Animal discovery theme is very meaningful to students.*
Teachers stoop to the child's eye level and position whole body facing the child for speaking	✓			*This is a definite area of strength for Ms. Miller.*
Teachers use a variety of inquiry strategies to guide the child's focus on learning	✓			*Excellent use of open-ended questions.*
Teachers encourage extended participation by consciously waiting for more talking after each participant speaks	✓			
Teachers support tools that are necessary for learning (e.g., language, problem solving, inquiry)		✓		
Teachers use cultural information to plan the learning environment and curricular experiences		✓		
Teachers use assessment information to plan experiences that are not too easy or too hard for the children	✓			
Teachers provide clear communication about the learning goals of various classroom elements	✓			*Yes—both verbal and visual directions are provided.*
Teachers orient children to expectations for use of learning centers and materials	✓			*Expectations are clearly outlined.*
Teachers integrate learning goals across content areas	✓			

Figure 5.5. Checklist for Guiding Engagement.

How to Use This Tool

The first step in using this tool is to analyze how a curriculum is planned. Think about the information used to develop themes, projects, and experiences. Think about how decisions are made to select materials and about the expectations for use of those materials. Then, look for evidence that the conditions described in the tool are met or not met. If they are met, check *Yes.* If not, check *No.* Write the evidence or example of how the condition is met in the appropriate column.

Suggestions for Using This Tool

1. Children come to the classroom with a variety of learning styles and histories. Without proper planning for the variety of styles, skills, and understanding levels, behavioral challenges can arise. Analyzing the curriculum for its potential to engage children can be one of the most important tools for preventing challenges. Teachers must expect to make modifications to themes, projects, and curriculum frames based on the children in the class.

2. The only way to provide an engaging curriculum is to gather information about the children in the classroom and consciously plan for them. It is very important that teachers honestly evaluate the engagement opportunities in the classroom.

3. After implementing plans, teachers must evaluate how children interact with learning centers, peers, and activities. Sometimes what is intended is not what takes place. When challenges arise, teachers must ask themselves about difficulty levels, timing issues, learning styles, and interests. Curriculum modifications can then provide better connections for children with the content.

4. Integrating learning goals across the classroom increases the number of opportunities children have to practice skills. In addition, by providing different types of opportunities, teachers add to a child's repertoire and increase the likelihood that skills will be generalized across settings.

Even after much thought, planning, and follow-through, teachers may find that some children are less engaged than others. Some children may need more support than others to evidence any meaningful level of engagement. When this happens, teachers must closely evaluate the skill levels of individual children. Teachers can scaffold engagement by gathering information about what skills children have and building on them. The tool below provides a template for gathering and analyzing information about engagement for specific children.

Event Sample of Time Engaged

Teachers need systems of collecting information about the types and the quantity of engagement children experience. Along with the quality of engagement, the quantity of time children engage is one indicator of the level of a child's engagement. Figure 5.6 gives teachers a way to collect information about the quantity of engagement children experience.

Purpose of This Tool

The purpose of using this tool is to gain a picture of the amount of time a child engages in an activity, interaction, or other experience. This tool also provides information about the types of experience that generate shorter and longer engagement. In addition, teachers can use this tool to set goals to increase engagement overall or for specific events.

When to Use This Tool

This tool is used in the classroom in real time. It should be used when questions arise about the amount and quality of engagement for a given child.

How to Use This Tool

One team member must agree to step outside of the classroom role and become the observer. The observer uses a timer or watch with a second hand to time the beginning and end of each incidence of engagement. For the purposes of this observation, the timer begins each time the child attends, converses, manipulates objects, or otherwise focuses in an intentional way. Wandering around the room or staring into space does not count.

For consistency, the number of seconds the child is engaged is recorded. This requires undivided attention. The start and end times of the engaged event are recorded. Continue this procedure for each event in which the child is engaged across the observation period.

Suggestions for Using This Tool

1. Research is showing that the more children are engaged in classroom experiences, the less frequently they will engage in challenging behavior. For this reason and many more, finding ways to engage children in experiences that are meaningful to them is critical. Increasing the amount of time children are engaged should be a goal. In addition, increasing the time engaged in nonpreferred activities is a goal.

2. Some children move about the room very quickly. It can be difficult to keep up with them while recording the time they are engaged. It is not unusual for a child to move from activity to activity several times in one minute. If possible, it is helpful to ask more than one person to observe children with high activity levels. This will aid in the collection of information over time.

3. It is best to observe at more than one time in a day. It is also best to observe more than one day. This way, observers will get a more accurate picture of the engagement levels.

4. When more than one observer is used, common definitions must be used. Observers should talk about what they will mark as engaged and what they will not mark as engaged.

Event Sample of Time Engaged

Directions: Have one team member be the observer. The observer uses a timer or watch with a second hand to time the beginning and end of each incidence of engagement. For the purposes of this observation, the timer begins each time the child attends, converses, manipulates objects, or otherwise focuses in an intentional way. Wandering around the room or staring into space does not count. For consistency, the number of seconds the child is engaged is recorded. This requires undivided attention. The start and end times of the engaged event are recorded. Continue this procedure for each event in which the child is engaged across the observation period.

Child's name: _Dylan A._

Observer: _Ms. Rapp_

Date	Start time	End time	Total seconds	Type
11/9/09	9:30	9:33	180	book
	10:15	10:17	120	water
	10:27	10:28	60	truck/blocks
	10:28	10:28	45	book
	10:47	10:50	180	art/markers
	10:53	11:19	960	train
11/10/09	3:00	3:15	900	sandbox
	3:20	3:22	120	climber
	3:27	3:38	660	sandbox

Figure 5.6. Event Sample of Time Engaged.

This will make the information more consistent from observer to observer. This is called interobserver reliability.

Supporting Inquiry

Teachers can support positive behavior of children in their classrooms by providing children with skills to ask questions and solve problems. This is because authentic approaches to inquiry provide children with opportunities to gather information and solve problems at their own pace and level. These approaches enhance engagement and teach skills needed to solve social *and* academic problems. The questions that teachers ask provide them with insights into the interests and skills of children in the class. In addition, the questions children ask enable children themselves to play an active role in their learning (Berdoussis, Wong, & Wien, 2001).

Authentic inquiry is a skill that both teachers and children can learn. In fact, research indicates that inquiry skills do not naturally develop but must be taught across school experiences (Kuhan & Pease, 2008). Teachers and children learn more when questioning focuses on content that is real to children and activities that expand skills. Rather than focusing on one-sided questioning from the teacher, teachers and children together can look for paths to engage children in rich problem solving and skill development over time.

It takes time and patience to develop a classroom community that values and accepts "trying to find out" the answers to questions. It is well worth the effort when children begin to use their own interests to attend and engage in experiences that develop social and academic skills. Some children develop these skills more rapidly. Some children, however, will need more intentional scaffolding of skills to do this.

Teachers support the development of inquiry skills by modeling, prompting, and directly teaching children how to develop questions. To be successful, it is extremely important to communicate an acceptance for questioning and problem solving. Acceptance is communicated when teachers slow down, sit with children, and focus on where children are in developing this new skill.

Sometimes, teachers are learning questioning skills themselves. It is then helpful for teachers to understand their own inquiry styles and abilities. The following tool provides information for collecting information about the questions teachers ask.

Event Sample of Teachers' Questions

Teachers can intentionally plan their questions while still leaving the opportunity for spontaneous questioning. Figure 5.7 helps teachers reflect on their own questioning skills by providing information about the type and quantity of questions they ask.

Purpose of This Tool	The purpose of this tool is to provide teachers with information about their own inquiry skills. Information gathered should be used to plan specific questions for specific planned experiences to

Event Sample of Teachers' Questions

Directions: Use this tool in pairs of either classroom teachers, parents and teachers, or administrators and teachers. One person observes while the teacher interacts with children. When the teacher asks a question, the observer records the time, the types of experiences in which the children were engaged, the specific wording of the question asked, and the type of question asked. Observers should use the types of questions listed on the tool as a guide.

Name of teacher: *Kim Welch*　　　　　　　　　　Date: *2/27/10*

Name of observer: *Ali Gurbaz*

Types of questions:

1. Requests for specific information (e.g., who, what, where, when)

2. Analysis (e.g., why, how, what do you think about)

3. Prediction (e.g., what if, what happens when)

4. Synthesis (e.g., what would/if [putting together information from different sources])

5. Other

Time	Learning experience/center/activity	Question	Question type
9:16	*Making pudding—table in art area*	*How much milk?* *How should we mix it up?*	*Specific info* *Analysis*
9:17		*What will happen when we add the milk?*	*Prediction*
9:19		*Remember when we made butter? The bowls we used were different than these. Why?*	*Analysis*
3:30	*Dramatic play—Grocery store*	*What do we need at the grocery store for our pudding?*	*Specific info* *Synthesis*

extend the learning of children and to scaffold questioning skills of others.

| When to Use This Tool | This tool should be used several times across the year. Because old habits die hard, it is recommended that teachers use this tool every 3–4 months. |

| How to Use This Tool | Teachers use this tool in pairs. The pairs can be made up of classroom teachers, parents and teachers, or administrators and teachers. One person observes while the teacher interacts with children. When the teacher asks a question, the observer records the time, the types of experiences in which the children were engaged, the specific wording of the question asked, and the type of question asked. Observers should use the types of questions listed on the tool as a guide. |

| Suggestions for Using This Tool | 1. Modeling inquiry is one of the most important types of support teachers can provide children. Look to determine the types of questions used. Intentionally try to extend the types of questions used. |

2. Notice which children seem to respond to different types of questions. This will help to determine some of their skills.

3. It is very important that the questions be geared to the interests of children. Rather than coming off as a "grilling" of children, questions should be developed to help children focus on higher levels of understanding. They should generate more engagement rather than decreasing engagement.

When children develop the skill of asking questions, they also develop ways of thinking about problems. Teachers provide models that help children engage in content but also teach children how to use their interest and curiosity to manage their own learning. This helps children in social and academic areas. Once teachers observe children, they can begin to plan experiences that help children practice their questioning and problem-solving skills. The following tool provides a method for gathering information about the inquiry skills of children in the group.

Event Sample of Child's Questions

For children to become good problem solvers, they must be good questioners. Questioning is something that should be facilitated. Figure 5.8 facilitates reflection on the questioning skills of children. Challenging behaviors can be forestalled when children take initiative for their own learning and problem solving.

| Purpose of This Tool | The purpose of this tool is to provide teachers with information about the inquiry skills of children in the classroom. Information gathered should be used to plan specific questions for specific |

Event Sample of Child's Questions

Directions: Use this event sample as children interact in the classroom. Record the name of the child and the date. Write down the times the observations take place. Describe what the child is doing in the second column. Record the question and the type of question the child uses.

Child's name: _David Segaur_   Date: _3/7/10_

Types of questions:

1. Requests for specific information (e.g., who, what, where, when)
2. Analysis (e.g., why, how, what do you think about)
3. Prediction (e.g., what if, what happens when)
4. Synthesis (e.g., what would/if—putting together information)

Time	Learning experience/center/activity	Question	Question type
3:15	Dramatic play—grocery store	Can I have it?	Specific info
3:21	Dramatic play—grocery store	Why did you do that?	Analysis? Don't know if he was really asking a why question
3:22	Dramatic play—grocery store	Is he playing with it?	Specific info

Figure 5.8. Event Sample of Child's Questions.

planned experiences to extend the learning of children and to scaffold questioning skills of others. This tool can also track growth.

When to Use This Tool

This tool should be used several times across the year. It is especially helpful to use this tool in conjunction with planned experiences. Dramatic play, cooking, art, science, mathematics, book reading, writing, and construction activities provide especially rich opportunities for gathering information about inquiry.

How to Use This Tool

Teachers use this tool as they interact with children. Teachers can observe one child or more than one child at a time. Teachers record the types of questions children ask in real time. This tool can be used in conjunction with a planned activity or spontaneously as questioning emerges in the classroom.

Suggestions for Using This Tool

1. Children need help to develop their repertoire of inquiry strategies. Children can ask questions verbally or nonverbally. For example, experimenting by mixing colors to see what happens is a type of inquiry. Teachers can help children learn what they are doing by verbalizing for them.

2. We give children replacements for challenging behavior when we support their inquiry. When children explore materials, engage with constructs, and problem-solve, we are teaching learning strategies that will benefit them for years to come. As such, the questions must be developed for the child's own engagement and advancement. Teachers use what they know about children to be available if needed.

3. Communicating acceptance for the questions of children is essential. This means taking time to listen and encourage. Children are encouraged when teachers smile, describe, position their bodies to listen, and build on what they have heard. That is, teachers must actively engage with the learning they see in children.

4. Young children can be fooled by their perceptions and react accordingly. Noticing the first attribute that appears and responding to it can actually provide misinformation on which children build learning. Teachers must help children see more deeply to circumvent misleading reactions.

Supporting Language

Teachers support positive behavior by teaching acceptable behaviors that replace previous behaviors (Neilson, Olive, Donovan, & McEvoy, 1998). Once teachers understand the purpose of a child's unacceptable behavior, they can teach children a behavior that meets the child's purposes but is more appropriate for the situation. Often, teaching children to appropriately communicate their wants and needs is the desired replacement behavior. Children may need to learn to use words, signs, or gestures to express themselves.

Children learning language may act out their needs rather than speaking them. For this reason, it is important to know the skills and levels of understanding of the children in the group. Teachers must think about the replacement skills that the child can do easily and quickly. In addition, they must be sure that the language planned to replace the behavior meets the needs of the child.

All young children should be screened by a licensed speech-language pathologist (SLP). Screening is brief and can determine whether a child's skill levels warrant a closer look. A speech and language evaluation may be needed to determine whether the child would benefit from prescribed language intervention. When children need speech and/or language therapy, it is important for teachers to be part of the intervention team.

One very important aspect of language development is self-talk. Self-talk refers to the language that people use to speak to themselves. This language helps to provide a method for framing thoughts and problems. Self-talk can provide a "prompting" function for children whose behaviors are impulsive. Fostering self-talk can also become a replacement for children who need adults to constantly prompt and remind them. Children can talk to themselves to remember the steps for working through problems or tasks. They can also provide their own source of positive feedback.

Language support in the classroom touches many areas of the child's life for years to come. Children need language for many academic pursuits. They need language to initiate and sustain friendships. Language also is important for employment later in life. For all of these reasons, teachers must pay close attention to the skills children possess and plan experiences to support them.

Language Support Plan

It is very easy to miss specific elements of a child's use of language while moving about the classroom. Developing language as a social tool can prevent and intervene in challenging classroom dynamics. Figure 5.9 is a tool that teachers can use to help them systematically plan to support language.

Purpose of This Tool	The purpose of this tool is to help teachers plan intentional language supports for specific children.
When to Use This Tool	This tool should be used for any child whose learning or social interactions are limited by the amount and type of language skills he or she possesses. This tool should be used weekly for children needing intensive support.
How to Use This Tool	The first step in using this tool is to develop objectives for language learning. Place an X next to the specific objective. Think about the experiences you will design to support the child's area

Language Support Plan

Directions: The first step in using this tool is to develop objectives for language learning. Place an *X* next to the specific objective. Then, think about the experiences you will design to support the child's area of need. Place an *X* next to the area of the classroom in which you will implement your plan. In addition, place an *X* next to the specific strategy you will use to support the child. Describe the experience. Be sure to note which materials you will need. Also note the individuals involved. Will other children be involved? Which teachers will be involved? Circle the days of the week on which the plan will be used and note the time of day the supports will take place.

Child's name: _Miles Simon_   Date: _3/15/10_

Objectives:

_X_ Practice familiar vocabulary

____ Use new vocabulary

____ Use specific vocabulary _____

____ Initiate conversations with peers

____ Make requests

____ Increase the length of communication

____ Increase turn taking

____ Use language to express needs and feelings

____ Use language to request a toy or material

_X_ Use language to enter a group

____ Stay on topic

____ Make inferences

____ Make predictions

____ Increase sentence length

____ Increase sentence complexity

Area of the classroom:	Strategy:
_X_ Dramatic play	_X_ Modeling
____ Art	____ Targeted differences in sounds, words, and structures
____ Reading	____ Play-by-play narration
____ Writing	____ Expansion of expressed language
____ Block building	____ Restatements
____ Sensory	____ Prompts
____ Group game	____ Redirection
____ Muscle room	_X_ Scripts of familiar activities
____ Outdoor	____ Open-ended questions

Description of activity and resources needed:

Dramatic play is set up as doctor's office. Invite T.L. to play. Say, "I am going to ask T.L. to play. Would you like to come with me?" Walk to T.L. Say, "I am going to move so he can see me. Then I will say his name and ask him to play." Say, "T., would you like to play in the doctor's office with Miles and me?" Next time encourage Miles to do this.

Days per week: (M) T W Th F   Time: _10:00_

Figure 5.9. Language Support Plan.

of need. Place an *X* next to the area of the classroom in which you will implement your plan. In addition, place an *X* next to the specific strategy you will use to support the child. Describe the experience. Be sure to note which materials you will need. Also note the individuals involved. Will other children be involved? Which teachers will be involved? Circle the days of the week on which the plan will be used and note the time of day the supports will take place.

<table>
<tr><td>

Suggestions for Using This Tool

</td><td>

1. If speech or language delays are suspected, it is important to refer to a qualified speech-language pathologist. Planning supports for language are not a substitute for obtaining an assessment by a professional.

2. It is important to be as detailed as possible. The more detail, the more likely that the plan will be able to be implemented thoroughly. The plan provides an important tool for communicating among team members.

3. Follow-through is very important. If the plan is not implemented completely, no one will know how to modify supports if interventions do not work.

</td></tr>
</table>

Language learning should take place in every area of the curriculum. Children learn language by listening to books, composing silly words, talking with adults, and talking with peers. Each of these elements of the curriculum provide a forum for learning to communicate, taking turns, sharing, and empathizing (Carr et al., 1994; McConnell, 2002). Opportunities for teaching language to support appropriate, prosocial behavior abound in the early childhood classroom.

Any type of group activity provides a good source of content for language development and social learning (Yuill, Strieth, Roake, Aspden, & Todd, 2006). However, dramatic play provides an exceptional source of content due to the nature of the groups, the ability of teachers to manipulate the themes, and the appealing aspects of self-directed play. As children interact, they develop an understanding of the meaning of words, the ways that words are spoken in their culture, the social expectations for language, and the many purposes and structures of language. In addition, children take roles that give them an opportunity to practice multiple perspectives and social strategies (Goncu, Patt, & Kouba, 2002).

One important outcome of dramatic play is that children learn scripts for how to use language in specific situations (McAloney & Stagnitti, 2009). These scripts help children extend play, develop concepts, solve problems, and navigate social interactions. When children learn to use a variety of scripts, they are better able to move in and out of different social scenarios.

Teachers can help children learn appropriate replacements for behavior by carefully planning play themes, props, and social supports. Teachers should consider the child's culture, learning history (previous experiences), and interests when designing dramatic play environments. Children may need to start with simple, concrete play scripts or routines. As they develop, the complexity, types of themes, and materials should increase. The tool in Figure 5.10 provides a way to plan a continuum of supports using dramatic play.

Dramatic Play Planning Tool

Directions: Delineate the props that will be used as well as the conversations, social supports, and extension of the experiences that will occur during specific instances of dramatic play.

Theme/Project: _Doctor's office_

Date	Props	What will the children talk about?	Social support (e.g., prompt, model, gesture, sign)	Other areas in the classroom that will be integrated
9/16/09	Lab coats Gowns Gloves Masks 2 stethoscopes Waiting area Dolls Paper/pencils/clip boards	Staying healthy Hand washing The heart Helping each other	Prompt discussion about helpers Role play turn taking—patient, doctor Doctor office script—sign in, waiting, call name, go to doctor Model through use of homemade book about pretending doctor's office that details turn taking	Book corner Emergency vehicle, block props, and body puzzles in large play area. Children dictate stories about doctor's office in writing center.
9/17/09	Books about hospital, bones, skin, eyes, mouth, blood	Bones Skin Eyes Mouth Blood	Prompt children to initiate roles—redirect children to include each other Model questioning Photograph children interacting	Emergency vehicle visits program.
9/18/09	Add: X rays Bandages Splints Props for ambulance (chairs, cot)		Turn taking—prompt shared use of materials and changing roles Facilitate children's conversation about health	
9/19/09	Homemade books about children's stories of visiting the doctor	Visits they have made to the doctor	Model solving medical problems. Prompt with questions that require children to analyze illness to diagnose and treat	Medical worker visits (nurse, doctor).

Figure 5.10. Dramatic Play Planning Tool.

Dramatic Play Planning Tool

Dramatic play is incredibly useful in teaching social skills. Figure 5.10 helps teachers intentionally plan to scaffold social experiences in the dramatic play area.

Purpose of This Tool	The purpose of this tool is to provide a way to intentionally plan for language learning in the dramatic play environment.
When to Use This Tool	This tool can be used to plan more than one dramatic play theme. This tool should be used any time a new dramatic play environment is needed.
How to Use This Tool	Teachers should use this tool in their planning team to discuss the ways to enrich the dramatic play environment to increase language and social skill development. During planning time, teachers delineate the props, conversations, vocabulary, and extension of the experiences. This tool also can be used to plan experiences in the block area.

Suggestions for Using This Tool

1. Dramatic play themes should be based in experiences familiar to the children. It is not unusual for children to use materials inappropriately if they do not have an understanding of the script needed to engage in particular play themes.

2. While remembering to plan familiar themes and materials, teachers must also think about how to extend learning experiences. Teachers can introduce new themes, materials, and methods of interacting by starting with the familiar and adding.

3. Often, children communicate spontaneously when interacting in the dramatic play environment; however, it is not sufficient to rely on those natural interactions alone to support needed language learning for children. Teachers need to be present to encourage the extension of skills. While not intruding into the play, teachers can help children focus on language and social skills that will extend the interaction and create far more learning.

4. It is possible to engineer the dramatic play environment to obtain the types of interactions needed by children. For example, children learning to take turns, stay on the play topic, or learn social scripts may need to start off with a smaller group. Places for dyads to play provide a way for children to learn social skills more effectively. When children are very skilled, complex themes for larger numbers of children provide challenges for learning cooperation and negotiation.

Conclusion

Tapping into a child's natural tendency to solve problems, communicate, and seek higher levels of information is an important tool for teachers to support learning in the short and long term. When teachers thoughtfully design and execute a curriculum that meets the needs of the individuals in the classroom, they provide an important source of protection for those children. Challenging behaviors can be prevented and ameliorated by attending to the individual differences of children in the classroom.

Teachers must expect that some modification of the curriculum will take place to promote learning. It is important for teachers to evaluate how they plan the curriculum. They must also evaluate the experiences provided to the students. They must be sure that the curriculum in the classroom is based on specific information about the children in the group. When children are engaged with rich curriculum experiences, they learn more than just the focus of the activity. They learn interaction skills and behaviors to replace those that create challenges.

CHAPTER 6

Using Routines and Schedules to Support Positive Behavior

How teachers structure time in the classroom can have a great impact on the development of relationships, skills, and understanding in the classroom. The daily schedule, transitions from activity to activity, and transitions within activities provide a foundation for the use of materials and interpersonal exchanges (Yarbrough, Skinner, Lee, & Lemmons, 2004). Individual children respond differently to the sequence of experiences, the duration of experiences, and transitions between and within specific activities (Sainato, 1990). For all of these reasons, it is important to plan schedules and transitions that fit the needs of the children in the group (Buck, 1999; Fudge, Reece, Skinner, & Cowden, 2007; Polloway & Patton, 1997).

Planned Schedule versus Actual Schedule

Research reveals that schedules and routines designed by teachers contribute to the type of instruction, social interaction, and levels of engagement children experience (Powell, Burchinal, File, & Kontos, 2008; Smith & Dickinson, 1994). Research also demonstrates that the amount of time teachers believe they have planned for specific experiences does not necessarily represent the actual time provided. For example, researchers found that children spend more time in large groups than teachers think they do.

Even when teachers think they have scheduled the optimum amount of time for free play and small- and large-group experiences, they must double check by paying close attention to what actually happens during the day. The belief that what is planned is actually taking place can fool teachers into misunderstanding the behavior of children in the classroom. It is important for teachers to compare the planned schedule for the day with what actually takes place. The tool below helps teachers see these differences clearly.

Planned and Actual Classroom Schedule

Sometimes what takes place in the classroom is not what is planned. Figure 6.1 provides information for teachers to reflect on what takes place as compared to what is planned for the classroom.

Purpose of This Tool	The purpose of this tool is to provide information for teachers to analyze the schedule they have planned and the schedule as it actually takes place. Teachers can use this tool to compare the ideal schedule with the actual schedule.
When to Use This Tool	This tool should be used whenever teachers believe the daily schedule may be negatively affecting the behavior of children. It should be used before decisions are made to change the schedule.
How to Use This Tool	This tool is divided into two sections. Write the classroom schedule on the left-hand side of the tool. Then, ask an observer to write the time and activities that actually take place on the right-hand

side of the tool. Talk about any differences that you note. Repeat this activity for several weeks.

<table>
<tr><td>

Suggestions for Using This Tool

</td><td>

1. Schedules should be flexible to meet the needs of children in the group; therefore, when differences are observed, there may be good reasons. Teachers must use judgment to know whether the differences in schedules warrant changes.

2. Sometimes the schedule is difficult for one child but is fine for everyone else. Before changing the schedule think about the impact for all of the other children in the class. If the schedule can be changed without substantially affecting other children negatively, teachers should consider changing the schedule.

3. Teachers should consider the length of time allocated to experiences when designing the schedule. Most children need long amounts of time to engage with peers and materials. Some children, however, will need extra help with this. For these children, breaking the time into smaller increments with teacher support may be helpful.

4. It is easier for children to transition from quiet to active play than from active to quiet play. Special attention should be paid to children's responses when schedules require moving from a loud, active activity to a quiet, slower activity (Sainato, 1990).

5. Picture schedules are useful for reminding children of the order of activities. Seeing what comes next also can help children wait for their preferred activities when they see that they are coming shortly. Picture schedules can be made and posted for an entire group, or they can be made for individual children who struggle with knowing what comes next.

</td></tr>
</table>

Many studies of quality programming recommend scheduling long periods of time for children to engage in play. Often times, eating, washing hands, taking attendance, waiting, and transitioning take up a much larger portion of the day than is recommended (Howes et al., 2008; Pianta et al., 2005; Pianta & LaParo, 2003). Schedules that allow children to explore, pretend, and problem solve have been shown to have a positive impact on impulsivity (Bodrova & Leong, 2005). Schedules that allow children to move freely in small groups for extended periods of time have been shown to improve language development and social skills (Smith & Dickinson, 1994).

Because children need time to learn the schedule and corresponding expectations for behavior, it is important to give the schedule time to work. Too many changes can create a chaotic situation for everyone. Carefully planning and communicating changes can decrease anxiety and confusion.

Some children struggle with specific aspects of classroom schedules. Waiting, transitioning, and large-group instruction are elements of the classroom schedule with which many teachers report having difficulties. These times can trigger concerning behavior for some children. Teachers can decrease waiting, transitions, and the amount of time children spend in large-group, teacher-directed instruction by manipulating the schedule.

Planned and Actual Classroom Schedule

Directions: This tool is divided into two sections. Write the classroom schedule including time and planned activities on the left-hand side of the tool. Then, ask an observer to write the time and activities that actually take place on the right-hand side of the tool. Talk about any differences that you note. Repeat this activity for several weeks.

Classroom: _Eagle_   Date: _9/27/09_

Teacher's name: _Ms. Jane_   Observer's name: _Mrs. Quinn_

Time	Planned activity	Time	Actual activity
8:00	Breakfast	8:10	Breakfast
8:30	Free choice	8:30	Free choice
9:00	Outside	8:55	Clean up–Not outside until 9:00
9:30	Group time	9:35	Group time/Bathroom time
9:50	Transition to free choice/special art	10:05	Group discussion/ transition
10:00–11:15	Special art activity	10:15	Free choice/special art
11:15	Free choice		
11:20	Transition to cooperative learning groups	11:30	Clean up
11:35	Transition to lunch	11:55	Lunch (late)

Figure 6.1. Planned and Actual Classroom Schedule.

Decreasing Wait Time

Many teachers report concerns about behavior during times that children must wait. *Wait time,* in this instance, refers to the time during which children are expected to engage in acceptable behavior while no activities are planned. Research shows that children actually do become more active, restless, noisy, and distracted and exhibit more challenging behavior while waiting than they do during times they are not waiting (Antrop, Buysse, Roeyers, & Oost, 2005). Often, teachers do not realize how much time their students spend waiting. Objective observations can help teachers understand the frequency and the length of time that children wait.

It is important to know the natural points in the schedule that children wait. Once the reasons for waiting are known, teachers can work to decrease this challenging time. Teachers must be objective, however, in analyzing the real amounts of time children wait throughout the day. Rather than trying to retrospectively reconstruct the ways children spend their time, teachers should observe the students in real time. It may also be helpful for teachers to ask a co-worker to observe and specifically look for times in the day during which children wait. The tool below can help teachers gather information about the actual wait times that children experience.

Wait Time Event Sample

Children become more restless, active, and distracted during times in which they must wait. Figure 6.2 provides a mechanism for gathering information to analyze the time children spend waiting.

Purpose of This Tool	This tool provides an overview of the times in the classroom that children are observed waiting. It gives teachers a baseline of information from which to plan.
When to Use This Tool	Teachers should use this tool when they observe conflicts or concerning behaviors that seen to occur around the same times during the day.
How to Use This Tool	This tool should be used to document real-time observations. Teachers can sit for periods of time and observe or they can keep this template within reach and record information each time they notice a child is waiting. If teachers are not able to sit and observe, it is helpful to have more than one person document the information.
Suggestions for Using This Tool	1. Wait time in classrooms typically represents time when children are not engaged in meaningful learning. This time is especially critical for children who require extra support for learning social and academic skills. From this perspective, each segment of time spent waiting is a missed opportunity for learning. It is important for teachers to decrease wait time so that they can use that time to support appropriate behavior.

Wait Time Event Sample

Directions: This tool should be used to document real-time observations. Teachers can sit for periods of time and observe or they can keep this template within reach to record information each time they notice a child is waiting. If teachers are not able to sit and observe, it is helpful to have more than one person document the information.

Classroom: _Preschool 1_   Date: _11/05/09_

Time of day	Activity	Location	Length of time
8:00	Waiting for breakfast—children sit down when teacher goes for cart, then wait while teacher prepares	Tables in classroom	12 minutes
9:25	Children sit near door with coats on waiting to go outside.	Classroom door	9 minutes
11:15	Children wait to wash hands.	Sink in classroom	Last child waited 7 minutes

Figure 6.2. Wait Time Event Sample.

2. Once teachers have objectively identified times in the day that children wait, they can begin to plan to reduce the wait time. This can be done by changing the routine, changing the ways that children are grouped to move through the schedule, or providing interesting activities for children while they wait. Knowing the children in the group helps teachers determine which strategy to use.

3. When teachers see patterns in the times that children wait, they can target those times. Teachers should evaluate each period of waiting and ask themselves what alternatives are possible. Oftentimes, the solution is as easy as getting materials for activities ready before the children are sitting at the table. Sometimes the alternatives to waiting are more subtle. For example, for the situation in which children have to wait to go outside until each student puts on his or her coat, teachers may need to think about how to group children differently or how to assign adults to help particular students to decrease the wait time. These alternatives require that teachers organize their own time more effectively. The following is a list of strategies to manage wait time:

- Prepare all materials ahead of time.
- Change the schedule to decrease the need for waiting.
- Change the location of the waiting activity to an area where children can engage in acceptable activities (e.g., book area).
- Find a way to engage smaller groups of children in waiting for shorter amounts of time.
- Position adults to help specific children based on their needs.
- Provide positive feedback.

Plan for Decreasing Wait Time

Once teachers have identified the times of the day children wait, they can begin to plan to decrease these specific wait times. Figure 6.3 guides teachers to develop strategies to rethink when and how children wait.

Purpose of This Tool	The purpose of this tool is to provide an overview of the strategies teachers will use in their classrooms to decrease wait time. It can be used as both a discussion guide and a communication tool so that all classroom staff members follow through on alternatives.
When to Use This Tool	This tool should be used when there are times during the day that conflicts or concerning behaviors recur. It also can be used when observations of wait time indicate a need for decreasing wait time.

How to Use This Tool

To use Figure 6.3, teachers should summarize information they recorded using Figure 6.2. Write the time of day, the specific activity, and the length of time children wait on Figure 6.3. Talk about each period of the day during which children spend time waiting. Identify the specific children who are challenged by the time waiting. Brainstorm strategies for alternate sequencing of the schedule, experiences that can be integrated into the routine, or different areas of the classroom to be used. Write new strategies on the form (Figure 6.3).

Suggestions for Using This Tool

1. Children have different tolerances for the amounts of time they are able to wait. Some young children can wait for 10 minutes with nothing to do. Other children, however, can only wait 1 or 2 minutes. It is important to know the limits of the amount of time children can sit idly.

2. There will always be times in the day that children need to wait. These times should be few and very short. In these instances, it is important for teachers to understand the needs of children and teach appropriate waiting behavior. Teachers should explicitly discuss the expected behavior.

3. Some children will need more support than others. Teachers should plan to stay in close proximity to these children. They should provide positive feedback for appropriate behavior and should think of ways to engage children in acceptable activities.

4. Teachers should analyze all of the times during the day that children wait. Some children become increasingly agitated or stressed if there is a great deal of noise and stimulation during the waiting period. This is especially true when large groups of children wait at the same time. Teachers should plan to lower stimulation levels by designing schedules that reduce the number of children who have to wait at any given time. For example, children can move in small groups of two or three to wash their hands for lunch.

One way that teachers can minimize wait time difficulties is to think of ways to keep children occupied while they wait. Throughout the day there are periods that children may need to wait their turn for the use of highly preferred materials and equipment. Disputes among children are frequent in classrooms that do not provide systems for waiting. One quick and easy way to help children understand the idea of waiting for a turn is to create waiting lists. Once children begin to use waiting lists, they can monitor their progress. In addition, this allows children to engage in other experiences while they wait. The tool in Figure 6.4 is a template for a waiting list for using the computer. The title can be changed so that the list can be used for any highly preferred equipment or area of the classroom.

Plan for Decreasing Wait Time

Directions: Summarize information from the Wait Time Event Sample on this form. Write the time of day, the specific activity, and the length of time children wait on this form. Talk about each period of the day during which children spend time waiting. Identify the specific children who are challenged by the time waiting. Brainstorm strategies for alternate sequencing of the schedule, experiences that can be integrated into the routine, or different areas of the classroom to be used. Write new strategies on the form.

Classroom: _Preschool 1_   Date: _4/14/09_

Time of day	Activity	Location	Length of time	Alternative strategy
8:00	Waiting for breakfast—children sit down when teacher goes for cart, then wait while teacher prepares.	Tables in classroom	12 minutes	Develop new morning routine—one teacher invites children to book area while breakfast is set up. While teaching the new routine, use very interesting books and props for the transition.
9:25	Children sit near door with coats on waiting to go outside.	Classroom door	9 minutes	Each teacher takes a group outside as they are ready. One teacher sits with waiting children while singing transition songs until the small group is ready to go outside.
11:15	Children wait to wash hands.	Sink in classroom	Last child waited 7 minutes	One teacher facilitates washing hands in smaller groups.

Figure 6.3. Plan for Decreasing Wait Time.

Waiting List Template

Waiting lists are easy to make and use. Figure 6.4 provides one way for teachers to quickly generate a waiting list.

Purpose of This Tool	The purpose of this tool is to provide children with a way to conceptualize the idea of waiting for a turn. It provides a visual that enables them to track their progress on the list. It also provides an important literacy experience.
When to Use This Tool	This tool should be used when more than one child wishes to use the same materials, equipment, or areas of the classroom at the same time. It also can be used to prevent disputes by systematizing how these disputes will be handled.
How to Use This Tool	Teachers can proactively place waiting lists in areas that are highly desirable. A photo of a child using the equipment or materials in question helps children quickly see to which area or activity the list applies. Children write their name on the list to indicate their desire for a turn. If children cannot write their name, a teacher can help. As children finish using the material, they cross their name off the list.
Suggestions for Using This Tool	1. Many children will need to be taught to use a waiting list. Teachers should be available to help children by explaining, modeling, and prompting as the waiting list is introduced.
	2. There is a tremendous amount of value in facilitating problem solving between children in disputes of property. Waiting lists should not be used to prevent all disputes. They should be used as one method of solving problems when disputes over particular materials are regular and frequent.
	3. One important goal for social learning is for children to manage conflict and disputes themselves. The waiting list system gives children opportunities to practice a system that they can use in many situations in the future.

Providing Choices

Preference, learning history, social groupings, classroom design, and teacher-designed schedules play an important role in the choices that children make. When teachers offer choices to a child, they take advantage of the child's natural inclination to explore and learn. Offering choices increases a child's engagement and cooperation in the classroom (Dunlap & Liso, 2004).

Waiting List for the Computer

1) James

2) Sydney

3) Aiesha

4) Peter

5) Stephan

Figure 6.4. Waiting List for the Computer.

In addition to providing opportunities to become engaged in the classroom, it is important for children to learn how to make choices because it is a way for them to manage their own behavior and learning. Making choices in the classroom is a form of self-determination. Children learn to move independently through the classroom and regulate their behavior (Elias & Berk, 2002). In addition, when children make choices, they are practicing the crucial skills of decision making and problem solving (Erwin et al., 2009).

Research has shown that providing extended classroom time for children to make choices helps them in several areas. Teachers who reported giving children long amounts of self-directed, unrestricted free play provided children with rich language experiences (Smith & Dickinson, 1994). In another study, teachers providing longer amounts of time for self-directed play showed evidence that children used more problem-solving and self-management strategies (Palmer & Wehmeyer, 2003). Language development, problem solving, and self-management are enhanced when children learn to make appropriate choices.

Some children need more support for making choices than others. Although many children can manage their transition into and out of self-initiated activities easily, some cannot. In addition, although many children thrive in an environment with many materials, social groups, and learning challenges, some become overwhelmed. Children who have difficulty making and following through on choices may wander aimlessly in the classroom, act silly, use materials inappropriately, or withdraw. It is important for teachers to know the tolerances of children in the classroom and plan ways to scaffold skills.

It may be necessary for teachers to scale back the number and types of choices for some children. Some children may do well with an hour and a half of uninterrupted free play. This amount of time may be an excellent way to provide ample choice-making opportunities for these children. However, this amount of time could be too much for a child who has difficulty making choices. It may be necessary to provide shorter amounts of time in unstructured settings for some children.

Altering schedules and routines to meet the needs of children in the group should be done by observing and documenting children's responses to the existing schedule. When children struggle with choice making, teachers can alter the schedule *or* provide more physical support. Teachers must think about the needs of the individual child and balance those with the needs of the group when designing supports. Teachers should always carefully plan to increase abilities by adding choices and decreasing adult structure.

The first step in planning for choice-making is to observe and analyze the skills of children for whom there is a concern. The abilities of children to make choices can be influenced by classroom factors.

Analysis of Choice Time Tool

A child's ability to make choices has a significant impact on his or her success in the classroom. Teachers can use Figure 6.5 to review the types of choices children make so that they can provide the appropriate supports.

Analysis of Choice Time Tool

Directions: Write the name of the child and the date of the observation on the tool. It may be helpful to place copies of the tool around the room. Then, record all situations in which the child makes choices. The time of day, the situation, and the location should be briefly noted. Teachers should then make a judgment as to whether this situation was a concern or not and check the corresponding box.

Name of child: _Caroline L._   Date: _10/3/09_

Time	Situation	Location	Concern	No concern
8:30	Moving from breakfast to free play— Clean up and transition	Classroom— table to books	X	
8:45	Making transition to go outside	Moved from book corner/area to door		X
9:30	Wandered in the classroom. Prompted by teacher to engage.	Window area to art area	X	

Figure 6.5. Analysis of Choice Time Tool.

Purpose of This Tool	The purpose of this tool is to summarize information about a child's skills in participating in choice time.

When to Use This Tool

This tool should be used whenever teachers have concerns about a child's skills in engaging in self-directed experiences in the classroom. This tool should be used as children move through the schedule during the day. Teachers may forget important information if they complete the tool retrospectively.

How to Use This Tool

Write the name of the child and the date of the observation on the tool. It may be helpful to place copies of the tool around the room. Teachers should record all situations in which the child makes choices. The time of day, the situation, and the location should be briefly noted. Teachers should then make a judgment as to whether this situation was a concern or not and check the corresponding box.

Suggestions for Using This Tool

1. Much can be learned when children make appropriate choices. When choice time goes well, teachers should reflect on the reasons. Is there a pattern to the types of situations that do not cause concern? Are there characteristics of the situation that encourage positive choice making? Is this a preferred activity? How can what is learned about this situation be transferred to a situation in which the behavior was concerning?

2. When choice-making behavior is concerning, teachers should analyze the schedule and the specifics of the experience to determine how to scaffold appropriate choice-making behavior. The length of time and the sequence of activities can have an effect on the experience for children.

3. Learning history, temperament, preferences, and peer culture play a role in the success of time planned for making choices. All of these factors interact. It is important to reflect on all aspects before making changes in the schedule.

4. The schedule may work for some children in the classroom but not for others. When this happens, it is important to think about ways to manage the needs of all children. It is possible to create shorter intervals of uninterrupted time by something as simple as prompting the child who needs more help.

5. Teachers should stay in close proximity to a child who needs extra help making choices at critical intervals (Ponitz, Rimm-Kaufman, Grimm, & Curby, 2009). By analyzing the patterns of choices children make, teachers will begin to predict when children will need help. They will also be better able to see the beginnings of concerning behavior and intervene proactively.

One strategy for helping a child learn to make choices is to provide a smaller number of choices from a selection of equally beneficial options. For example, a child may be able to make a choice from three activities but not from all of the possibilities in the room. Or, it may be easy for a child to select from activities that are preferred but not so easy when the activities are disliked.

Making a Choice Board

Some children may be aided by pictures of the activities or materials from which they are to choose. In this case, a *choice board* may be helpful. A *choice board* helps a child to visualize the available choices so that the choices seem more concrete. When the child begins to develop choice-making skills, additional choices can be added. For example, in the beginning, the child may select one activity from three that are offered. Once this is mastered, the child may select more than one activity and place them on the board in the order they will be done.

Materials Needed

- Small clipboard
- Velcro
- Pictures of materials in the room
- Tag board

Steps

1. Glue a strip of Velcro vertically down the center of the clipboard.

2. Cut strips of tag board the same width as the clip board and at least 2 inches tall.

3. Glue a picture of an acceptable material or activity in the classroom on each tag board strip.

4. Laminate the strip with the picture (optional).

5. Place strips in a basket for selection.

When a child needs help making choices, teachers should provide supports and set goals for increasing the numbers and types of choices a child makes in a day. Teachers also should increase the variety of choices a child makes, helping the child to increase the number of times he or she chooses nonpreferred activities.

Longer periods of complex, self-directed play support the development of many skills. Free play may seem to be a time that requires little thought and interaction by teachers; however, this is deceptive. During free play, teachers work to understand the play skills of all children in the class. They move around the room to provide prompts, models, and cues so that children will learn to engage in longer periods of self-determined behavior. They facilitate problem solving and engagement. This extended period of choice making is an ideal time of the day for enriched social learning.

Planning Transitions

The process of transitioning from one activity to another, or from one part of an activity to another, can be stressful for children and teachers alike. Teachers report that transition times create stress for them because these are times when challenging behaviors surface (Bell, Carr, Denno, Johnson, & Phillips, 2004). Transitions can be stressful for children because they can create higher activity levels, adults are less available, and expectations are often ambiguous (Ostrosky, Jung, & Hemmeter, 2002). For transitions to run smoothly, teachers must plan them carefully.

Two types of transitions take place in classrooms. One type of transition involves stopping one activity and beginning another. A second type involves transitioning from one step or process in a given activity to another step or process in the same activity. Each of these types of transitions exists in the context of the classroom routine. It is important to think about the specifics of those contexts to provide positive support for both types of transitions.

Many young children benefit from knowing what activity or step comes next and the expectations associated with the activity (Dooley, Wilczenski, & Torem, 2001). This is true for the general classroom schedule and also for transitions within and between activities. Transitions should be planned and predictable, and expectations should be communicated clearly. Once children become familiar with the transition routine and its associated behaviors, transitions run more smoothly.

Transitions between Activities

Transitions between activities take place for many reasons. One primary reason relates to the classroom schedule. Children transition to go outside because that is when they are scheduled to do so. Children transition to group instruction from outside because it is time. These transitions may not seem logical or intuitive to children. Children may perceive transitions as intrusive and disruptive. It is a time that the schedule interrupts a child's focus. For this reason, transitions should make sense from the child's standpoint and should be limited to only those that are necessary.

Typically, transitions between activities affect large groups of children at once. Teachers expect that students will stop one activity and begin another. This requires a shift in attention, engagement, and behavior. Depending on the types of activities involved, large numbers of children may need help from teachers at the same time, leaving some children with no support.

One strategy to create smooth transitions is to break down the size of the group. This is not always possible, but the schedule should be analyzed to ensure that smaller numbers of children transition with smaller numbers of teachers when it is possible. Examples of times the group can be made smaller include the following:

- Washing hands before going to the lunch table

- Getting on coats to go outside

- Moving to another activity after clean up

This strategy lowers the stimulation level in the classroom, decreases wait time, and prevents disruption (see section on waiting in this chapter). Opportunities to transition smaller groups are more prevalent than readily apparent.

Whether transitioning in small or large groups, teachers must cooperatively move to the areas of need. For example, one teacher may help with clean up while another moves to help children enter the next activity. Planning the roles of the teachers is essential to fostering smooth transitions.

Cleanup, personal care routines, and moving to different locations require that a lot takes place in a short period of time. Teachers should think about each type of transition and their role in making it run smoothly. It is helpful to assign roles. This is especially true when children and teachers are learning the routine. Then, teachers must follow through on their assignment to be sure that the children who need help receive it.

Communication is critical during transitions from activity to activity. When children are familiar with the schedule, they can predict the sequence of activities. Knowing what time a transition will take place, however, is more difficult for them. They depend on teachers to communicate that the transition is about to happen. A consistent cue provides a predictable way for children to know that it is time to move to another activity.

When children are engaged in learning experiences, it helps to give them a warning that the transition time is coming. Some children require more than one warning. Teachers should be guided by their knowledge of the needs of the children in the group.

Cues for transition can be verbal or nonverbal. Some children are more sensitive to sensory stimulation than others; therefore, decisions about the type of cues used for transition should be based on the sensitivities of children in the classroom. Because transitions can become chaotic at times, it is important to think about ways to signal the transition that will be well tolerated by the children in the group. Some examples of cues for transitions include the following:

- Singing or playing a particular song

- Turning the lights off

- Walking to small groups and telling children that it is time to transition

- Providing cards for children to move from area to area

One signal that has been validated as a useful tool for transitions is a color wheel (Fudge et al., 2007; Fudge et al., 2008). The color wheel is a homemade device with two circles of paper laid on top of one another. The bottom circle has a section of red and a section of green. The top circle is white with a wedge removed so that when turned, either green or red shows through. The top circle can then be turned to signal a transition by showing red. Once children in the research study learned the system, they were observed to make transitions with fewer distractions. The system also was used to decrease the time children spend in transition.

When transitions between activities are problematic, the following suggestions may be tried:

- Change the schedule to decrease the number of transitions.

- Change the schedule to decrease the amount of time for the transition.

- Change the activities to provide preferred activities during or after transition.

- Decrease sensory stimulation.

- Provide clear guidance for what comes next in the transition—cues, prompts, models, proximity of adult, or feedback.

Transition periods are frequently teacher-directed times during which children are not engaged in productive activities. It is important to find ways to decrease the numbers of and time spent in transitions. The following tool provides a method of planning for transitions, teacher roles, and cues.

Schedule with Intentional Transitions

It is important to build intentional transitions into the classroom schedule. Smooth transitions are created through reflection and implementation of plans.

Figure 6.6 details plans and roles so that teaching teams may analyze and implement the best ways to transition children in their group.

Purpose of This Tool	The purpose of this tool is to aid planning and communication of the specific transition times, roles of teachers, and cues. This tool also can be used to analyze schedules to determine whether the length of time and sequence for each element is appropriate for the group.
When to Use This Tool	This tool should be used whenever a new schedule is developed or when transitions become problematic.
How to Use This Tool	Write the time that each scheduled daily routine or activity will take place in the column labeled *time*. Write the name of the activity and describe the expected behavior for the activity or routine in the white sections of the column labeled *activity*. Describe the transition and expected behaviors in the gray section of the *activity* column, making sure to describe the areas of the room the children will move from and to. Also, note the cue that teachers will use to signal the children that the transition is taking place. Assign roles to teachers for the transition. Write the teachers' names and assigned roles in the columns indicated.
Suggestions for Using This Tool	1. Although planning schedules and transitions will help most children in the classroom, there may still be children who require more assistance. These children may require an adult to be near them to help during transitions.
	2. Some children benefit from picture schedules so that they can see the schedule and know the order of activities. Teachers may need to remind children of the schedule by looking at the pictures and talking about what comes next. Some children benefit from a personal photo album that helps them predict the transition. This strategy is most helpful when the child already knows the skills for the transition but needs cues to help

Schedule with Intentional Transitions

Directions: Write the time that each scheduled daily routine or activity will take place in the column labeled *Time.* Write the name of the activity and describe the expected behavior for the activity or routine in the sections of the column labeled *Activity.* Describe the transition and expected behaviors in the *Activity* column, making sure to describe the areas of the room the children will move from and to. Also, note the cue that teachers will use to signal the children that the transition is taking place. Assign roles to teachers for the transition. Write the teachers' names and assigned roles in the columns indicated.

Classroom: *Preschool 3*

Observer's name: *Janet K.*

Time	Activity	Teacher name	Responsibility
From: 8:00 To: 8:30	Arrival transition description: Children put things in cubby	1) Sarah 2) Terri	Sets up breakfast Engages children
From: 8:00 To: 8:30	Breakfast		
From: 8:30 To: 8:45	Transition from breakfast to free play Cue: Children begin to scrape plates	1) Sarah 2) Terri	Assists clean up Engages children
From: 8:45 To: 10:00	Free choice/special art		
From: 10:00 To: 10:30	Transition from free choice to outside Cue: 10 and 5 minute warnings Clean-up song on CD player	1) Sarah 2) Terri	Helps with clean up Helps with coats
From: 10:30 To: 11:15	Outside		
From: 11:15 To: 11:35	Transition from outside to large group Cue: 5- and 10-minute warnings Teacher gathers some children and walks to door.	1) Sarah 2) Terri	Moves to door Directs children to door
From: 11:35 To: 11:50	Group time		
From: 11:50 To: 12:00	Transition from group time to lunch Cue: Songs with names	1) Sarah 2) Terri	Sits with group Moves to lunch tables

Figure 6.6. Schedule with Intentional Transitions.

him or her remember and follow through (Stromer, Kimball, Kenney, & Taylor, 2006).

3. When children have difficulty with transitions, it may be helpful for teachers to sit with children and help them talk about the expectations and provide feedback about behavior during the transition.

Transitions within Activities

Just as some children need support to move from one activity to another, other children need support to move from step to step within an activity. These children may get stuck at the beginning, middle, or end of an activity. They may not be able to complete multiple steps. For these children, concrete guidance to know what comes next within the activity is helpful in order to be successful.

Within-activity transitions are different than between-activity transitions because they are usually not teacher-directed and they typically involve small groups rather than large groups. Often, within-activity transition challenges involve only one child. Although the context is different, many of the strategies used for between-activity transitions can also be used for within-activity transitions.

It is important for teachers to plan support for children who struggle with within-activity transitions. Planning should include a thorough analysis of the types and frequency of behaviors the child needs to learn. Knowing the types of behaviors helps teachers then know the targets for the support they provide. Knowing the frequency helps teachers monitor progress across time.

One strategy that has been used successfully is that of providing *activity schedules*. These schedules are sometimes called *work plans*. Activity schedules have been shown to reduce tantrum behaviors (Dooley, Wilczenski, & Torem, 2001) and increase on-task behavior. Research shows that activity schedules can be used to support children's successful progress from step to step within an activity and also between activities. (Bryan & Gast, 2000; Dauphin, Kinney, & Stromer, 2004; Dooley et al., 2001; Morrison, Sainato, Benchaban, & Endo, 2002). Once children learn to use them, they also can be used to teach social skills.

Activity schedules provide visual support for transitions. They are made up of pictures or photos that cue the child that a transition is coming. The pictures show the child what comes next. The following steps may be part of an activity schedule that helps young children know how to begin to build with blocks:

1. Think about what you would like to build.

2. Think about the blocks you will need.

3. Remove the blocks from the shelf.

4. Place the blocks where they are needed.

5. Continue until you are finished building.

6. Put the blocks back on the shelf.

A photo of a child completing these steps is included next to each step. The photos can be mounted on tag board and attached with rings or placed in a photo album. Smaller photos can be made into a bracelet that a child wears.

When these types of supports are needed, it is important to remember that we are teaching appropriate behavior. The cues provide a mechanism for signaling children when the transitions occur and provide a cue to the appropriate behavior. Such supports should be removed gradually as children learn the expectations for transitions, become more independent, and can manage their own transitions.

Conclusion

Classroom schedules and routines play an important role in setting up success for children and teachers. Teachers who know the sensitivities and tolerances of the children in their classroom can design an overall routine that provides optimal amounts of time for children to become engaged with their peers and the curriculum. Even when schedules are planned carefully, some children will still need additional support. Then, planning at the individual or small-group level becomes necessary. Teacher presence and concrete cues may be needed for these children. As children learn the routines and corresponding behavior, they can begin to function independently and monitor their own behavior.

CHAPTER 7

Centerwide Support

MARC GIVES
NEW MEANING
TO DRAWING
A LINE IN THE
SAND.

To support all children in early childhood settings, teachers and families need support from everyone in the school or center. Carr, Johnson, and Corkwell (2004) described principle-centered leadership as a best practice for administrators and supervisors. However, these principles apply to everyone in early childhood care and education. Essentially, the habits we develop for working with others and obtaining the support we need to be successful in our positions require that we become proficient with communication practices that are effective, be ethical and considerate with our actions and words, organize our days to address the important and urgent items first, collaborate with others instead of floundering on our own, and figure out where we need to improve our skills and enhance our knowledge through practice and/or professional development (Carr et al., 2004; Covey, 1990).

Being clear with our communication about the frustrations and needs we have in caring for children must be based on reflections and data. If a child is challenging you or displaying inappropriate behaviors, complaining about the situation *will not* be effective for obtaining support. However, presenting data about what you have tried and the resulting outcomes is a very effective way to obtain assistance. Data can be descriptive, numerical, or couched other ways, so long as it is collected and presented professionally and systematically.

Requesting Help

Documenting concerns to obtain assistance is the best way to ensure that your needs and the needs of the student are not ignored. The Request for Collaborative Centerwide Support in Figure 7.1 provides a template for doing just that.

Request for Collaborative Centerwide Support

A request for centerwide support is typically initiated by a teacher or caregiver, but anyone who is in place to support—disability coordinator, counselor, psychologist, family services worker, director, and so forth—would also need to document what action was taken to address the problem and the outcome from that action. For example, an action could be a call to the family to describe the challenging classroom behavior. The outcome may be that the family agreed to come in for a meeting. This meeting, then, becomes another action taken. Perhaps the outcome of that meeting is an agreement to shorten the child's day to help her become more successful within a shorter time frame. This may lead to an intervention plan or script that is clearly planned to support the child. It is undertaken by the adult in the classroom, supporting personnel, and families. At this time, progress would be documented on the intervention plan. However, should another incident occur unrelated to the intervention, this tool may be used again.

Request for Collaborative Centerwide Support

Directions: Document the child's behavior that is concerning. Also document what you have done in the classroom to meet the child's needs. List the specific assistance that you may need. Examples of support requiring resources outside the typical classroom include 1) extra classroom coverage, 2) observation from a psychologist or administrator, 3) meeting with the center intervention team, 4) help determining what strategies to try, and 5) help working with the family to resolve issues. The first action step should be completed by the person filling out this form. This form should be circulated among all stakeholders in the particular child's care and education.

Date: *5/29/09*

To: *Terri Stuart, principal*

From: *Patty Newman, classroom teacher*

Concern: *AG has bitten several children and two teachers. He seems to react quickly and intensely when having disputes.*

Need: *The child needs to be observed and brainstorming sessions need to be conducted to resolve this behavior.*

Action previously taken by person initiating this request: *Met with parents to discuss concerns. Instructed AG to use his words to express himself.*

Outcome: *I have not seen a decrease in the targeted behavior.*

Date: *5/29/09*

Action taken as a result of this request: *Met with parents to discuss observations. I observed AG for 5 days and then conducted a functional assessment.*

Outcome: *I developed an intervention for AG based on teaching appropriate ways for him to acquire materials. Positive feedback for AG's success was included in the intervention.*

Date: *6/10/09*

Follow-up needed: *Implement intervention with observation for 3 weeks and then meet to evaluate.*

Figure 7.1. Request for Collaborative Centerwide Support.

Purpose of This Tool	The purpose of this tool is to provide a method for obtaining and tracking centerwide assistance. This tool also can be used to frame the request for support by eliciting specific information about needs of the child, family, and teachers.
When to Use This Tool	This tool should be used after classroom-specific interventions have been initiated and the need for more centerwide help is needed. This tool is the first step to begin the process for documenting a concern that requires something more than can be supported in the classroom alone, which may or may not lead to a referral for an intervention plan.
How to Use This Tool	Document the child's behavior that is concerning. Also document what you have done in the classroom to meet the child's needs. List the specific assistance that you may need. Examples of support requiring resources outside the typical classroom include 1) extra classroom coverage, 2) observation from a psychologist or administrator, 3) meeting with the center intervention team, 4) help determining what strategies to try, and 5) help working with the family to resolve issues. The first action step should be completed by the person filling out the Request for Collaborative Centerwide Support. The form is circulated among all center stakeholders in the particular child's care and education.
Suggestions for Using This Tool	Use this tool to begin collaborating with other staff, administrators, and supporting professionals. Once a level of acceptable resolution is obtained, file the form. It may be that a strategy begins to work for you and the child in the classroom; the parents become more involved, which helps the child's concerning behavior dissipate; or a referral for an intervention is made.

It is possible that challenges require more attention and specialized intervention than is available within the center. For example, an observation may be needed from someone with "trained eyes." This may be a master teacher, center director, social worker, or psychologist, all of whom should have extensive child development knowledge and well-developed observational skills. It is important that the teacher, or person with a concern, communicate the challenge clearly so that the observer can focus on the specific behavior and all of the factors that may affect the behavior either positively or negatively.

When outside support in requested, agreements should be developed that describe the roles each will play and the actions they will take. The agreement should specify the resources (financial or personnel) each party will commit. In addition, the agreement should specify a timeline (Branson & Bingham, 2009). A complete agreement will prevent misunderstandings that can stall progress during an important time in the development of the intervention.

Sometimes an additional staff member is necessary for the success of the classroom. This is an expensive solution but one that is needed in many programs across the country. While adult-to-child ratios typically are maintained according to state or district standards, these are minimum standards and not specifically optimal ratios. To really meet the needs for all children, adults must be available when the child is in need, and the adults must have the support needed to perform as a professional educator and caregiver throughout the day. This usually requires higher adult-to-child ratios than are mandated.

Using Data

Everyone involved with a child with challenging behavior needs information about the child to know how to respond. Often, teachers take much of the wealth of information they have about the child for granted. They are with the child and have a deep sense of how the child responds in certain situations, what type of events may be difficult for the child, and what seems to be soothing for the child. It is easy for others who spend little or no time with the child to miss important cues and details. When it is necessary to ask for assistance from administrators or outside consultants, information will need to be gathered and written down. Accurate information about the child and interactions with the environment is necessary for help to be effective.

Individuals coming from the outside to support classroom teachers will need to know specific information about the frequency and the duration of the behaviors that are challenging in the classroom. They also will need to know a detailed description of what the behavior looks like. They will need to know what has been tried in the past and the outcomes of those attempts. It is helpful if teachers collect the information prior to requesting support. If this information has not been documented in detail, it is likely that the consultant or program administrator will devise a system to collect the information. This may slow the process of developing interventions.

Most of the information teachers will need to communicate to outside professionals is found through observing the child in the classroom environment. Teachers can observe and record everything that happens in the classroom, or they can observe only at certain times or during certain events. Each of these types of observation and recording methods provides critical information when designing intervention plans. Types and uses of some helpful observation methods are listed in Table 7.1.

Often, teachers try many things before requesting help from outside the classroom. These attempts and their outcomes should be documented. Examples of things that teachers can do to support children include modifying materials to make them easier or more difficult, changing the length of activities, positioning teachers closer to a child, changing the sequence of events, or using concrete cues to signal transitions. This list is but a small fraction of the types of steps teachers may take to support children in the classroom. They are valid modifications.

Table 7.1. General observation methods

Type	Description	Pros	Cons
Narrative record	This method is best used when there is not a very good understanding of what is happening and why. To complete the record, the teacher sits and observes, writing everything that is seen and heard: Language, body position, other children, routine, materials, and position in the classroom are included.	This method provides details about what happens just before, during, and after the concerning behavior. All classroom influences can be noted.	This method can be very time consuming and give much useless information. This may not be manageable while teaching an active group of children.
Event sample	When teachers are only concerned about specific events, they can zero in on these events. For example, if a teacher wants to know if interventions decrease a child's kicking, she will first need to know how many times the child has kicked before the intervention. The kicking behavior is the *event* that is being recorded. Event samples tell us how many times something happens.	This method provides accurate information about well-defined events.	This method is very focused on the event in question, which may cause the observer to miss important information.
Time sample	Time samples are used to gather information for a specified amount of time. The intervals should be designed to give information that will generalize the day or routine of the day in question.	This method provides more complete information about what happens before, during, and after a specific event than an event sample. This method can be designed to make ballpark judgments about the frequency of a behavior.	This method will not record all of the behavior. This could yield inaccurate information if the time intervals observed are not well selected.

Classroom Modifications to Support Behavior Tool

It is important for outside professionals to know how each modification was implemented and how it worked. The Classroom Modifications to Support Behavior Tool in Figure 7.2 will help teachers collect information on the modifications they implement.

Purpose of This Tool	This tool provides a template for teachers to briefly communicate what they have done in the classroom to support children with challenging behaviors.
When to Use This Tool	This tool can be used to document supports and/or modifications made in the classroom regardless of whether a request for outside support is made. It can be used after modifications have been tried and as a planning document to discuss and record modifications with team members.

Classroom Modifications to Support Behavior Tool

Directions: After deciding which classroom modifications to make, document them in the first column. Document the date the modifications were put in place. Observe to determine whether the modifications seemed to change behavior. Describe what you did to implement the modifications.

Modification type	Date	Outcome	Description of implementation
Move location of breakfast	4/1/09	(o Change) o No change	Children ate within direct sight of all classroom staff. Moved shelves to make area less stimulating.
Begin breakfast set-up routine earlier	3/10/09	o Change (o No change)	Started breakfast set up. at 8:00. Now start at 7:15.
Use familiar music as transition cue	4/7/09	(o Change) o No change	Played classical music CD beginning at 7:45
		o Change o No change	
		o Change o No change	

Figure 7.2. Classroom Modifications to Support Behavior Tool.

How to Use This Tool

After deciding which classroom modifications to make, document them in the first column. Document the date the modifications were put in place. Observe to determine whether the modifications seemed to change behavior. Describe what you did to implement the modifications.

Suggestions for Using This Tool

1. Many times teachers make modifications in the classroom without thinking about them. Adaptations are made to assist the children and teachers as they work through the day. When these modifications are written down, it saves time for a consultant who may inadvertently recommend some of the very modifications that have been tried. It also saves frustration and the "I already tried that" response.

2. Often, it can be difficult for teachers to ask for help. They feel bad about the fact that they have not found ways to support the child. When the attempts are documented, it can give teachers a sense of accomplishment rather than feelings of inadequacy.

3. Trying many modifications without a real plan for how to make them work can inadvertently make matters worse. For example, making too many changes in materials, routines, and groupings could make target behaviors increase. It is important to see the modifications as a whole.

Professional Development

To be able to depend on the program or district resources to provide help when it is needed, all stakeholders must know and understand evidence-based practices. To assure that administrators and co-workers are current in their understandings of research and practice, professional development should be available to early childhood stakeholders on a continuing basis. A theory of instruction and care must guide what is done in early childhood settings to achieve positive outcomes. Research-based, or evidence-based, practices should be implemented with fidelity to promote positive outcomes for children.

Centerwide Professional Development Needs Tool

To reach the professional standards outlined above, support for those who are working in the field is critical. The DEC specifically stated that many services should be available to address challenging behaviors in early childhood environments, including "external consultation and technical assistance or additional staff support" (1999, p. 4). Professional development and support, however, can occur by using internal and local resources, early childhood study group participation, college

Centerwide Professional Development Needs Tool

Directions: Give this survey to teachers and caregivers to complete. Then review and compile the results. Professional development content and schedules can then be developed from the survey.

Name: _A. Dill_   Date: _11/28/09_

1. What supports do you need in your classroom to address challenging behaviors?

   I do not know what to do to extend attention and slow impulsive behavior. I need to learn what to do to help children engage in the learning experience. I would like to get some ideas to help G.A. play with others rather than alone. And, I would like to learn how to help children become more accepting of G.A.

2. How have staff members with whom you work addressed challenging behaviors in the past?

   We basically try to redirect children who are exhibiting impulsive behaviors, but we find that we spend a great deal of time on redirecting.

3. With whom do you discuss your needs for support in addressing challenging behaviors?

   We discuss concerns among ourselves. And, we discuss them with our education coordinator.

4. Where do you find information about working with children who have challenging behaviors?

   From our education coordinator.

5. What was the most informative professional development session and/or class you have ever attended, and why was this so?

   I took a class that focused on child development and the needs of young children. This class was really helpful.

Figure 7.3. Centerwide Professional Development Needs Tool.

courses, seminars, video, and professional conferences. Figure 7.3, the Centerwide Professional Development Needs Tool, outlines centerwide needs for support in addressing challenging behaviors.

Purpose of This Tool	The Centerwide Professional Development Needs Tool should be used to elicit information from teachers regarding their and their co-workers' concerning skill levels.
When to Use This Tool	Administrators should use this tool at least once a year, when new staff members are just starting or on an as-needed basis.
How to Use This Tool	Give this survey to teachers and caregivers, then review and compile the results. Professional development content and schedules can then be developed from the survey.
Suggestions for Using This Tool	Once data is collected from staff, administrators should use the information to design professional development opportunities that meet the specific needs noted in the survey. For example, if additional help is needed in the classroom as a support and no funds are available, perhaps a session on using volunteers in the classroom to work with children or a session on creating a more autonomous environment for children would be helpful. Or, it may be that a session for administrators on fundraising to support additional staff would be necessary. If guidance strategies appear to be a theme from staff, then finding a coach from within or outside the center to work with individual staff may be the professional development strategy needed. If a certain co-worker seems to be listed as the "go-to" person in question 3, then perhaps providing individual professional development for that person who would, in turn, coach others would be the best course to take. Overall, attending to the generalities and specifics from staff answers will be helpful in creating professional development opportunities to make individuals and the center more successful in addressing challenging behaviors.

Conclusion

In summary, it is the responsibility of the center administrator to ensure that staff professional development needs are met and that supports and resources are provided for classrooms when needed. Staff must be systematic in communicating the specific concerns they have and communicate their needs effectively. It is the professional responsibility of the entire center to support all the children and all the staff. In this way, a sense of place that is nurturing to all, collaborative in nature, and respectful of the profession can be developed and maintained.

Transactional Contexts

Young children grow up within a complex system of family and early childhood education or child care environments with a myriad of expectations, opportunities, and restrictions. They must learn to negotiate each environment to be successful or resilient if they are vulnerable or at risk. This is not particularly easy, especially for children with disabilities or mental health concerns. Adults and other children interact with children who have challenging behaviors according to their own senses of understanding and skill sets. It is important to note that when too many risk factors are present, children's emergent intellectual capacity and ability to negotiate the curriculum are jeopardized (Sameroff, Seifer, Barocas, Zax, & Greenspan, 1987). Protective factors can be enhanced in the early care and education environment to support children who are at risk.

A transactional model of development acknowledges that individuals are continually being shaped through interactions with others and environmental influences. Rather than seeing all children develop through set stages, an *organismic* world view, or that behavior is shaped systematically, a *mechanistic* world view, seeing children through a contextual world view, or one that acknowledges the impact of culture on development, allows the teacher to build communities of learning that foster collaborative relationships between the adult and the child. It may even foster a transformational relationship whereby both the child and teacher are positively influenced. Guidance, then, is significant: it can be explicit and clear or tacit and implied, and language is the mediator. As Rogoff (2003) emphasizes, life and learning rely on the presence of diverse improvisations. We see these improvisations as transactional occurrences in the classroom. To view child development through a transactional perspective, one must take into account individual and environmental conditions as well as the impact each person has on one another (Sameroff & Chandler, 1975; Sameroff & Fiese, 1990). Within this framework, teachers can respond to children's behavior, talk with families, and empower a child's peers so that the understanding of the behavior is reframed. Thus, consistent, effective responses to an undesirable behavior may help a child become more successful within the early childhood environment. Studying this and reflecting upon one's own interactions can make improvisation seem second-nature.

The chapters in Section III focus on the transactional contexts of factors that are under a teacher's control and how teachers can influence those that are not. It presumes that changing one's own behavior influences the behavior of another.

CHAPTER 8

Teachers' Reactions to Children's Behaviors

Effective teachers are introspective. They must contemplate their own feelings toward a child who is disrupting the classroom harmony. It is possible to reframe situations so that teachers may respond differently to the classroom situation and problem solve with families to ensure that all adults are helping the child learn to be more successful in the classroom. It is important for teachers to use direct, honest, and respectful communication with children and families. This chapter provides strategies to assist teachers with self-reflection and to reframe an understanding of a situation.

Goodness of Fit

Think about how a quartet sounds when all the notes are in harmony. Then consider how it sounds when the notes are discordant. It is most delightful when harmonious. This is one way to perceive the value of determining whether teacher temperament is harmonious with a child's behavior. We all have temperaments that are part of who we are; however, we are also greatly influenced by our environment and culture and our innate temperaments are manifested accordingly. We tend to interact with others given the nature of our own temperament; in addition, how we behave toward others influences how they behave toward us. Together, we create harmony or discord, depending on our goodness of fit. Although we cannot change the innate sense of who we are, we can reflect on who we are and why we may perceive a child's behavior as challenging. For example, some teachers highly value active, inquisitive children. Other teachers find these same children annoying.

Temperament scales, based on the early work of Thomas and Chess (1977) and Thomas, Chess, and Birch (1968), essentially look at nine temperament characteristics and how these traits manifest themselves along a continuum for individuals, beginning at birth. These characteristics are who we are, influenced by our environmental and cultural expectations. As we mature, we are much better able to recognize how we respond and modify our own behaviors to adjust to stressful situations. More importantly, consider how this might be problematic if a child leans toward the high or low end of the scale and/or if our own temperament and behaviors lean in a different direction. Given that teachers are the adults in these transactions, it is imperative that the "goodness of fit," or match or mismatch, between the adult and the child or the child and the environment be acknowledged. A mismatch may be the underlying reason the teacher perceives that child as having a behavior problem. Temperament continues into adulthood, and these characteristics continue to influence our behavior and adjustment throughout the life span. The specific behaviors determined to be innate to our temperaments are *activity level, regularity of sleeping and eating patterns, initial reaction, adaptability, intensity of emotion, mood, distractibility, persistence and attention span,* and *sensory sensitivity.* Teachers who are able to reflect on their own temperament and understand a child's temperament may also be able to reframe how they communicate with that child, creating constraints that better fit the child's temperament so that the child is more successful in class.

Temperament Scale to Determine Goodness of Fit

Although temperament is not an excuse for misbehavior, recognizing temperaments may help to prevent and manage problems that may arise from our differences. The Temperament Scale to Determine Goodness of Fit in Figure 8.1 lists the continua of behaviors for the nine temperament characteristics. Chart yourself and the child whose behaviors are of concern to you. You should solicit input from families to determine whether your perceptions are accurate. It also may help families determine where some of the issues lie within the home environment as well.

Purpose of This Tool

The purpose of this tool is to determine whether there are significant differences in temperament between the teacher and the child perceived as having challenging behaviors in the classroom. It may also be a useful tool for parents to use when they struggle with parenting a child who is innately different than they may be.

When to Use This Tool

Consider using this tool when a child "drives you crazy" with activity or inactivity, rigidity or lack of organization, intense emotions or passivity, and so forth. It may be that the fit between the adult and child is a mismatch, requiring a conscious effort to mediate the differences.

How to Use This Tool

Read the temperament category on the left. Reflect on your own typical behavior and preferences, then put an *X* on the continuum, from 1 to 5, where you think your innate preferences lie. There are no right or wrong answers. (You may also want to refer to the temperament scales in Chapter 1.) Then, go back and fill in the tool for the child who is difficult for you to work with in the classroom. It is best to solicit input from families because they know their child best. Note where there are obvious differences and obvious similarities between the two of you. You may want to circle the areas where there are differences and write some examples of how these differences have been noticeable in the classroom.

Suggestions for Using This Tool

Using the information gleaned from completing the tool in Figure 8.1, think about how some of your areas of fit or areas of differences affect your own behavior. Reflect on how you respond in situations where these differences or similarities are evident. How do you treat the child in each of these situations? Note your reflections on the tool. Acknowledge and address your feelings toward the child and the challenging situation. The following vignette is an example of how the Temperament Scale to Determine Goodness of Fit might be applied.

Temperament Scale to Determine Goodness of Fit

Directions: Read the temperament category on the left. Reflect on your own typical behavior and preferences, then put an *X* on the continuum, from 1 to 5, where you think your innate preferences lie. There are no right or wrong answers. Then, go back and fill in the tool for the child who is difficult for you to work with in the classroom. It is best to solicit input from families because they know their child best. Note where there are obvious differences and obvious similarities between the two of you. You may want to circle the areas where there are differences and write some examples of how these differences have been noticeable in the classroom.

Teacher's name: _____ Child's name: _____

Temperament characteristic	Temperament rating scale		
How active are you during the day? Can you sit through long meetings? ACTIVITY LEVEL *Does the child wiggle and move around when being read to, sitting at a table, or playing?*	Calm and content, inactive much of the time	You 1----X--------3--------5 Child 1-----------3-------X---5	Highly active, always on the go
How regular are you in your eating, sleeping, and bowel habits? REGULARITY *Does the child prefer regular meal and snack times, nap and bed times, and a consistent number of sleep hours and have bowel movements about the same time daily?*	Habits are regular	You 1-----------X--3--------5 Child 1--------------3-X--------5	Habits are irregular
How do you react the first time to new people, places, activities, or things? INITIAL REACTION *How does the child usually react the first time to new people, new foods, new toys, and new activities?*	Willing to try new things and usually comfortable in social situations	You 1---X---------3--------5 Child 1--------------3-X--------5	Unwilling or reluctant to try new things and often withdraws in social situations
How quickly do you adapt to changes in schedules, routines, new people, places, or things? ADAPTABILITY *How quickly does the child adapt to changes in schedules, routines, new people, places, or things?*	Adapts easily to change	You 1------X--------3--------5 Child 1--------------3----------X----5	Does not adapt easily to change
How strong are your reactions to new or unexpected stimuli? INTENSITY OF EMOTION *How strong or violent are the child's reactions to new or unexpected stimuli? Does the child laugh and cry with intensity, or does he or she just smile and get a bit irritated or fussy?*	Emotional reactions are mild, low key	You 1-----------X-3--------5 Child 1--------------3---X----------5	Emotional reactions are intense, even exaggerated

Figure 8.1. Temperament Scale to Determine Goodness of Fit.

Temperament characteristic	Temperament rating scale		
How much of the time are you pleasant and joyful compared with being in a grouchy or sad mood? MOOD How much of the time does the child exhibit pleasant, joyful behavior compared with crying or fussing behavior?	Typical mood is pleasant, positive, and happy	*You* 1 -X----------3-----------5 *Child* 1 -----------3-X---------5	Typical mood is negative, often angry, cries often
Are you easily distracted by sounds, people, or environmental stimuli? DISTRACTIBILITY Is the child easily distracted, or does he or she ignore distractions such as other noises or other children?	Highly focused, can concentrate well, not easily distracted	*You* 1 --X----------3-----------5 *Child* 1 -----------3-----------X---5	Easily distracted, unable to ignore distractions, daydreams
How long will you continue working on a difficult task? PERSISTENCE AND ATTENTION SPAN How long does the child continue with one activity, even if it is difficult?	Sticks with projects until they are done, does not give up	*You* 1 -----------3-X----------5 *Child* 1 -----------3---------X----5	Does not stick with projects until they are done, gives up easily
How aware are you of slight differences in noise level, temperature, visual stimuli, taste, or touch? SENSORY SENSITIVITY How aware is the child of slight noises, lighting, touch, pain, temperature differences, and, differences in taste and clothing?	Not overly sensitive	*You* 1 -----------X--3-----------5 *Child* 1 -----------3-----------X--5	Highly sensitive

Note obvious similarities and differences here. _____

_____

_____

_____

_____

_____

Joellen is highly sensitive to touch and at the opposite end of the temperament scale from the teacher with regard to sensory sensitivity. She does not like other children sitting too close to her or having people bump into her or even hold her hand walking through the hallway. All tags are removed from her clothing. The teacher loves hugs, often reaching out to pat children on the shoulder or head, and enjoys loads of stimulating activities. Joellen withdraws or may even cry when she perceives too much stimulation. The teacher sees this as atypical behavior and wonders whether Joellen may be on the autism spectrum. At other times, however, Joellen is very engaged and appears to be enjoying the activities in the classroom. After using the Temperament Scale to Determine Goodness of Fit for herself and Joellen, the teacher also realizes that she and Joellen differ in several other areas. She did not understand Joellen's responses because they were not how she would respond. This tool helped the teacher reflect on how differently she approaches life in general than does Joellen. She realizes it is her responsibility as a teacher to target specific activities that may be uncomfortable for Joellen; therefore, she decides to do some additional planning. Thus, the teacher realizes that for Joellen to feel comfortable participating in class activities, she needs to monitor her own feelings and behavior, be sensitive to Joellen's needs during group situations or while reading a story, and be thoughtful about planning activities for the classroom that may require physical closeness among the children and staff or that may be too stimulating for Joellen.

Reframing Perceptions

Once you have determined where the differences between you and the child lie, where there may be temperament risk factors, or whether the child has any extreme temperament characteristics, you have the information necessary to begin to reframe how you view the child.

For example, Schick (1998) clusters children deemed "difficult" into five groups according to temperament-based behaviors: those who 1) are difficult to manage, 2) are difficult to keep healthy and safe, 3) are difficult to be around, 4) have difficult attitudes, and 5) have difficulty focusing.

For those children who are challenging to manage, consider that they may have low adaptability, may be emotionally sensitive, or may perhaps have a pessimistic mood. These may be protective factors in many ways. For example, these students may not make impulsive decisions and have numerous regrets. However, if this is not your temperament, you may find that those children often seem defiant, stubborn, or timid.

Some children appear to be gullible, take too many risks, focus on competition, follow others mindlessly, or appear flippant. These characteristics may result from temperaments that are optimistic, highly adaptable, not very intense, and very active. These children may be difficult to keep safe in that they give up items too quickly, do not stand up for themselves, or seem to continually put themselves in harm's way or be victims of bullying behaviors. You may find these traits unacceptable and aggravating, particularly if you cannot relate to them yourself.

If you are a fairly optimistic person yourself, you may also find children who are highly sensitive, pessimistic, and not very good at adapting to new situations difficult to be around. Realize that these children may need more time than others to adjust to new situations.

You may get into power struggles with children who are very active, not easily distracted, persistent, and not very sensitive to others' feelings. If you are also intense, you may end up adding to the drama that surrounds children who have these traits. You may need to learn strategies for waiting and communicating positively to teach these strategies to children like yourself.

If children are sensitive to their own feelings but not as much to other's feelings, are highly active, very intense, and highly distractible or some combination of these traits, they may have difficulty focusing or be very excitable.

Reflection Questions to Focus on Reframing Perceptions

Although not every challenging behavior, such as tantrums, procrastination, attachment, and manipulation, is directly related to temperament, the manner in which behaviors are displayed often is (Schick, 1998). Therefore, if you can predict the behavior and how it might be displayed, you can plan a way to address it. You also can determine what types of skills children may need to be taught to be successful. Considering how your basic temperament fits with the child's temperament may help you reframe your perceptions of the child and challenging situations to create plans that will make the classroom more pleasant for both of you. The Reflection Questions to Focus on Reframing Perceptions Tool in Figure 8.2 can help with the process of changing your perspectives.

Purpose of This Tool	Variations in temperament often affect teacher perceptions of a child's teachability (Chess & Thomas, 1996). Thus, the questions in Figure 8.2 help you reframe your own perceptions of challenging situations and the children you see as challenging.
When to Use This Tool	Use this tool after acknowledging where you have goodness-of-fit and temperamental differences to help guide your thoughts about your perceptions of children and classroom situations.
How to Use This Tool	Think about your responses to children, the feelings you experience when challenging situations arise, and your natural reactions to situations. Then answer each question thoughtfully.
Suggestions for Using This Tool	Once you have considered and reconsidered your perceptions of children who have temperaments that differ from yours, you can then begin to make a plan to reduce stress and build on the assets of both your characteristics and the child's. For example, you may develop scripts and constraints for promoting positive outcomes and reducing challenging behaviors. *Scripts,* or consistent responses to children, can be developed and used by teachers, parents, and peers in response to behaviors that are unacceptable,

Reflection Questions to Focus on Reframing Perceptions

Directions: Consider the following questions to help reflect on and reframe your perceptions about a child.

1. How well do you work with children who you perceive as easy, slow to warm up, or difficult?

   I prefer to work with children who are easy. Those who are slow to warm up seem difficult as do the ones who are too active. However, the active ones seem to push my buttons.

2. What might you say to and do for each child in the classroom with these varying temperaments to make the classroom pleasant and accommodating for all children?

   I could try to be more patient with those children who are slow to warm up. I could provide more wait time for them to answer or perhaps use a toy to play near the child until he is ready to approach me. For those children who are extremely active, I could try to schedule the day so that there are more periods of high activity for the active children. Maybe I could use some signals to indicate that I would like for them to calm down before I try to communicate.

3. What do you do or say to exacerbate situations for a child given the child's innate temperament?

   I think I sometimes get frustrated, particularly with active children. Then I forget to sit down on the floor to work with children. I am up moving around so this seems to make ALL the children become more active instead of engaging with the classroom materials and activities.

4. What might you do or say differently to bring out the best in both you and the child?

   Maybe I could model taking deep breaths and try to remain calm—with a smile instead of a grumpy, frustrated look. I think I need to gain trust to get cooperation. I need practice!!

5. In what way does culture and environment affect temperamental characteristics for both you and the child?

   I think our goals are often different. I am thinking of one child whose family does not want to squelch his creativity. So, he has no limits set for him at home. He is a very active child so keeping him on task is challenging. Since this is not my nature or my philosophy, I need to try to understand the family's culture a bit better and maybe have more conversations with them about my expectations and typical reactions to what they see as creative behaviors.

6. Under what conditions are temperament-based characteristics most displayed or inhibited?

   During transitions and late in the afternoon, this is the most difficult. Mid-mornings seem to go more smoothly, particularly when there are fewer transitions and more opportunities for child-directed activities.

7. In what ways can you modify your own perceptions to understand the temperament-based behaviors of the child?

   I think I need to find the strengths in all the children and focus on these. I sometimes see differences as weaknesses, but maybe it's because I am just uncomfortable. I also think I could do some more reading about children who are highly active so that I can learn to value what they can bring to the classroom community.

8. How can you help the child understand how he or she responds based on individual temperament—emphasizing not a "good" or "bad" temperament, but that we all have characteristics about which we must be aware to better use our own strengths to succeed?

   Maybe it's about building empathy and doing loads of problem-solving. I think if we try to get children to understand how their behavior affects others, they may be able to better understand what not to do in some situations. At least, I hope so.

9. How can you adapt situations for individual children, freeing the child from stress and supporting individual variations in development?

   I think this is tough. I am trying to implement a universally designed curriculum, but this actually causes me some stress, too. However, every child does need someone to really "get" him and who will figure out what is supportive, both emotionally and academically. I am willing to put more time into planning the curriculum and using problem-solving and other communication strategies to promote learning and alleviate some of the tensions caused by a poor temperament fit.

10. Knowing that attention problems and high activity often can have a negative effect on academic performance (and not just in children diagnosed with attention deficit/hyperactive disorder) what might you do to help children focus and relax?

    I need to be aware of when the children seem to be getting to the end of their attention span and do something before there is a meltdown. Maybe I could create special activities that vary in length and encourage children with attention issues to start small and move to more complex and longer activities.

Figure 8.2. Reflection Questions to Focus on Reframing Perceptions.

such as foul language, hitting, or crying. *Constraints* can be built within the curriculum and environment to guide the child toward appropriate choices and acceptable behavior. These concepts also are addressed in other parts of this book. The use of these tools is very important because temperament characteristics noticed early in preschool, particularly high activity levels and attention issues, may affect later school success (Martin, Gaddis, Drew, & Moseley, 1988). These challenges can be addressed by making plans to focus on your behavior. As a result you may transform the interactions between the child and yourself. Then, the line in the sand is drawn around you instead of between you.

Conclusion

In summary, there are many temperament variables within ourselves and within children that make interactions difficult or easy, depending on how well we "fit" together and/or tolerate one another's behavior. However, as adults, it is our responsibility to assess these traits and plan for children's success. Finding ways to do this assists with professional growth and reduces the stressors and power struggles that may arise from intolerance and temperament mismatch. When adults reframe perceptions about working with children they perceive as difficult, it is possible to positively transform the teacher–child relationship.

CHAPTER 9

Teacher Language

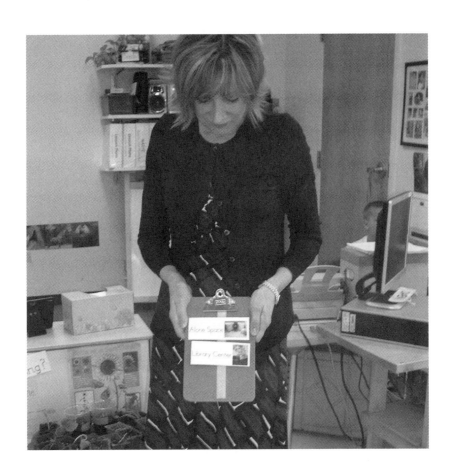

The language that teachers use is important for teaching and learning. Most of the language we use is verbal, but children also understand the messages we send via nonverbal or body language. This chapter describes methods for using language as a teaching tool. Instructional and caring contacts are introduced, and ways to build the teacher–child relationship are presented. Templates for developing scripts for consistent communication and tools for practicing clear, consistent language in challenging situations are included. The impact of teacher language toward and communication with families is also discussed in this chapter.

Transactional and Transformational Teachers

Positive guidance and discipline techniques are designed to teach children skills they need to be successful in school and group situations. These techniques work best when strong relationships exist between the adult and the child. This is why teachers need to address their own "goodness of fit" (see Chapter 8) with individual children and reflect on their own individual set of beliefs and social experiences. These factors are the primary influences on how teachers interact with children. Thus, practicing positive and supportive transactional skills helps teachers build quality relationships with children. In this chapter, transactions refer to the dynamics within the interactions between adults and children. As adults, teachers can turn negative transactions into positive ones by the manner in which they communicate with children, plan the curriculum, set appropriate limits, and provide individually appropriate guidance toward positive outcomes with behavioral supports as warranted. Positive transactions are egalitarian and mutually respectful. Adults who offer empathic acceptance of all children with respect for their dignity *can* create successful learning relationships. When these relationships become mutually beneficial, they then become transformational.

Focusing on the dynamics of respectful communication is essential for teachers who work with children who are at risk for or who have challenging behaviors (Buyse, Verschueren, Doumen, Van Damme, & Maes, 2008). Otherwise, vicious cycles can occur in which challenging behaviors increase due to poor teacher interactions and teacher interactions become negative due to an increase in challenging behaviors (Pianta, Hamre, & Stuhlman, 2003). When teachers focus on the verbal and nonverbal messages they send to children with the intent to build positive relationships and foster learning and teaching, they become transactional teachers and very influential with regard to teaching, learning, and reducing the impact of challenging behaviors in the classroom. Teachers who have great capacity to reflect on teacher–child relationships, make continual conscious efforts to monitor their actions, and use language to help children construct positive ways of interacting may move beyond transactional and actually become a *transformational* teacher and leader in the classroom (Burns, 1978). Thus, whereas *transactional* teachers focus on the exchanges between themselves and children, *transformational* teachers focus on the potentialities of relationships, considering how both the teacher and child can have their own individual goals and needs met. For example, in a child care setting, a transactional teacher focuses on an efficient and kind way to change diapers. A transformational teacher finds innovative ways to change diapers that make the experience more pleasant for *both* the teacher and the child. Transformational teachers focus on intrinsic needs. They are generally charismatic, inspirational, intellectually thoughtful, and considerate of individual needs (Avolio & Yammorino, 2002). It is indeed a goal worth pursuing through reflection on language we use in practice and focus on the messages we send to children and other adults.

Brief Reflection Tool

The reflective process discussed above is critical to refining one's profession (Schön, 1996). It is important because in early childhood care and education settings, developing practitioners may take for granted aspects of their own teaching and consider only reflecting on broader matters, such as why families are not more involved or cannot parent or why children have such challenging behaviors (Dreyfus & Dreyfus, 1986). The Brief Reflection Tool (Figure 9.1) helps teachers through this relective process.

Purpose of This Tool	This tool is a brief checklist for beginning to reflect on the messages teachers send to children.
When to Use This Tool	Use this tool periodically to help reflect on the interactions, communication intent, and discourse that occurs in the teaching environment.
How to Use This Tool	Think about each statement in terms of whether it is a skill that is common practice in the classroom. Determine whether the item is not generally part of your routine even though you may have done this on occasion (circle *no*); done when reminded, periodically, or with some children, but not others (circle *sometimes*); or is part of your regular teaching style for all children (circle *yes*). Then consider whether this is a priority for you to focus on changing your own teaching behaviors. Circle *yes* or *no* for areas that you might choose to work on for professional growth.
Suggestions for Using This Tool	Given that there are numerous items for teachers to think about in the course of their teaching career, this is only a brief list of items that are important to teaching and learning. You may choose to add items as reflection becomes a part of your regular practice. It may be that you determine you need to engage in professional development activities related to building relationships or modeling appropriate language in the classroom. Continual reflection on one's habits and tendencies is a way to target areas to improve practice and elevate teacher effectiveness.

Brief Reflection Tool

Directions: Think about each statement in terms of whether it is a skill that is common practice in the classroom. Determine whether the item is not generally part of your routine even though you may have done this on occasion (circle *no*); done when reminded, periodically, or with some children, but not others (circle *sometimes*); or is part of your regular teaching style for all children (circle *yes*). Then consider whether this is a priority for you to focus on changing your own teaching behaviors. Circle *yes* or *no* for areas that you might choose to work on for professional growth.

Do I . . .		
1. Consider what I say before I say it?	No Sometimes (Yes)	I could work on this: Yes No
2. Take time to have pleasant conversations with *all* children?	No (Sometimes) Yes	I could work on this: (Yes) No
3. Avoid associating the name of a child who is challenging with a negative vision?	No (Sometimes) Yes	I could work on this: (Yes) No
4. Take time to get to know as much about a child and his or her family as possible?	No Sometimes (Yes)	I could work on this: Yes No
5. Use teachable moments to build empathy and teach appropriate behavior?	No (Sometimes) Yes	I could work on this: (Yes) No
6. Use fair, individualized practices in the classroom?	No (Sometimes) Yes	I could work on this: (Yes) No
7. Encourage autonomy and self-regulation of behaviors?	No Sometimes (Yes)	I could work on this: Yes No
8. Share humor (not sarcasm) with children?	No (Sometimes) Yes	I could work on this: Yes (No)
9. Apologize when I am wrong?	No (Sometimes) Yes	I could work on this: (Yes) No
10. Demonstrate sincerity?	No Sometimes (Yes)	I could work on this: Yes No
11. Monitor messages I send via body language?	No (Sometimes) Yes	I could work on this: (Yes) No
12. Provide guidance and feedback regularly?	No Sometimes (Yes)	I could work on this: Yes No
13. Model kind and appropriate school language and behavior?	No Sometimes (Yes)	I could work on this: Yes No
14. Communicate clear expectations?	No Sometimes (Yes)	I could work on this: Yes No
15. Use language that exudes positive regard for the classroom community?	No (Sometimes) Yes	I could work on this: (Yes) No

Figure 9.1. Brief Reflection Tool.

Instructional and Caring Contacts

Children who are taught by teachers with effective instructional skills spend more time in goal-directed activities, have fewer behavior problems in class, and demonstrate better social skills with their peers (Barnett, Lamy, & Frede, 2001; Burchinal, Peisner-Feinberg, Pianta, & Howes, 2002). Boat et al. (in press) present communication strategies that teachers may intentionally use to promote positive outcomes for children. These language-based skills, called *instructional and caring contacts* (ICCs; Nichols & Barnett, 2004) include important strategies for reducing challenging behaviors. Research shows that children's responses *are* alterable by making changes in instruction (Greenwood, Horton, & Utley, 2002). The definitions of the ICCs that are related to intentional instruction are provided in the following section.

Instructional and Caring Contacts for Promoting Positive Child Outcomes

Intentional Instruction

Teachers should not be passive when charged with facilitating learning. Lecturing, a very intentional instructional strategy, however, is not appropriate for young children. Yet, there are other ways to be intentional when providing learning experiences. The environment provides an intentional learning venue, but purposeful and thoughtful teacher interactions promote active learning experiences, inquiry, child engagement, and positive behavior within the educational setting. These strategies are called instructional and caring contacts.

Teacher-Directed Instruction	*Teacher-directed instruction* occurs when teachers overtly provide a direction to complete a task or provide information to a child or group of children by directly teaching or reteaching the information. A teacher might use directed instruction when pointing out the names of certain types of trees, stating the expectations for participating in a field trip experience, or transitioning children from one activity to another.
Prompting	*Prompting* occurs when teachers make a verbal statement to initiate a response. Prompts are typically used as a reminder or scaffold for demonstrating a skill or providing a verbal response. The verbal statement can be made with or without a physical prompt, such as pointing or gesturing. Teachers often use verbal prompts to help children identify letters and sounds. They typically use verbal and pointing prompts to assist children in finding their name in print or putting items away on shelves.

Modeling	*Modeling* occurs when teachers provide children with assistance or other type of adult-initiated opportunities to observe a behavior that will later serve as a tool for the child's own behavior. Modeling may occur in situations in which a new set of materials is introduced to the classroom. The teacher may want to excite children about the new items being placed in the classroom and/or demonstrate how to care for and store the new materials. Modeling might also be used by a teacher when a child struggles with a physical task such as positioning a puzzle piece so it fits or putting a glove on so all fingers are in the right spots.
Practice Opportunity	*Practice opportunity* is used by teachers to provide children with an opportunity to practice by having them perform a skill or verbally restate information that has been provided. Teachers may ask children to practice using words instead of physical means to show anger. Teachers also typically provide children with ample practice opportunities throughout the classroom to perfect a skill such as writing one's own name.
Incidental Instruction	*Incidental instruction* occurs when teachers use one of the above intentional strategies during natural interactions. The teacher may focus on what a child says or does and encourages the child to elaborate or provides elaboration him- or herself. Incidental instruction occurs often during free choice time and other child opportunities for unstructured play.
Corrective Feedback	*Corrective feedback* is used by teachers to provide instructional verbal feedback to children, giving information about the inappropriate behavior or replacing an incorrect child response with a specific replacement behavior or response. For example, if a child points to picture of an animal and wrongly identifies it as a "cow," the teacher says, "No, that's actually a horse." Or, at group time, a child may say, "I am sitting on the couch," to which the teacher responds, "No, at group time, we all sit on our mats."

Intentional Instruction Tool

This tool (Figure 9.2) will encourage you to consider how you use intentional strategies within educational settings. It is very important to consider the dynamics of the transactions and the purpose of the intentional communication. Thus, reflecting on what you do and say in your role as a teacher is critical to children's learning.

Purpose of This Tool	This tool is useful for thinking about how much intentional instruction you use with the children in your classroom.

Intentional Instruction Tool

Directions: Refer to the definitions of ICC intentional instruction in Chapter 9. Using the scale provided, rate yourself for each of the items in the tool. Then, provide one or two examples of how you have recently used this strategy in your practice. If you cannot list examples and would like to study this strategy more in depth, check the blank and consider listing this type of training in your individual professional development plan.

Scale:

1–2 I seldom, if ever, use this: Maybe you have tried this approach once or twice, but you do not use it and/or do not have confidence in it.

3–4 I use this some of the time: You have heard of this practice and have tried it on occasion or use it periodically, but it is not part of your everyday teaching style.

4–5 I use this most of the time: This is the primary way you teach and manage your classroom because you strongly believe in this practice.

1. When children are in group or circle time, I give direct and explicit instruction in teaching the objectives from our curriculum.

    1   2   3   ④   5

    Example: *At the beginning of the group, I told the children we were going to learn about rhyming words and gave them several examples before we read a book with rhymes.*

    _____ I would like to learn more about this technique.

2. When a child has difficulty with a task or does not provide an accurate answer to a question, I provide a prompt (e.g., hint, cue, wait longer for an answer, ask a question, give additional information) to elicit the correct answer or perform the task better.

    1   2   ③   4   5

    Example: *I try to do this most of the time, but sometimes I forget. When I am working one to one and I am not distracted, I can do this. Like when Joey was trying to count the little cars—I would give him hints on what number came next.*

    __X__ I would like to learn more about this technique.

3. I use modeling strategies to help children learn new tasks.

    ①   2   3   4   5

    Example: *I did not think we were supposed to model things for the children in preschool. I am not sure if I do or not.*

    __X__ I would like to learn more about this technique.

4. I incorporate creative and frequent practice opportunities for children who struggle with concepts or skills.

    1   2   ③   4   5

    Example: *When Stefan and Marlo were trying to play a math game using counting skills, I set out more games for them to play because they were having difficulty getting past 3.*

    __X__ I would like to learn more about this technique.

(continued)

Figure 9.2. Intentional Instruction Tool. (*Source:* Carr & Boat, 2006.)

Figure 9.2. *(continued)*

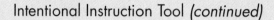

Intentional Instruction Tool *(continued)*

5. While a child is participating in an activity, I carefully listen to what he or she says and elaborate on what he or she is saying to extend his or her learning and/or I encourage him or her to elaborate on the topic being discussed.

  1 2 3 ④ 5

  Example: *Sasha was talking about her little sister when she was playing in the housekeeping area. She was talking about how little Elena wanted to play with all her toys. I talked to her about cooperation and living together—sharing, etc. She talked about sharing at school. I asked if this was something she could do with Elena. She then called one of the dolls Elena and we role played a bit, with me taking the part of Elena. Sasha directed the play, but the conversation did bring out what I would consider some jealousy of Elena. She seemed to like talking about it and I tried not to be judgmental. I reflected back to her the things she was saying.*

    __X__ I would like to learn more about this technique.

6. If a child gives incorrect information or gives an inappropriate response, I provide verbal feedback giving the child the appropriate response.

  1 2 3 ④ 5

  Example: *I told Jasmine that the letter she was calling b was d. I am not sure if I am too quick to do this sometimes or should be doing this when I do.*

    __X__ I would like to learn more about this technique.

When to Use This Tool	This tool is useful at any time during the school year to evaluate one's own teaching or to use for discussion with supervisory staff.
How to Use This Tool	Refer to the definitions of ICC intentional instruction in the sections above. Using the given scale, rate yourself for each of the items in the tool. Then, provide one or two examples of how you have recently used this strategy in your practice. If you cannot list examples and would like to study this strategy more in depth, check the blank and consider listing this type of training in your individual professional development plan.

Direction and Feedback

Direction and *feedback* are two areas teachers often use when providing guidance to children or managing the classroom. Unfortunately, there are steps to guidance that, when omitted, can turn it from a positive to negative situation. When steps are omitted, children may not get the message about what to change about the behavior in which they are engaged. Boat et al. (in press) found that teachers can change their interactions with children and use positive guidance if they focus on language that addresses the specific inappropriate behavior using a firm yet pleasant tone of voice, get the child's attention by making eye contact or by using some other culturally appropriate mechanism such as saying the child's name or using a signal, *and* providing *one* of the following:

- A replacement behavior: "Don't run in the classroom. You must walk."

- An explanation: "You cannot throw things; you could hurt someone."

- Practice: "Let me hear you practice using your words."

- Choice: "You can play with the puzzles or work in the science center. Which would you like to do first?"

Language used with young children needs to be specific, clear, and to the point when asking for compliance. It is not considered positive guidance if there is no verbal explanation of what the child did that was inappropriate and no replacement behavior is provided. Similarly, providing effective verbal feedback to a child following an incorrect or inappropriate verbal or physical response and providing the child with a specific replacement behavior or response will help the child understand the concept being taught. These strategies are helpful in scaffolding children's learning and promoting positive behavior and compliance in the classroom. By the time children reach preschool, they typically require less continuous adult support and guidance to maintain appropriate behavior. They also begin to internalize behavioral expectations and monitor their own behaviors (Bronson, 2000). They use language themselves to understand emotions, negotiate situations and experiences, and resolve problems. Teacher language can facilitate children's internalization of behavioral expectations.

Instructional and Caring Contacts for Positive Teacher Management

Having a positive teacher–child relationship is an important facet of classroom management. Such relationships can be achieved through ICCs.

Teacher Management

Positive classroom management is an essential element of teaching. Management is most effective when it is both positive and instructional.

| Positive and Instructional Management | Management is positive when the verbal reminder that a teacher delivers to a child who is engaged in an inappropriate behavior includes the following: 1) the teacher's using a firm yet pleasant tone of voice; 2) getting the child's attention in a discreet but clear manner; and 3) providing a replacement behavior, explanation, practice, or choice. Management of individual behavior should be directed to the child who is demonstrating the behavior as discreetly as possible without interrupting other children who are engaged in classroom learning activities. |

Noninstructional and/or Negative Management	Management can become negative when a teacher engages in negative scanning of the classroom or group or delivers a verbal reprimand (formal scolding) to a child engaged in inappropriate behavior that does not explain to the child what he or she did that was inappropriate or suggest an appropriate replacement behavior. Management is also negative when a teacher yells across the room and does not focus directly on the child in a discreet manner; uses an irritated or mean tone of voice; uses arbitrary punishment tactics unrelated to the behavior itself; and/or fails to provide a replacement behavior, explanation, practice, or choice.

Teacher Managerial Tool

This tool (Figure 9.3) will provide a mechanism for reflecting on how you manage your classroom. For children with challenging behaviors, it is critical that management strategies be purposeful and intentional, providing a replacement behavior, an explanation, practice, or a choice.

Purpose of This Tool	This tool is useful for reflecting on the managerial strategies you use in the classroom.
When to Use This Tool	This tool is useful at any time during the school year to evaluate one's own management strategies or to use for discussion with supervisory staff.
How to Use This Tool	Refer to the definitions of positive and negative managerial ICCs above. Using the given scale, rate yourself for each of the items on the tool. Then, provide one or two examples of how you have recently used this strategy in your practice. If you cannot list examples and would like to study this strategy in more depth, check the blank and consider listing this type of training in your individual professional development plan.

Instructional and Caring Contacts for Positive Relationship Building

A child's challenging behaviors, such as aggression, high activity levels, asocial behavior, and anxious or fearful behaviors can inhibit the quality of the teacher–child relationship. Having a positive teacher–child relationship is an important long-term protective factor for children who exhibit these behaviors (Hamre & Pianta, 2001). Positive guidance and management strategies and emotionally supportive teachers

Teacher Managerial Tool

Directions: Using the given scale, rate yourself for each of the items on the tool. Then, provide one or two examples of how you have recently used this strategy in your practice. If you cannot list examples and would like to study this strategy in more depth, check the blank and consider listing this type of training in your individual professional development plan.

Scale:

1–2   I seldom, if ever use this: Maybe you have tried this approach once or twice, but you do not use it and/or do not have confidence in it.

3–4   I use this some of the time: You have heard of this practice and have tried it on occasion or use it periodically, but it is not part of your everyday teaching style.

4–5   I use this most of the time: This is the primary way you teach and manage your classroom because you strongly believe in this practice.

When a child exhibits inappropriate behavior, I calmly obtain the child's attention and briefly discuss why the behavior is inappropriate, giving the child a more appropriate behavior (e.g., telling the child what he can do instead of just reprimanding him or telling him to stop)

1   ②   3   4   5

Example: *I usually just tell children to stop.*

___X___   I would like to learn more about this technique.

Figure 9.3. Teacher Managerial Tool. (*Source:* Carr & Boat, 2006.)

are essential to a classroom community that embraces all children. Teachers who are warm and respectful versus irritable or sarcastic are far more likely to create meaningful relationships with the children in their care. One way to do this is to use natural conversations and provide positive attention to children, even those who may be the most challenging. ICCs for conversations and positive attention are defined in the next sections.

Conversations

When a teacher and a child are engaged in a sustained conversation that is not instructional in nature, in which both the adult and the child take at least one turn engaging in verbal exchanges that have a positive or neutral valence, children are likely to perceive that the teacher is interested in his or her thoughts, ideas, and stories. These types of conversations typically follow the child's lead and focus on a topic of interest to the child.

Positive Attention

When teachers provide verbal encouragement or specific verbal feedback regarding the appropriateness or desirability of a behavior, children are more likely to continue to engage in those behaviors. The key is to focus on specific positive feedback and attention versus empty or general praise. It is important that children understand that what they did well was a direct result of the effort they put into something and not necessarily because it pleases the teacher. For example, refraining from saying "I like the way..." reduces the emphasis on the teacher as judge and jury. Instead, positive attention is more genuine when teachers use encouragement of efforts and statements that give feedback that helps children internalize the message that they have control over their behavior and efforts. Therefore, using "I noticed that you put all the books back on the shelf all by yourself" sends a different message than "I like the way you put all the books back on the shelf." In this case, it may also be appropriate to say, "Thank you."

Positive Relationship Building Tool

Building positive relationships with the children in your care is essential to learning. Figure 9.4 will guide you as you reflect on how you implement positive communicative transactions to bring out the best in both you and the children in your classroom.

Purpose of This Tool	This tool is useful for reflecting on how you build positive relationships with all the children in your classroom.
When to Use This Tool	This tool is useful at any time during the school year to evaluate one's own relationship-building strategies or to use for discussion with supervisory staff.
How to Use This Tool	Refer to the definitions of ICC conversation and positive attention ICCs above. Using the given scale, rate yourself for each of the items below. Then provide one or two examples of how you have recently used this strategy in your practice. If you cannot list examples and would like to study this strategy more in depth, check the blank and consider listing this type of training in your individual professional development plan.
Suggestions for Using This Tool	The ICC tool and definitions may serve as a framework for increasing effective instructional language and creating caring relationships with children. Practicing these strategies as defined and using them in teaching will help focus language toward improving outcomes for young children in the classroom.

Language for Problem Solving

For many classroom situations, generally developed teacher language scripts can often be used that become second nature when situations arise that are perceived as problems and need to be addressed. These types of scripts are essential problem-

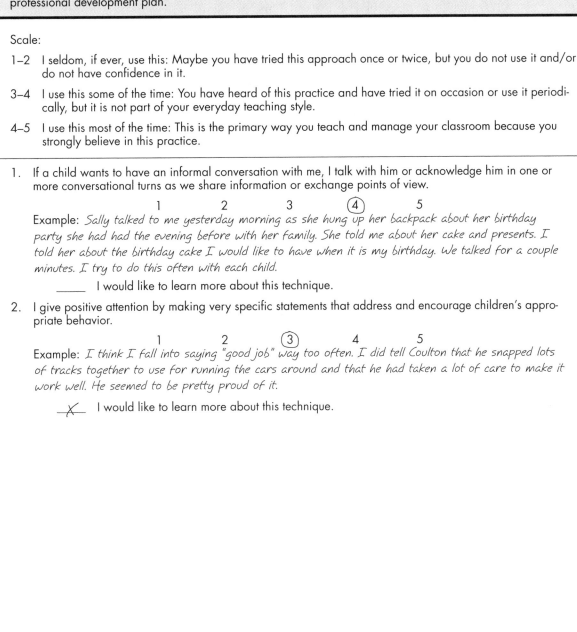

Positive Relationship Building Tool

Directions: Refer to the definitions of conversation and positive attention Instructional and Caring Contacts in Chapter 9. Using the given scale, rate yourself for each of the items below. Then provide one or two examples of how you have recently used this strategy in your practice. If you cannot list examples and would like to study this strategy more in depth, check the blank and consider listing this type of training in your individual professional development plan.

Scale:

1–2   I seldom, if ever, use this: Maybe you have tried this approach once or twice, but you do not use it and/or do not have confidence in it.

3–4   I use this some of the time: You have heard of this practice and have tried it on occasion or use it periodically, but it is not part of your everyday teaching style.

4–5   I use this most of the time: This is the primary way you teach and manage your classroom because you strongly believe in this practice.

1.   If a child wants to have an informal conversation with me, I talk with him or acknowledge him in one or more conversational turns as we share information or exchange points of view.

           1   2   3   ④   5

Example: *Sally talked to me yesterday morning as she hung up her backpack about her birthday party she had had the evening before with her family. She told me about her cake and presents. I told her about the birthday cake I would like to have when it is my birthday. We talked for a couple minutes. I try to do this often with each child.*

        _____   I would like to learn more about this technique.

2.   I give positive attention by making very specific statements that address and encourage children's appropriate behavior.

           1   2   ③   4   5

Example: *I think I fall into saying "good job" way too often. I did tell Coulton that he snapped lots of tracks together to use for running the cars around and that he had taken a lot of care to make it work well. He seemed to be pretty proud of it.*

        X   I would like to learn more about this technique.

Figure 9.4. Positive Relationship Building Tool. (*Source:* Carr & Boat, 2006.)

solving techniques based on Gordon's (1970, 1974, 1989) parent and teacher effectiveness trainings that are inherent in most early childhood settings and are aligned with positive guidance strategies. The use of the two basic scripts depends on *who* owns the problem, the child or the teacher.

If a child owns the problem, then a teacher typically uses reflective listening strategies to help the child identify the problem, generate solutions, implement a chosen solution, and evaluate the outcome. In this situation, teachers must avoid giving advice. The focus is on actively listening to assure the accuracy of the message the child is sending. This is accomplished through confirming the message the child is sending by reflecting the message back to the child in different words. The aim is to encourage the child to think about his or her own problems and identify potential solutions, a lifelong skill.

Reflective listening skills are also helpful when working with families who may have initial uncomfortable thoughts and feelings about the classroom, your teaching, child guidance, separation from their child, and so forth. Using reflective listening with families may be helpful for reframing their perceptions and problem-solving situations within the influence of both teacher and family. Reflective listening is essential to engaging families in the problem-solving process to address challenging situations. The premise is that self-insight and growth is a capacity we all have and that we are most likely willing to accept solutions or ideas that are self-generated. One does not have to be a therapist to engage in reflective listening. There are three wonderful advantages to using this technique: 1) You can increase your understanding of the other person's concern or problem; 2) you can help the other person clarify his or her thoughts, thereby reframing perceptions, and 3) you can genuinely show that you want to help solve the problem at hand.

Reflective Listening Checklist

Figure 9.5 will provide you with a mechanism to thoughtfully consider how well you listen to what children say. We are too often thinking about what we want or what we will say next to really listen to children. Yet, we may be very mistaken about the messages children send without carefully considering the communication intent. We must listen carefully and reflect on what is being said.

Purpose of This Tool	This tool is useful for evaluating your own reflective listening skills.
When to Use This Tool	This tool can be used to gain or reinforce an understanding of the principles of reflective listening.
How to Use This Tool	Check *Yes* for each of these strategies if you were successful in using them during a reflective listening encounter; check *No* if you were not successful. This tool also may be used as a review prior to meeting with a parent who has a concern to share about their child or your program.

Reflective Listening Checklist		
Directions: Check *Yes* for each of these strategies if you were successful in using them during a reflective listening encounter; check *No* if you were not successful. This tool also may be used as a review prior to meeting with a parent who has a concern to share about their child or your program.		

1. Did you do more listening than talking?   (Yes)   No

2. Did you respond only to what was important to the person with whom you were talking?   Yes   (No)

3. Did you restate what the person said for clarification and to expand his or her thoughts?   Yes   (No)

4. Did you hear the facts, probe for specifics, and focus on the feelings being shared?   (Yes)   No

5. Did you show genuine empathy, accepting what the person was saying and refrain from fake concern?   (Yes)   No

Figure 9.5. Reflective Listening Checklist.

When the teacher owns the problem, the strategy recommended in problem-solving situations is the "I" message. It is a sophisticated communication skill that communicates what you feel about a problem, tells the child why the behavior is a problem, and provides an opportunity for the child to problem-solve. It is not intended to blame or criticize or essentially send a "you" message. According to Gordon (1970), it is an appeal for help in solving the situation that is bothering you due to the behavior or lack of behavior of another person. The theory is that presenting your problem in this way will influence others to change more than sending a "you" message, as in "you are bad" as a critically communicated message. Although Gordon's work may be decades old, Cheung and Kwok (2003) found more recently that children are most receptive to "I" messages from their mothers that reveal distress and are most antagonistic toward the critical "you" message. The essence of an "I" message is thus:

- A nonblameful description of the child's behavior

- The effect that behavior is having on the teacher

- The teacher's feelings about that behavior

"I" messages may sound like this, "When you dump the cereal on the floor, I have to stop what I am doing to clean it up. This frustrates me." However, the word "I" does not need to be in an "I" message to make it effective. It is much simpler and more natural to say, "Ouch! That hurt me" when a child hits you than to say, "When you hit me, it hurt me, and I feel sad." Either way, refraining from "you" blaming messages provides the child with an opportunity to problem-solve a way to keep the relationship between the two of you positive.

"I" Message Checklist

Considering who owns the problem at hand is critical to communicating with children. The teacher should refer to Figure 9.6 for assistance with self-evaluation with respect to how well she or he conveys "I" messages to children.

When to Use This Tool	The teacher should use this tool during planning to gauge how well he or she is doing with conveying "I" messages to children and thereby "owning" problems.
How to Use This Tool	Cicle *Yes* for each of these strategies if you were successful in using them; circle *No* if you were not successful.
Suggestions for Using This Tool	The purpose of this tool is to evaluate your skill at using "I" messages. It is a reflective tool for developing "I" message language scripts that may be used often in the classroom with many of the children in the program.

Developing Individualized Scripts

It takes practice to be effective with "I" messages and reflective listening problem-solving strategies. For "I" messages to work, there must be congruence between the nonverbal and verbal message, and the tone of voice must match the message being sent. For individuals to be effective active listeners, empathetic sincerity must be evident to the person who is sending the message.

Teacher–Child Interactions in Challenging Situations Tool

Sometimes a more strategic script needs to be developed for specific, situational challenges in the classroom. Behaviors such as aggression, defiance, and disruptions may require more intense analyses and planning. Figure 9.7 poses a way to collect information to begin thinking about a scripted strategy to address specific challenging behaviors.

Purpose of This Tool	This tool helps the teacher identify the context and specific teacher behaviors that may elevate or exacerbate challenging situations.
When to Use This Tool	This tool is best used to help teachers "put their finger on" what is happening in the classroom to make a child act inappropriately or in a manner that the teacher perceives as disruptive to learning. It also helps teachers focus on their own behaviors so they can reflect on factors that can be changed to positively influence the situation.

"I" Message Checklist		
Directions: Circle *Yes* for each of these strategies if you were successful in using them; circle *No* if you were not successful.		
1. Did you send a clear message that indicated what behavior bothered or hurt you?	(Yes)	No
2. Were you clear about how this behavior affected you?	Yes	(No)
3. Did you refrain from blaming the child or telling the child that he or she was "bad"?	(Yes)	No
4. Were you clear about how you felt about being bothered or hurt?	(Yes)	No

Figure 9.6. "I" Message Checklist.

How to Use This Tool

Use this tool as soon as you can after a challenging situation occurs. Think about what the child did that created a challenging situation for you. Describe that situation. Note the time of day, daily routine, or other contextual information to help determine when and where this occurred. Where were you when this challenging situation occurred? How were you standing? Were your arms crossed? Was your face showing anger, disgust, or disappointment? Did you tower over the child? Then document what you said before, during, and after the behavior or challenging situation occurred. What was the tone of your voice?

Suggestions for Using This Tool

After completing this tool, consider what things you can change. How do your feelings about the child's innate responses influence what you say and do? Could some of the challenges be attitudinal from your perspective? What do you have influence over?

After studying the results from the tool in Figure 9.7, reflect on your own language that you typically use with young children and consider what message is being received by the child, particularly in situations that you perceive as challenging. How might the outcome change if you changed your verbal and nonverbal messages and self-monitored the language you used with the child? For example, can you change how you provide directions? Can you get down on a child's level to talk with her instead of towering over the child? Can you use simpler language with fewer words to provide guidance? Can you use a script to help transition from one activity to another to make the routine predictable and responses to inappropriate behaviors consistent? After thinking this through, use the Script Template in Figure 9.8 to make a plan for your own responses in situations that are similar and then be consistent on how you respond to the child in those situations. Document your efforts and progress, review progress periodically, and modify the plan as needed.

Teacher–Child Interactions in Challenging Situations Tool

Directions: Use this tool as soon as you can after a challenging situation occurs. Think about what the child did that created a challenging situation for you. Describe that situation. Note the time of day, daily routine, or other contextual information to help determine when and where this occurred. Where were you when this challenging situation occurred? How were you standing? Were your arms crossed? Was your face showing anger, disgust, or disappointment? Did you tower over the child? Then document what you said before, during, and after the behavior or challenging situation occurred. What was the tone of your voice?

Child: _Mandy_ Date: _11/14/09_

Teacher: _Jackson_

Challenging situation (describe situation or behavior)	Time and/or routine (context)	Teacher(s) location (proximity)	Teacher body position (nonverbal messages sent)	Teacher language—before, during, and after the situation (verbal messages sent)
Mandy threw herself on her stomach on the carpet next to the puzzle she was working with Terri to put together, screaming that she hated Terri. She then rolled over to her back and kicked the manipulatives off the shelf.	11:30; just as we were beginning to clean up for lunch	I was at the sink helping other children wash hands. Marcia was helping a third child clean up the manipulative area. Her back was turned away from Mandy.	Marcia was not looking or facing toward Mandy until she heard Mandy fall. She then reached toward her to stop her from kicking and put her hands on Mandy's legs, holding them down. I was looking over the manipulative shelf, scanning the room. I walked over to Marcia and Mandy after the kicking stopped. I had my hands on my hips.	I had just finished asking the children to clean up and wash their hands for lunch. Marcia turned and said "OH!" when Mandy started screaming. She then said to "stop kicking." Afterward, Marcia told Terri that Mandy did not mean it and asked Mandy to apologize to Terri. I said she did not need to apologize, but we needed to problem-solve the situation.

Figure 9.7. Teacher–Child Interactions in Challenging Situations Tool.

Script Template

Script for (child's name): _Mandy_

Date: _11/19/09_   Review Date: _12/1/09_

Describe the behavior that initiates the script:

Mandy falls to the ground and screams that she "hates" whoever she is playing with at the moment. (tantrum)

Describe what the adults do and say:

Before the behavior:

Say: *When positive behavior is occurring, say, "Mandy, you and _____ are working together on _____ . I see you are doing _____ and _____ (the other child) is doing _____ ." If tantrum occurs:*

Do: *Walk away from Mandy unless she is going to hurt herself or another child. Move between Mandy and the child who she is yelling at. Redirect that child positively to another area of the classroom saying that "Mandy is having a hard time playing right now."*

During the behavior:

Say: *We can talk when your body is calm. (Repeat as needed.) When calm or calming, say, "Let's talk."*

Do: *Wait for the behavior to subside, protect Mandy from physically hurting herself but restraining her only if needed. Look away from her until she shows signs of calming. Look toward her and say, "Let's talk," when she either stops moving and screaming OR when she takes a breath that provides a second of calming. Try to catch the moment when she may be likely to pay attention.*

After the behavior:

Say: *"I see something upset you. Tell me what that was. What would you like to have happened? What can you say to _____ to make that happen?"*

Do: *Ask her to practice what she might say. Take her by the hand and walk to the other child. Engage the two of them in a problem-solving dialogue. It can be brief. Model the words for Mandy and the other child if needed.*

Figure 9.8. Script Template.

Script Template

Having well-defined and consistent scripts (Figure 9.8) that all adults in the classroom use with children who have challenging behaviors is critical to success. Defined scripts should be purposefully designed to address the challenges and send a message that is clear and concise.

Purpose of This Tool	This tool is designed to help teachers create a script that is based on challenging situations in the classroom.
When to Use This Tool	Use this tool after collecting and documenting information that informs goodness of fit and reflections about how situations may be better addressed by the teacher or caregiver by using specific teacher language and behaviors. Consider how this might assist with helping the child understand what is expected in the classroom.
How to Use This Tool	Scripts should be designed for specific behaviors or situations. It is important that teachers target specifically defined behaviors for changing how they respond to children. The goal is to ensure planned, consistent responses to children over time. Teachers can change what they do or say before, during, or after the behavior occurs. The impact of these changes may influence the inappropriate or undesirable behaviors in a positive way. It may also be important for teachers to write in "take a big breath" or "count to three" prior to responding if this helps with positive guidance. Scripts are individualized. Make sure to consider the temperaments of both the teacher and the child when developing scripts; in addition, it is helpful to engage families in developing scripts and extend them into the home for consistency if the behavior occurs at home as well. The language used should feel natural for sending and receiving messages.
Suggestions for Using This Tool	Once a script has been planned and written, it is important to implement it with fidelity. This means that teachers (and all adults in the classroom) should say and do the same thing every time in the same way. It is also important to document progress and review it again at a set date and time. (See Chapter 11.)

Conclusion

Clearly, the development of teacher communication skills is complex and requires extensive practice and reflection. To be an effective communicator, we must rely on more than our natural inclinations to speak and respond to others. To facilitate learning and positive behavior, we must learn and practice effective communication skills.

CHAPTER 10

Peer Culture

FRIENDS APPLY LESSONS OF
CREATIVE PROBLEM SOLVING TO
EVERY DAY LIFE.

Whereas adults play a large role in the lives of infants and toddlers, peers become increasingly important to children during the preschool years. Adults still need to support the preschool child's efforts toward self-regulation, but they must also be responsive to children's growing independence and autonomy (Bronson, 2000). Young children need to understand what the limits are in the classroom and have peer models for appropriate behavior. Because children socially construct their own understanding and beliefs about the world, social ecologies are dynamic processes whereby reality is reproduced by children's interpretation of what they see and hear and how that relates to their own knowledge and experiences.

Social Construction of Peer Culture Knowledge

Children generally do not come to school knowing how to navigate the classroom culture. These lessons are typically socially constructed as they engage in interactions with their peers and get guidance from the adults in the classroom. The theoretical concept of *social constructivism* (Dewey, 1920, 1948; Vygotsky, 1978), or how meanings grow out of social encounters, supports the premise that children may be more actively engaged in constructing positive ways to participate in group settings if teachers clearly communicate expectations, are explicit about the language used for communication, and provide effective feedback to children (Atherton, 2005). (See Chapter 9 for an explanation of effective communicative language.) As children mature, these social encounters become more and more important to them. Groups such as children enrolled in preschool classes form their own peer culture and develop a set of within-group expectations for engagement in group play and other activities.

Children form their own peer culture rather quickly in early childhood settings. Their social ecologies, or the expectations they generate, are shaped by all the past experiences children have had in prior child care settings (Thompson, 2009). The social ecology is very different from home settings. For example, besides all the new "potential friends," there are strange adults in the group, often multiple adults who have a professional hierarchy that is unknown to the child and who are authority figures like parents but are not parents. Given that there may be numerous unfamiliar children, requiring a new set of interactions, the maintenance of the peer culture in preschool is critical to a child's social identity (Corsaro, 1988; Ladd, Herald, & Kochel, 2006). Thus, it is very important to consider peer influence on social-emotional growth and development.

Corsaro (1988) asserted that peer culture has five dimensions:

- Conceptions of status

- Conceptions of role

- Importance of play

- Friendship and social integration

- Protection of interactive space

Negotiations, conflicts, and problem solving occur within all these dimensions. The peer culture forms the structure in which the children play and provides opportunities for children to form their own rules, determine routines, decide on artifacts needed for play, and create meaning and direction within a group setting where the adult is not part of the experience (Corsaro, 1988).

Children who accumulate a pattern of rejection in early childhood tend to have ongoing adjustment issues in later academic settings. Long-term rejection can lead to increased aggression, substance abuse, internalization of problems, low grades, and other social-emotional difficulties (New & Cochran, 2007). Thus, the importance of teachers understanding how to help children succeed in early childhood settings cannot be underestimated.

In addition to supporting social success, it is also important for teachers to help parents understand that one way they can help their own children be more successful in group settings is to establish firm limits and clear boundaries at home, hold their children accountable for their behavior, teach children to manage feelings and control behaviors, communicate openly and effectively, and create an environment of responsibility and respect. When children understand these expectations and bring these experiences to school, they are more likely to enjoy a smooth transition to the classroom and positive experience within the peer culture.

Play

Play not only contributes to children's cognitive and creative development, it is a venue for the expansion of learning experiences within the classroom culture. Play promotes social skills, perspective taking, and understanding of social roles and cultural norms (Corsaro, 1985; McAloney & Stagnitti, 2009). Decades ago, Isaacs (1933) asserted that the pathway to socialization occurred through play. Later, Vygotsky (1976) described play as the mechanism for children to create and negotiate rules. Subsequently, Kantor, Elgas, and Fernie (1993) found that children needed to generate a shared understanding, fulfill specific roles, use play situation-appropriate language, coordinate roles and themes, and possess certain objects to be successful in play situations. Furthermore, children who are flexible, compromising, and cooperative in play negotiations are more well-liked by their peers (Harrist & Bradley, 2003). Therefore, helping children be successful in play can positively affect the outcomes for group interactions and individual esteem.

Helping Children Enter Play Tool

Elgas and Lynch (1993) described ways to be successful and unsuccessful as an adult when helping children enter social play. The most likely way to fail is to tell a child to ask the group if he or she can play. Essentially, a quick answer may be "no." Aggressive behaviors, using strategies that are unrelated to the theme, and misunderstanding the routine established by the players are also detrimental to entering a play group. Figure 10.1, however, lists strategies that have been shown to be successful for helping children enter play (Elgas & Lynch, 1998).

Helping Children Enter Play Tool

Directions: Think about the strategies in terms of whether you use them, understand the premise, or would need to learn more about the strategy through coaching or professional development. Provide an example of a time you may have used the strategy and what the outcome was for the child.

Help children...

1. Become aware of their own goals for socialization.	*Example:* I asked Xander if he wanted to play with three boys who were building with blocks and pointed to the tower they were building. He said yes but knocked their blocks down. So I said that he might want to just play next to them and tell me about what he was building. I think I need to work on this! My second strategy worked better.	*Outcome:* After he talked to me about his tower, one other boy started to help. Xander gave him specific blocks to use.
2. Understand peers may have incompatible play goals in mind.	*Example:* I typically try to talk to children when they are playing and ask them if another child can play. The children often say no. I needed another strategy. So, I tried to describe what I saw other children doing for Micah. I asked what he might like to do with the materials. It was different than what he saw.	*Outcome:* Micah chose another activity.
3. Reflect on how their behavior affects others.	*Example:* I try to build empathy by using I messages and problem-solving strategies with all the children. This has worked for me pretty well overall.	*Outcome:* Reduces conflict, but takes consistency and time (well worth it)
4. Explain and interpret other children's behaviors.	*Example:* Sadie was watching another girl put beads into muffin tins. I explained to Sadie what muffin tins might be used for and that I thought she was watching the preparation of cupcakes.	*Outcome:* Sadie said she wanted a cupcake and was given a bead.

Helping Children Enter Play Tool (continued)

Help children...

	Example	Outcome
5. Understand the play theme the other children are using.	*Example:* Several children were lining up chairs to make a train. Zachary pushed them out of line. I explained the concept of the train and suggested he find a seat on the train.	*Outcome:* Zachary sat down and watched the other children for approximately 3 minutes before leaving the area.
6. Determine what objects or artifacts are being used by the children in the playgroup and obtain them.	*Example:* When children were playing Spiderman, it appeared important that one needed a cape. I made 4 capes and put them into the dramatic play area. I directed children to the capes when they showed interest in joining the playgroup.	*Outcome:* Most children are included once they have a cape—unless they hit another child or bring in something that another child says does not "go with" Spiderman.
7. Obtain opportunities to work with children who are socially successful, especially if they have been rejected by a peer group.	*Example:* I directly ask Mattie and Holly to include Gregory, a child with autism, into play about once a day. These two are more patient than some of the other children.	*Outcome:* Gregory is given an object and/or a role most times. He does not, however, engage with the other two children verbally or with eye contact.
8. Practice as they play with you as a co-player to build their repertoire of skills.	*Example:* Gregory is often left out of play and does not take turns with materials. My assistant teacher and I try to engage him in activities with materials that other children seem interested in. We use language and gestures to work on turn taking.	*Outcome:* Gregory wants something in his hand almost all the time. He has, however, given a toy back to me twice this week.

Figure 10.1. Helping Children Enter Play Tool.

Purpose of This Tool	This tool describes strategies for helping children enter play.
When to Use This Tool	Use this tool to determine what strategies work with which children with regard to fostering successful play interactions.
How to Use This Tool	Think about the strategies in terms of whether you use them, understand the premise, or would need to learn more about the strategy through coaching or professional development. Provide an example of a time you may have used the strategy and what the outcome was for the child.
Suggestions for Using This Tool	Reflecting on teaching strategies is a way to target areas to improve practice and elevate teacher effectiveness. It is also a way to document those strategies you try with consistency in the classroom to determine if they worked for the individual child and/or to reflect on whether you use teaching strategies with fidelity. You may want to review your responses on this tool with your supervisor or contemplate how you help children enter play on your own.

Strategies for Problem-Solving Complex Interactions

Not all children experience positive group interactions. The teacher can set the stage by creating a positive, physically and emotionally safe classroom environment where children have ample opportunities to engage in rich curricular activities as discussed earlier in this book. When children are engaged, they are less likely to exhibit challenging behaviors. To maintain child engagement in groups, teachers typically use direction and instruction (Powell, Burchinal, File, & Kontos, 2008). As teachers monitor the classroom, it is important that they use affirmations and encouragement to promote or maintain child engagement. Yet, Powell and colleagues found that children are far more likely to be engaged when they are left to play with peers or alone than when they are in a whole group or child–teacher setting, particularly during times when teachers are providing verbal direction. Therefore, the importance of social ecology of the peer culture that is created by the children themselves is of great value to children's development. For most children in high-quality classrooms, this is a positive experience and the classroom dialogue fosters intellectual engagement (Rogoff, 2003).

Children with disruptive behaviors, on the other hand, may make some children feel like victims in their own classroom, creating anxiety and fearfulness within the peer culture (Holt & Espelage, 2007). When this happens, it is critical that the teacher takes the situation seriously and addresses any behaviors that resemble bullying. Teachers can influence the peer culture by monitoring behaviors and providing children with language and problem-solving strategies that empower children, thereby reducing victimization. Strategies include the following:

- Proximity controls

- Flexible grouping

- Individual and group problem solving

- Powerful scripted language

Engaging in *proximity control* essentially means that the adult is close to the child in order to help the child follow the rules, problem-solve situations, keep the child and others safe, model appropriate behavior, and provide guidance through words and gestures. It is a way to intervene early and with little disruption to the rest of the children in the classroom if things get out of hand. Sometimes, just an adult's nearness helps children maintain appropriate behavior. It is also helpful to be near children who are likely to have difficulty during transition times to assist with the transition in a proactive manner.

Designing productive *peer groupings* is another method for influencing the peer culture within a classroom setting. Receiving social support from a peer or friend has been found to provide protection from feelings of victimization. For example, it may be that a child is targeting another child in the classroom with aggressive behavior or foul language. Reducing the interaction time for the two children may help the behaviors dissipate and/or give you more opportunities to be present to problem-solve when the two children are interacting within the classroom. In addition, working to group children who are likely friends provides a source of social support.

Strategies for creating flexible groupings include limiting the number of children who can play in learning centers in the classroom by setting out a limited number of materials (e.g., aprons for the water table), providing time for small groups to go to the large motor room versus having the entire group go together, engaging small groups in reading, fostering small-group projects, and so forth. In putting children together in groups, redirect those who need time apart, organize groups to include good "mixes" whereby children can learn socialization skills from one another, and promote engagement with projects and other interesting activities. When working with children in groups, be alert to opportunities to help children problem solve and build on one another's ideas.

Problem solving between children is a skill many early childhood teachers learn early on. However, some teachers tell children what to do and how to feel. This may have been learned from one's own parenting or it could be that problem solving was not something to which those teachers have been exposed. Gordon (1974) asserted that adults often use "roadblocks" to effective communication, particularly with young children. Unfortunately, teachers often use these strategies when addressing challenging behaviors in the classroom. Using these strategies can be detrimental to helping a child internalize appropriate behaviors because they are disrespectful and do not teach the child how to behave. These roadblocks that shut down communication and problem solving include the following:

- Ordering or commanding

- Admonishing or threatening

- Moralizing or preaching
- Criticizing or blaming
- Ridiculing or shaming
- Interrogating or humoring

To help children solve the problems they are having as individuals in the classroom as well as with one another, it is important to encourage children and help them learn appropriate classroom and interactive behaviors. Adults can help by reframing an understanding of the situation and by modeling effective responses to undesired behaviors. Commenting on a child's feelings or someone else's feelings helps children focus on the situation at hand. Addressing the behaviors that are disruptive, disconcerting, or inappropriate versus telling a child he or she is "bad" is key to maintaining respect and focusing on the behavior that needs to be modified. The process is more important than the result because it takes time to change habits and behavior.

Recognizing what the child has contributed to a situation to make things go smoothly is important. Then you can talk about the mistakes that have been made or the behaviors that are inappropriate. In this way, you can help children engage in inductive reasoning and problem solving by helping them define the problem and think of possible solutions. In this way, children have ownership of the problem and may be more committed to the solution. With consistency and practice, even very young children can learn to solve problems among themselves. The basic strategy for problem solving is this:

1. State that you notice there is a problem that needs to be solved.

2. Acknowledge that the children are upset, and help them cool down if needed.

3. Ask children to speak directly to each other or to you to identify the problem, paraphrasing their words to ensure understanding.

4. Kindly ask what might be done to solve the problem, and accept all solutions.

5. Help children generate several possible solutions.

6. Guide children through an evaluation of potential solutions stating that a solution must be agreed on to try out between or among themselves.

7. Back away when the children have agreed to try a solution to give them the opportunity to make the solution work.

8. Check back with the children to discuss if the solution worked and to acknowledge that they were successful in using the strategy to come to a solution that they both or all could accept.

It takes time to teach children the process for problem solving, but it is well worth it. Experienced early childhood teachers show respect for children and understand that assisting children to learn such invaluable tools as problem solving is a life skill that helps children become more independent in their daily interactions with others. These teachers do not solve problems for the children, but they do facilitate the children's problem-solving processes.

At times, children need assistance to develop specific *scripts with powerful language* to counteract unwanted behaviors from other children. Teachers can assist children to communicate by empowering them with language or gestures to reduce victimization. Behaviors that are hurtful, inappropriate, or unacceptable are more likely to be reduced when all stakeholders in the setting give the same corrective feedback to children who are demonstrating the unwanted behaviors.

Teachers may use a number of steps to support a child with challenging behaviors. They may use the strategies already discussed in this book. They may work individually with a child who is using foul language, hitting other children, or doing other harmful things; or they may obtain the assistance from mental health or disability specialists to work with the child. The other children in the class are at risk of becoming victims of the unwanted behaviors, too, so they need to be prepared to send a strong message that discourages the unwanted behaviors. For example, if a child is likely to grab toys from other children, work with those who are playing to develop a scripted response that sends a clear message indicating a dislike for the grabbing behavior. Teachers might say, "I cannot let you grab toys from others. You will have to choose another toy." The children may be encouraged to say, "I don't like it when you grab the toys. It makes me not want to play with you." This would be an effective strategy if the goal for the child who grabs is to enter play groups. Another example in response to foul language might be for the children to learn a script such as, "We don't talk like that at school."

In addition to helping peers communicate powerfully, the teacher might provide a child who uses foul language with alternative expressions, expanding on the message the children send. When all are responding similarly to a child who is demonstrating unwanted behavior, the message is loud and the expectations are clear. Given the powerful impact of the peer culture, having all the children in the classroom respond in a scripted manner may be most effective in eliminating the behavior. It also empowers the other children to be assertive, thereby minimizing the potential for becoming victimized by other children.

Strategies to Reduce Challenging Behaviors

Figure 10.2, Strategies to Reduce Challenging Behaviors, provides a mechanism for planning responses to challenging behavior that addresses the behaviors with the peer culture.

Purpose of This Tool	This tool describes strategies for reducing challenging behaviors.
When to Use This Tool	Use this tool to determine what strategies work in specific situations to reduce challenging behaviors.
How to Use This Tool	Document examples of a child's challenging behaviors and choose a strategy to address it with the overall culture of the classroom. Document the outcomes of the strategy used.
Suggestions for Using This Tool	Documentation of intervention strategies is a way to determine if what you are trying to accomplish is working. This is particularly important when the behaviors not only affect an individual child

Strategies to Reduce Challenging Behaviors

Directions: Document examples of a child's challenging behaviors and choose a strategy to address them with the overall culture of the classroom. Document the outcomes of the strategy used.

Child's name: ___Derrick___   Date: ___9/22/2009___

Describe the challenging behavior.	Does this occur frequently, for a long period of time, or is it intense?	Who does it affect (individual, whole group)?	Document the baseline frequency, duration, or intensity of the behavior.	Outline a strategy to implement (proximity control, grouping, problem-solving, scripts).	Document the results of the use of the strategy.	Document results after a targeted time frame (e.g., 2 weeks). Should you continue this strategy?
Takes toys and objects from other children	Frequently	Other children from whom he is taking the toys	During choice time (30 minutes) an average of 8 times	Teachers will stay close to Derrick during choice time. Use a scripted problem-solving strategy. Placing a hand over and holding onto the object just taken away during the problem-solving conversation between Derrick and the other child.	Derrick does not resist the teacher intervention.	Sept. 30–Oct. 4 Choice time average incident of taking away toys 4 times in 30 minutes. Continue strategy!

Figure 10.2. Strategies to Reduce Challenging Behaviors.

but also the entire classroom community. It shows planning and progress monitoring. This information is essential for sharing with families and using to determine if a child should be referred for further evaluation.

Conclusion

People are not always good matches for one another and consequently do not always bring out the best in each other. As educators, we must always seriously consider why we do what we do in the classroom to ensure that all children can learn; how we plan curricular activities and communicate expectations for using materials in the classroom; what we say to children to be proactive about potential hot spots and guidance strategies; how we present material, new ideas, and changes in the routine and environment; and how we individualize for children who have varying temperaments and individual differences. To best help children prepare for long-term academic success, teachers can support children's task orientation or find ways to increase persistence, decrease distractibility, and reduce excessive activity. To build children's personal flexibility, teachers can help children learn strategies to respond to new situations, learn how to shake a bad mood, and adapt to new situations without undue stress.

Language and the context within which it is used is a framework for facilitating scripts that support positive behavior. This is useful for helping children self-regulate within their peer culture. Techniques used in quality classroom environments respect the peer culture and foster self-control while encouraging desired behavior and discouraging unacceptable behavior.

Individualized Plans to Address Challenging Behaviors

O nce teachers have collected and analyzed information about the intrachild, classroom, and transactional contexts of challenging behavior, some children will need specific behavior plans to ensure more harmonious patterns of behavior. Data collected with regard to influencing changes within the classroom as discussed in previous chapters will provide the basis for developing, evaluating, and revising individual behavior plans. It is expected that only a few children in inclusive classrooms will need specific plans. However, to maintain harmony, plans are necessary for these children and their teachers to feel successful within the educational setting.

All of the observations, interviews, record reviews, and discussions can be summarized into a hypothesis that posits the events that make the behavior more likely, the function or purpose of the behavior, and the goals and methods for teaching replacement behavior. Positive behavioral support plans are developed based upon the hypothesis.

It takes a while to collect all of the information necessary to make a hypothesis. This is because teachers must use real observation and interview data as a foundation for the hypothesis. Jumping to intervention before a comprehensive analysis of information can lead to ineffective interventions. Worse yet, when interventions do not work, it is easy to feel frustrated and give up. The time spent collecting the information saves time and eases frustration in the long run.

Behavioral support plans are based upon the best judgments of a team of stakeholders. They must be followed consistently in order to effect change. When plans do not work, they must be evaluated to understand what parts of the plan need to be revised. For the benefit of children, families, and staff, plans must become working documents. Section IV provides guidance in developing and evaluating support plans.

CHAPTER 11

Developing an Individualized Behavior Plan

UNLESS YOU HAVE THE SKILLS,
IT'S HIGH ANXIETY.

When an individual child's choices are disruptive despite carefully planned and consistently implemented general classroom strategies, then it is time to develop an individualized behavior plan (Bell & Carr, 2004). The behaviors of these children typically stand out as identifiably different from that of peers of the same age and gender (Bell & Barnett, 1999). They take up excessive amounts of teacher time because the teacher has to 1) directly intervene with the child; 2) communicate with administrators, other children, and parents; and 3) plan activities to avoid future meltdowns.

The most successful individual interventions follow a highly focused assessment of the individual child and the classroom variables that are involved in the problem situation. Teachers and parents must specify alternative behaviors and skills that will meet the child's needs in a classroom-sanctioned and less disruptive manner. Interventions involve changes in teacher plans to 1) prevent the occurrence of problem behaviors; 2) instruct appropriate, less disruptive alternative behaviors; and 3) support changes in child responses by the use of specific reinforcing consequences.

Prioritizing Problem Behaviors

Many children come to the classroom with multiple behavioral challenges. Prioritizing these for plan development and implementation can be a difficult process. Durand (1990) suggested selection of behaviors that 1) pose safety issues, 2) interfere with classroom participation and learning, 3) prove resistant to routine classroom educational strategies, and 4) hinder broader community acceptance. As part of the assessment process, teachers must identify, analyze, and prioritize child behaviors that are targeted for intervention.

Collaborating with Fellow Stakeholders

It is important to collaborate with parents and other individuals in the child's life. If required, these individuals will thrash out the specific details of an individual plan and ensure that it is implemented faithfully across activities and settings. Stages in effective plan development include 1) involvement of parents, teachers, and other stakeholders in all stages of plan development; 2) careful definition and analysis of the problem using observations, interviews, and data-based decision making; 3) selection of fundamental problems from prioritized areas of concern; 4) development of individualized strategies; 5) implementation of a consistent plan; and 6) revision based on ongoing progress monitoring (Bell & Carr, 2004; Hemmeter, Ostrosky, & Fox, 2006).

Tool for Assessing Challenging Situations

Teachers can use this tool to record information from each step of the problem-solving process. This tool should be completed in collaboration with all stakeholders (i.e., teacher, assistants, administrators, parents), documenting the specifics of the problem situation. The Tool for Assessing Challenging Situations (Figure 11.1) has been completed to provide illustrations of the types of information that might be helpful as the teacher specifies the problem, collects confirming information through observations and communication with others, and begins to generate initial strategies for addressing the problem.

Purpose of This Tool	The purpose of this tool is to guide the teacher and other members of the intervention team through the assessment process. The tool suggests specific areas for assessment and strategies for intervention.
When to Use This Tool	This tool can be used when the challenging behaviors first emerge—typically within a few weeks of enrollment. It also can be used to plan further interventions as additional problems arise over the course of the classroom year.
How to Use This Tool	This tool can be completed by the teacher alone or in conjunction with the center director, teaching assistant, and/or parent(s). Sections I–III should be completed by the individual team member. It is often instructive to gather different perspectives on the same problem situation. The teacher and/or team should work through Sections IV and V in a collaborative fashion, prioritizing the problem behaviors and planning observations to collect baseline information. This tool lists essential steps for caregivers to follow in assessment and plan development.

Developing Intervention Scripts

By the time the team has decided that an individual intervention plan is necessary, the members will have completed repeated observations and provided detailed documentation of the child's behavior and the specific settings in which it occurs (i.e., Steps I–IV of the Tool for Assessing Challenging Situations in Figure 11.1). An effective intervention plan dictates the specific steps that have been selected to address the problem situation. These action plans, frequently called scripts (Ehrhardt, Barnett, Lentz, Stollar, & Reifen, 1996), dictate a series of caregiver words and actions, individualized to prevent (or respond to) the challenging behavior. Advantages of scripts include 1) clarity in communication of planned strategies across caregivers, 2) incorporation of naturally occurring teacher language and classroom activities, 3) consistency of plan implementation across caregivers, 4) ease of data

Tool for Assessing Challenging Situations

Directions: This tool can be completed by the teacher alone or in conjunction with the center director, teaching assistant, and/or parent(s). Sections I–III should be completed by the individual team member. It is often instructive to gather different perspectives on the same problem situation. The teacher and/or team should work through Sections IV and V in a collaborative fashion, prioritizing the problem behaviors and planning observations to collect baseline information. This tool lists essential steps for caregivers to follow in assessment and plan development.

I. Defining the problem elements

Assessment question	Teac...
A. What is the most difficult aspect of the problem situation (e.g., activity, time of day, setting, impact on other children in the classroom)? Provide a specific description.	Coral has difficulty interact... play—she doesn't like to sh... play initiations of other chi... prefers time with adults to... *[handwritten: H snatches toys to see other's reaction She runs and smiles. She gets aggressive. Doesn't Know how to play yet.]*
B. How long has this problem been going on (i.e., Is it a new problem? Has it escalated over time?)?	Cor... atte... (ab... ...ten a child (or has ...rolled in the center *[handwritten: 3 weeks in new classroom but ongoing problem in previous classroom]*
C. What emotions do I experience during interactions with this child (or while anticipating or reflecting on them)? What automatic reactions, thoughts, or beliefs are generated?	*[handwritten: She is on a 1½ yr level. Doesn't do well because of her dev. age and mother doesn't want her to have rules boundries@home]* ...ee w. ...r ...ave to... *[handwritten: I feel frustrated bec' Parents knew she was not ready for new classroom with her delays but push her up. Now she is struggling w/advanced peers]*
D. If I had a magic wand and immediately could change this situation, I would change _____. (Use specific, positive, attainable goals.)	Coral n... child wi... Coral e... support... incident... *[handwritten: More positive peer and teacher interactions. It to enjoy her time w/o tantrums over transitions]* ...eside or with another ...e. First, I'd like to see ...centers with adult ...dependently with no ...her children.

Figure 11.1. Tool for Assessing Challenging Situations.

Tool for Assessing Challenging Situations *(continued)*

II. Analyzing the problem elements

Assessment question	Teacher response
A. Do I have enough information to determine that no preexisting health or developmental problem (e.g., health condition, sensory impairment, identified developmental disability, medication side effect) is related to the situation in Section I? Record any relevant medical or developmental screening information contained in the files, or note the need to investigate this further (e.g., I wonder if the child has an undiagnosed hearing, language, or attention problem.). Record the contact information for any relevant health care providers.	*Coral uses very little verbal language in the classroom. She is a young 3-year-old, but she seems to speak with limited vocabulary in one- to two-word sentences. I wonder if she has a speech delay. I would like to refer her for a speech-language evaluation.*
B. What temperamental tendencies might affect the problem situation?	*Coral definitely displays many of the characteristics of the difficult temperament.*
C. Does the child seem to lack developmental skills that should be taught in an individual or small-group setting (e.g., language, play initiation, self-regulation, turn taking)?	*Yes. She uses little verbal language, responds in an immature fashion to the play initiations of other children, and acts out impulsively. Coral tantrums when teachers intervene in play.*
D. What preferences might be important to consider (e.g., play areas in which the child is engaged for the longest period of time)?	*Coral spends most of her time in the manipulatives and book areas. She prefers to have teachers read to her.*

(continued)

Figure 11.1. *(continued)*

Tool for Assessing Challenging Situations *(continued)*

II. Analyzing the problem elements *(continued)*

Assessment question	Teacher response
E. What home factors (e.g., parenting style, sibling interactions, recent changes) might contribute to the problem situation? What topics should I address in a parent conference?	*Parents are both very busy physicians and Coral stays with a nanny much of the time. I wonder if she gets enough attention at home from her parents.*
F. What classroom characteristics might be contributing to the problem situation?	*We only have a teacher and one assistant at the present time. It's difficult to watch all areas of the classroom effectively to prevent Coral's aggression.*

1. Are curriculum and/or classroom materials appropriate and available for child's skills, interests, and abilities? Ⓨor N

   If not, what is the problem and what action might be taken?

2. Is the classroom furniture and/or the activity areas arranged in a way to promote self-regulation and designate safe, separate play for this child? Ⓨor N
   But we may need to move some shelving so that the teachers can always see Coral when she is playing in the manipulatives area.
   If not, what is the problem and what action might be taken?

3. Is the length and order of activities in the daily schedule arranged in a way to engage this child? Ⓨor N

   If not, what is the problem and what action might be taken?

4. Are guidelines for expected classroom behavior obvious to this child? Y orⓃ

   If not, what is the problem and what action might be taken?
   Coral seems to only visit the manipulatives and book area without direct adult scaffolding to choose and participate in another area. Maybe a picture schedule at greeting time would help.

Tool for Assessing Challenging Situations *(continued)*

II. Analyzing the problem elements *(continued)*

5. Are sufficient personnel available to maintain near proximity to support this child?   (Y) or N
Yes, but it is a stretch and I feel that the other children are sometimes neglected.
If not, what is the problem and what action might be taken?
Ask the director for a floater to help during free play.

6. Does the classroom provide sufficient areas of choice to take into account this child's   (Y) or N
preferences and characteristics?

If not, what is the problem and what action might be taken?

III. Zeroing in on and/or confirming the elements of the problem situation

Assessment question	Intervention suggestions (circle all that apply)
A. Is this mostly a group-time problem? Y or (N)	Is the area used for group time away from other classroom distractions? Would it help to modify the length, content, or sequence of group-time activities? Would it help to modify the time at which the child enters group? Would it help to use preferential seating for the child? Beside preferred or nonpreferred peers? Near the leader? By the assistant? Should I consider offering the child a more active role in the group? Would it help to give the child a group-related item to hold? Should I incorporate child preferences into group-time activities? Others?
B. Is this mostly a transition-based problem? Y or (N)	Is the transition signal effective? Is the transition routine effective? Should I consider transitioning the child individually? In a small group? Should I consider a transition-based teaching scheme? Should I implement a "save note" strategy? Should I use a picture schedule? Should I allow the child to preview the next activity? Others?

(continued)

Figure 11.1. *(continued)*

Tool for Assessing Challenging Situations *(continued)*

III. Zeroing in on and/or confirming the elements of the problem situation *(continued)*

Assessment question	Intervention suggestions (circle all that apply)
C. Is this mostly a naptime problem? Y or (N)	Do I have a consistent, concrete routine? Is the naptime environment conducive to sleep (e.g., lights dim, music playing, preceded by quiet activity)? Do I provide quiet books or toys to the children? Do I allow security objects (i.e., blankets, toys, pictures)? Do I provide individual attention to the child? How? Others?
D. Are child groupings a problem? (Y) or N	(Can I use small groups to separate problem pairings?) Can I use skilled peers to scaffold classroom skills? Should I change the child's classroom assignment? (Others?) *Make sure that Coral is with an adult when she is near other children.*
E. Would more teacher support be helpful? (Y) or N	(Can I provide structured lessons or cues?) *Yes—prompt her with a word or two to indicate her wants and needs.* (Do I scaffold play entry?) *Yes* (Do I prompt necessary skills?) *Yes—but need more here* Others? *Need to respond to her aggression immediately with reminders of the rules.*
F. Would a calm-down area be helpful? (Y) or N	(Is there space in the classroom for an individual retreat?) *Yes, we can block off an area by the books.* (What books or soft toys would be appropriate?) *Books, especially ones about dogs* (How will I introduce this to the class?) *This is a place to feel better when you're sad or mad.* Can more than one child use the area at a time? *No* What are the limits? *Teacher permission* Others?
G. Would pictorial and/or material prompts in an area be helpful? (Y) or N	(What materials should I use?) *Pictures of current classroom activities* (When should I introduce the schedule? At the beginning or throughout the day?) *Beginning* Would a picture exchange system be helpful (forewarning each specific activity)? *Not at this time* (Should the child take an active role in creating the daily picture schedule?) *Yes* What degree of child choice can be introduced into the daily schedule? *She must choose four to six centers each day* Others?

Tool for Assessing Challenging Situations *(continued)*

III. Zeroing in on and/or confirming the elements of the problem situation *(continued)*

Assessment question	Intervention suggestions (circle all that apply)
H. Is participation in some activities optional? (Y) or N	What activities might the child refuse? *Writing/art, math games, dramatic play* What skills will be affected by this choice? *Okay at this time—focus is on social skills and language use* What developmentally appropriate activities might be substituted? Others?
I. Have I invited parents to share their insights about the problem situation? (Y) or N	Does the parent see these behaviors at home? *No, she is never around other children* If so, how do parents typically respond to these behaviors? *N/A* If not, why not? What aspects of the home environment prevent these behaviors? Can this be duplicated in the classroom? *Right now this is only a classroom problem.*

IV. Summarizing and prioritizing the problem behaviors

Give a precise description of the elements of the challenging situation(s) by filling in the blanks below (use as many as necessary, addressing each in prioritized order):

1. _____*Coral*_____ typically _____*hits/bites/scratches/pushes*_____ during _____*free-play activities*_____

   (name of child)   (action verb)   (time of day/activity)

   and this leads to *fear/anger in other children, avoidance of Coral during free play. Coral is unable to develop social skills because she never plays with other children. Teachers have to devote exclusive time to watching Coral.*

   (implications of the action for other children, the child of interest, the success of the classroom activity, the teachers)

This concerns me because of (circle all that apply):

(the number of times this occurs throughout the day)
(the severity of the behavior when it occurs)
(the length of time that I have to spend dealing with the behavior)

V. Documenting observations of the challenging behaviors

A. Statement of the problem:

   _____*Coral*_____ typically _____*hits/bites/scratches/pushes*_____ during _____*free play activities*_____

   (name of child)   (action verb)   (time of day/activity)

   This leads to: *fear/anger in other children, avoidance of Coral during free play. Coral is unable to develop social skills because she never plays with other children. Teachers have to devote exclusive time to watching Coral.*

   (implications of the action for other children, the child of interest, teachers)

(continued)

Figure 11.1. *(continued)*

Tool for Assessing Challenging Situations *(continued)*

V. Documenting observations of the challenging behaviors *(continued)*

B. Observation during targeted time (should be repeated for different times and/or observers):

1. _____ *Bill* _____ observed _____ *Coral* _____ for _____ *30* _____ minutes

    (name of observer)   (name of child)   (duration of observation)

    during _____ *free play* _____ . Date: *10/9/09* Time: *9:30-10:00*

    (activity/routine)

2. Observed frequency of the challenging behaviors (be specific): *Attempted to hit a child who entered the manipulative area. Teacher caught Coral's arm and removed her to the book area. Scratched a child's face who approached the book area to listen to the teacher reading to Coral.*

3. Observed severity of the challenging behaviors (give details): *Scratches left marks. Both children cried and the child who was scratched said, "I wish Coral would go away!"*

4. Classroom modifications and/or strategies used and results:

    1. *Having a teacher or assistant shadow Coral seems to be effective in reducing the physical aggression and preventing harm to the other children.*

    2. *Coral does attempt to imitate the teacher or assistant when they give her specific words to express her needs/desires. She can imitate two words. She said, "No, Brady!"*

    3. *Coral's mom has begun asking about her day and requested communication. She indicated that she would like to come and spend some time in the classroom with Coral about once a week.*

VI. Determining the need for an individualized intervention plan

A. Observation results: Summarize information about the frequency, duration, and severity of the challenging behaviors across times and observers: *Coral exhibits physical aggression toward other children daily (or attempts to do so until prevented by the teacher). This happens during free play. It is severe because the scratches and bites leave marks. The other children have started avoiding her. They complain about her.*

B. Response to intervention: Summarize the child's response to classroom modifications and changes in teacher strategies across times and observers: *Coral will use words instead of physical aggression when prompted by the teacher.*

C. Summarize communication(s) with parents about problems in the classroom: *Mom has begun picking Coral up one day a week. She asked for a daily note. She would like to begin coming to the classroom one day a week for a short visit. She is very concerned about Coral's aggression. She says that Dad is concerned as well. Teachers have only had contact with Mom.*

D. Determine the need for development of an individualized intervention plan and/or script: Ⓨor N

E. Other actions/comments:

Sample Script to Prevent Biting	
Date: _1-19-10_	Step completed?
1. Greet ____Coral____ individually upon his or her arrival to the classroom.	(Y) or N
2. Introduce ____Coral____ to the activity choices and schedule for the day.	(Y) or N
3. Remind ____Coral____ of the classroom rules. a. Teachers keep the children safe. b. You can say "no" when children bother you. c. It is not okay to hurt other children.	(Y) or N
4. Always stay within arm's length of ____Coral____, monitoring his or her play.	(Y) or N
5. Give ____Coral____ specific, positive feedback for use of words during play with other children.	(Y) or N
6. If ____Coral____ attempts to bite, hit, or push another child during play, say, "Stop, no biting (hitting, scratching, pushing)!" and remove ____Coral____ to the calm-down area.	Y or (N) *Step not needed today*
7. After 3 minutes, invite ____Coral____ to return to play, reminding him or her that he or she has "lost his or her turn" in the previous area because it is "not okay to bite (hit, scratch, or push)."	(Y) or N
8. Record ____Coral____'s success or difficulties on a parent communication note.	(Y) or N
9. Mom, Dad, or caregiver provides ____Coral____ with a "special activity" if he or she has been successful (no incidents of aggression), affirming his or her success. OR Mom, Dad, or caregiver encourages ____Coral____ to "try again tomorrow" if he or she has been unsuccessful and reminds him or her of the special activity.	(Y) or N (By report)

Figure 11.2. Sample Script to Prevent Biting.

Sample Script for Preventing a Child from Running Away	
Date: _1-14-10_	Step completed?
1. Arrange the classroom furniture and activities to provide natural barriers for each play area.	(Y)or N
2. Incorporate high-interest activities and preferred toys into the daily schedule. Make sure that these are activities that are at _____ _Eli_ _____'s developmental level.	(Y)or N *(blocks, small) cars and books*
3. Upon entry into the classroom, go over the picture schedule, allowing _____ _Eli_ _____ to use hook-and-loop tape to secure photographs of his or her play choices, in order, to the board. If _Eli_ _____ was successful the previous day, his or her first activity can be a preferred center (such as the computer).	(Y)or N
4. Remind _____ _Eli_ _____ of the classroom rules: a. Teachers keep the children safe. b. Teachers and children stay together. c. It is not okay to leave the group.	(Y)or N
5. Pair _____ _Eli_ _____ with a preferred peer to rotate through the daily activities.	(Y)or N
6. Upon _____ _Eli_ _____'s first attempt to leave the classroom, take him or her to review the picture schedule and say, "See, you chose to play in the _____ _book_ _____ area. Are you finished? Would you like to change?" Provide two choices for change.	(Y)or N
7. Return _____ _Eli_ _____ to the chosen area, reminding him or her of the classroom rules.	Y or N
8. If _____ _Eli_ _____ again attempts to leave the classroom, take him or her to the time-out area, saying, "No, that's not safe. Remember, you have to stay with the group."	Y or (N) *Step not needed today*
9. If _____ _Eli_ _____ attempts to leave the playground, return him or her to the classroom saying, "No, that's not safe. I wish that you could have fun playing outside, but you forgot to stay with the group."	Y or (N) *Step not needed today*
10. Review _____ _Eli_ _____'s progress at the end of the day and record it on the home–school note. a. If he or she has had NO incidents of running away, praise him or her, give him or her a hug, and remind him or her that he or she will be able to have extra time to play at a preferred activity (such as on the computer) the next day. (b.) If he or she has ONE incident of running away, praise him or her for staying in the specific areas, give him or her a hug, and remind him or her that he or she will not be able to have extra time at a preferred activity (such as the classroom computer), but he or she will get to choose another activity and he or she will still be able to play on the computer at home. c. If he or she has MORE THAN ONE incident of running away, tell _____ that he or she did not remember to follow the rules and he or she will not be able to play on the computer at home or at school.	Circle the step used

Figure 11.3. Sample script for preventing a child from running away.

collection, 5) opportunities to specify caregiver responses to "if-then" scenarios, and 6) beneficial effects for other children with similar needs. These scripts are works in progress and can be replanned when necessary. Figures 11.2 and 11.3 provide sample scripts: Figure 11.2 is a script to prevent biting and Figure 11.3 is a script to intervene when children try to run away.

Conclusion

Solving a problem depends on the accuracy of the definition and analysis of that problem. There are a variety of child, teacher, peer, and classroom variables that may be influential in determining the child's behavior at school. This chapter discussed methods for defining, analyzing, prioritizing, observing, and summarizing the elements of the problem situation. This process assists the teacher and/or team in deciding whether an individualized intervention plan is necessary. The chapter ends with a discussion of specific action plans called scripts.

CHAPTER 12

Evaluating and Revising Behavior Plans

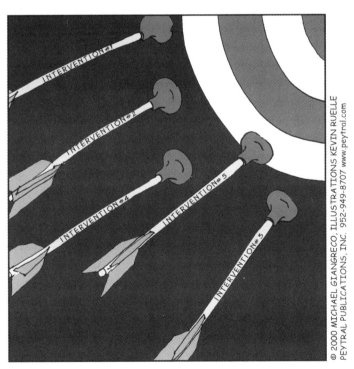

SHOOTING IN THE DARK:
WHAT HAPPENS WHEN YOU SELECT
INTERVENTIONS WITHOUT GOOD
ASSESSMENT DATA

Implementation of positive behavioral support plans has been demonstrated to prevent and reduce challenging behavior while increasing prosocial behavior (McLaren & Nelson, 2009). For implementation to work, however, plans must be well designed and consistently implemented (Crone & Horner, 2003). Even when stakeholders have used their best judgment to develop the plan, revisions may be needed. It is then important to take a thorough look at the function of the behavior, goals of the plan, and the steps used in the implementation.

Positive behavioral support plans can be legal documents. The Individuals with Disabilities Education Improvement Act of 2004 (PL 108-446) requires that plans be developed when children with individualized education programs require more behavioral support. Plans also are required when children are placed in a more restrictive environment or a manifestation determination meeting takes place. In these circumstances, a functional behavioral assessment and an intervention plan that uses positive supports must be completed. Many school districts and lead education agencies require specific forms and processes so that all legal obligations are met.

When implementation of behavioral support plans does not reduce targeted behaviors or increase prosocial behavior, they must be revised. Lack of positive outcomes could be the result of incomplete plans or insufficient implementation of the plan. First, it is important to study the implementation of the plan to be sure that the plan was followed as intended. The plan itself must be studied to be sure that the goals and strategies are appropriate to original judgments about the behavior. Finally, stakeholders should look at the hypothesis to determine whether judgments about the ecological context of the behavior have been correct.

Tracking Progress

Once an intervention plan has been put in place, it is extremely important to track progress so that decisions can be made. This requires gathering more information across time. Data, specifically about the frequency and duration of the behavior in question, should be collected and summarized. These new data should then be compared with data collected before the intervention to know whether progress is being made.

There are several ways to collect information about progress. Observation provides the central source of real-time information about changes children make over time. All of the stakeholders involved must make a commitment to data collection so that the information is accurate. Otherwise, erroneous decisions could be made.

Observations should be conducted before the intervention begins to establish a baseline from which progress will be judged. After the intervention begins, observation information should again be collected at regular intervals and compared with the baseline information.

Observations can be as simple as a tally of the behavior and the dates it occurs. Or, observations can include duration and intensity information. Which type of information to collect depends on the targeted behavior and the goals of the intervention plan. For example, if the goal of the intervention is to decrease hitting, a simple tally may be all that is needed. However, if the goal is to increase the frequency and duration of self-initiated play, information must be collected about both frequency and duration. The following tools provide templates for collecting both types of information.

Frequency Tally of Targeted Behavior

Interventions take time and attention. It is important to know if they are working. Simple tallies of behavior (before and after an intervention is implemented) provide basic information about progress. Figure 12.1 provides a method for collecting information to analyze progress.

Purpose of This Tool	The purpose of this tool is to provide information about whether an intervention is associated with decreasing the average number of times specified challenging behaviors occur.
When to Use This Tool	This tool should be used before the intervention has begun and again after the intervention has begun. It should be used across enough time intervals so that stakeholders agree that information gathered is sufficient to make comparisons and base judgments.
How to Use This Tool	Record the name of the child and the setting (e.g., group time, outside time, free play) in which the observation will occur. Record the targeted behaviors. Space for three behaviors has been provided. Place the tally sheet where it can easily be used. For this type of observation, it is best to designate someone as the observer and allow that person time and freedom to collect the information. Before the intervention begins, conduct a series of observations. Record the date for each before-intervention observation. Make a tally mark each time the behavior occurs. Once the baseline information has been recorded, total the number of times the behavior was observed. Calculate the average by dividing the total by the number of observations. Once the intervention has begun, conduct a series of observations. Tally the number of occurrences of the behavior for each day the same as the before-intervention tallies. Total the number of incidents and calculate the average just as for the before-intervention tallies. Compare the totals and the averages of the tallies. Discuss the comparison of the tallies with the stakeholder team. Write any thoughts or comments in the comments section.
Suggestions for Using This Tool	1. For the information recorded to be accurate, it is important to have clear definitions of the behavior so that everyone knows what to count and what not to count. Any questions about what to count should be discussed. 2. If a child's behavior changes dramatically from day to day, the average may be a helpful number to look at. It may be hard to make comparisons from only the totals. In addition, it is impossible to make comparisons if the number of observation

Frequency Tally of Targeted Behavior

Directions:
1. Record the name of the child and the setting (e.g., group time, outside time, free play) in which the observation will occur. Record the targeted behaviors. Space for three behaviors has been provided. Place the tally sheet where it can easily be used. For this type of observation, it is best to designate someone as the observer and allow that person time and freedom to collect the information.
2. Before the intervention begins, conduct a series of observations. Record the date for each before-intervention observation. Make a tally mark each time the behavior occurs. Once the baseline information has been recorded, total the number of times the behavior was observed. Calculate the average by dividing the total by the number of observations.
3. Once the intervention has begun, conduct a series of observations. Tally the number of occurrences of the behavior for each day the same as the before-intervention tallies. Total the number of incidents and calculate the average just as for the before-intervention tallies. Compare the totals and the averages of the tallies.
4. Discuss the comparison of the tallies with the stakeholder team. Write any thoughts or comments in the comments section.

Name of child: __Molly Sierra__

Setting: __Classroom—9–10:30 and 3–4; 17 children; 3 adults__

Before intervention (baseline)

	Date	screaming (Behavior 1)	taking toys (Behavior 2)	engagement > 2 minutes (Behavior 3)
1	10/12/09	19	7	3
2	10/13/09	19	5	4
3	10/14/09	19	8	5
4	10/15/09	17	6	4
	Total	74	26	16
	Average	18.5	6.5	4

Intervention progress tracking

	Date			
1	10/16/09	5	2	5
2	10/19/09	4	1	4
3	10/20/09	4	2	4
4	10/21/09	4	2	5
5	10/22/09	5	1	6
6	10/23/09	4	1	6
7	10/26/09	3	0	7
8	10/27/09	3	1	6
	Total	32	10	43
	Average	4	1.25	5.38
	Progress	(Y) N	(Y) N	(Y) N

Comments: *The intervention required teachers to give thumbs up every 3 minutes. It also required the use of a choice board for transitions between activities. This took a lot of teacher time.*

She may not understand the use of the choice board as a transition to an activity. However, she loves to use the choice board.

Figure 12.1. Frequency Tally of Targeted Behavior.

periods are different before the intervention begins from after the observation begins.

3. When challenging behaviors are dangerous, just a few incidents can be very powerful. It is critical that each individual incident be considered. In this situation, a total of the tallies rather than the average may be the important number to consider.

4. The stakeholder team should look at the information gathered to determine whether the intervention should continue as is or revisions should be made. It is important to observe as many times as are necessary for the team to have confidence that they understand the impact of the intervention over time.

A Picture of Progress

Graphing observation information creates a picture of a trend in a child's behavior. Figure 12.2 gives a very basic picture of a trend before and after an intervention is implemented.

Purpose of This Tool	The purpose of this tool is to produce a visual graphic of the frequency of the targeted behavior before and after beginning an intervention.
When to Use This Tool	This tool should be used when decisions about the effectiveness of the intervention are being made. This tool also can be completed when team members need to know the rate of progress being made.
How to Use This Tool	Write the name of the child, the targeted behavior, and the time frame for the observations in the top section of the tool. Using Figure 12.1, complete a graph of the frequency of the targeted behaviors by completing the following steps:

- For the first baseline observation, go to the number *1* of the *dates of observation* section. Also, look for the number on the left-hand column that matches the number of tallied behaviors for the first baseline observation. Find the place on the grid where the number *1* for *dates of observation* crosses the number for *tallies*. Place an *X* on that intersection.

- Continue the above process for all of the observations from the baseline observations.

- Continue the process for all of the intervention observations.

- Draw a line to connect the *X*s.

A Picture of Progress

Directions:
1. Write the name of the child, the targeted behavior, and the time frame for the observations in the top section of the tool. Using the Frequency Tally of Targeted Behavior, complete a graph of the frequency of the targeted behaviors by completing the following steps:
2. For the first baseline observation, go to the number *1* of the *dates of observation* section. Also, look for the number on the left-hand side of the table that matches the number of tallied behaviors for the first baseline observation. Find the place on the grid where the number *1* for *dates of observation* crosses the number for *tallies*. The line above each number corresponds to the number. Place an *X* on that intersection.
3. Continue the above process for all of the observations from the baseline observations. Continue the process for all of the intervention observations.
4. Draw a line to connect the *Xs*.

Name of child: _Molly Sierra_

Targeted behavior: _Screaming_

Time frame: _9–10:30 and 3–4:00; 10/12/09–10/15/09 (baseline); 10/16/09–10/27/09 (intervention)_

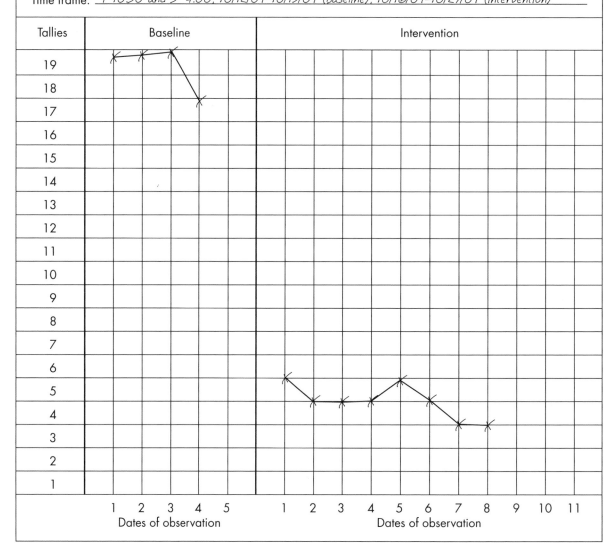

Figure 12.2. A Picture of Progress.

Suggestions for
Using This Tool

1. The complete graph provides a picture of the progress the child made at the time of the observation. It is based on real-time information.

2. More than one behavior can be graphed by using different colors for each targeted behavior. Or, each can be graphed on a different tool. When more than one behavior is targeted, it is possible that one or more may change differently than others.

3. The question of how much progress is enough must be answered by the stakeholder team. The data collected provide the information from which judgments must be made. Stakeholders must use what they know about the child, evidence-based practice, and thoughts about future placements to decide whether the intervention should be faded or revised or an entirely new intervention should be initiated.

Tool for Tracking the Frequency and Duration of Targeted Behavior

Progress can be made in many different ways. Sometimes the amount of times a child exhibits the behavior can change. And, sometimes the amount of time the behavior lasts can change. Figure 12.3 provides a tool for documenting and analyzing the frequency and the duration of the behavior.

Purpose of This Tool

The purpose of this tool is to provide information about whether an intervention is associated with decreasing the average number of times and the duration for which specified challenging behaviors occur.

When to Use This Tool

This tool should be used before the intervention has begun and again after the intervention has begun. It should be used across enough time intervals so that stakeholders agree that information gathered is sufficient to make comparisons and base judgments.

How to Use This Tool

Record the name of the child and the setting (e.g., group time, outside time, free play) in which the observation will occur. Record the targeted behaviors. Space for three behaviors has been provided. Place the tally sheet where it can be used easily. For this type of observation, it is best to designate someone as the observer and allow that person time and freedom to collect the information. Because you will record the duration of the behavior, you will need a stopwatch or a watch with a second hand.

Before the intervention begins, conduct a series of observations. Record the date for each before-intervention observation. When the behavior begins, start the stopwatch or note the time on a watch. Record the length of time the target behavior occurs in the duration section. Make a tally mark each time the behavior occurs.

Tool for Tracking the Frequency and Duration of Targeted Behavior

Directions:
1. Record the name of the child and the setting (e.g., group time, outside time, free play) in which the observation will occur. Record the targeted behaviors. Space for three behaviors has been provided. Place the tally sheet where it can be used easily. For this type of observation, it is best to designate someone as the observer and allow that person time and freedom to collect the information. Because you will record the duration of the behavior, you will need a stopwatch or a watch with a second hand.
2. Before the intervention begins, conduct a series of observations. Record the date for each before-intervention observation. When the behavior begins, start the stopwatch or note the time on a watch. Record the length of time the target behavior occurs in the duration section. Make a tally mark each time the behavior occurs. Once the baseline information has been recorded, total the number of times the behavior was observed. Total the number of minutes or seconds the behavior lasted. Calculate the average frequency and duration by dividing the total by the number of observations.
3. Once the intervention has begun, conduct a series of observations. Complete steps the same way as for the before-intervention observations. Compare the totals and the averages. Indicate whether progress has been made.

Name of child: _Jason Klein_

Setting: _Classroom; 20 children; 2 teachers; free play and group time_

Before intervention (baseline)

Date	Tantrum (Behavior 1)		(Behavior 2)		(Behavior 3)		Comments
	Frequency	Duration	Frequency	Duration	Frequency	Duration	
10/26	1	20 min					
10/27	2	34 min					
10/28	2	31 min					
10/29	3	45 min					
10/30	2	32 min					
11/2	3	21 min					
Total	13	183 min					
Average	2.17 per day	30.5 min per day					

Intervention progress tracking

	Frequency	Duration	Frequency	Duration	Frequency	Duration	
11/3	3	30 min					
11/4	2	15 min					
11/5	2	10 min					
11/6	2	10 min					
11/7	3	15 min					
11/8	2	12 min					
Total	14	92 min					
Average	2.3	15.34 min					
Progress (circle)	Y (N)	(Y) N	Y N	Y N	Y N	Y N	

Figure 12.3. Tool for Tracking the Frequency and Duration of Targeted Behavior.

Once the baseline information has been recorded, total the number of times the behavior was observed. Total the number of minutes or seconds the behavior lasted. Calculate the average frequency and duration by dividing the total by the number of observations.

Once the intervention has begun, conduct a series of observations. Complete steps the same way as for the before-intervention observations. Compare the totals and the averages. Indicate whether progress has been made.

Suggestions for Using This Tool

1. Sometimes intervention team members may wish to increase the amount of time a given behavior occurs (e.g., on-task behavior). Sometimes they may wish to decrease the amount of time a behavior occurs (e.g., self-stimulation). Many times the intervention team may wish to do both. This tool helps team members make decisions about whether the stated goals have been met.

2. The stakeholder team must agree that there is enough information to make decisions about the intervention. It is helpful to discuss up front how many observation intervals will be needed. Sometimes the behavior occurs more infrequently than stakeholders thought. In these cases, additional observation may be required.

When stakeholders believe that the intervention is not working, revisions need to be made in the plan. A thorough review of the plan is needed to diagnose which areas of the plan need revision. The next sections provide templates that may be used for making decisions about revisions.

Acceptability of the Plan

Before making changes to the intervention plan, it is important to ascertain whether the plan was implemented as intended. If elements of the plan were not fully implemented, it is hard to judge whether the lack of outcomes was due to the plan or incomplete implementation. It is easier to determine which elements of the plan are implemented when scripts are clear, specific, and provide a place for team members to check off steps once they have been completed. (See Chapter 11.)

Team members must feel comfortable implementing the plan. It should be easy and efficient. If team members do not believe the steps are necessary, they may skip some. In addition, if team members are philosophically opposed to implementation of some of the steps, they may not complete them. Finally, if the steps of the script cannot be implemented in real situations because they are too complicated or based on unrealistic expectations, it is unlikely all stakeholders will follow through.

Acceptability of Scripts Tool

Many problems with acceptability of the plan can be circumvented by involving team members in development of the scripts. Even so, it is important to evaluate the acceptability of the scripts. The Acceptability of Scripts Tool in Figure 12.4 provides information for understanding stakeholders' views regarding scripts.

Purpose of This Tool	The purpose of this tool is to provide information to determine whether the intervention scripts were acceptable to all of the stakeholders. This will help stakeholders understand the information they get regarding the effectiveness of the intervention.
When to Use This Tool	This tool should be used after stakeholders have had a chance to implement the script. It is important to use the tool as early as possible so that changes can be made before time is lost. Conversely, it is important not to make changes too soon. It sometimes takes time to learn the script.
How to Use This Tool	Stakeholders should rate each element and discuss their ratings. Stakeholders should then discuss whether changes should be made.
Suggestions for Using This Tool	1. It is more likely that scripts will be implemented completely if the activities required are easy and efficient. That is, given the setting of the intervention, the script must require as little effort as possible with the highest outcomes possible. If stakeholders do not feel the script is easy enough for the results they see, they may not implement the script consistently. 2. Deciding whether a script is efficient enough is a judgment call. This judgment often depends on the alternatives for intervention that are available. There is no hard and fast standard for the level of acceptability; however, if the script is so unacceptable that it is not used consistently, the script should be revised.

Elements of Effective Behavioral Support Plans

One of the most important elements of a positive behavioral support plan is the correct identification of the targeted behavior. Sometimes, interventions may show decreases in the targeted behaviors but, on reflection, stakeholders may still feel that the plan is not working.

Often, behaviors come in streams of movement or are associated with other behaviors that can make it difficult to see the target clearly. Stakeholders must clarify

Acceptability of Scripts Tool

Directions: Rate each element and discuss the ratings. Then, discuss whether changes should be made to the script.

Acceptability of script for <u>*Gabriel Levin*</u>

(name of child)

Date: <u>*11/28/09*</u>

Completed by <u>*Lori Cornish*</u>

Circle the number that best reflects your agreement with the following statements:

All of the steps of the script were easy for me to do.

1	2	3	④	5
Disagree		Neutral		Agree

It was easy for me to complete the steps for providing a consequence for challenging behavior.

1	②	3	4	5
Disagree		Neutral		Agree

I found no unnecessary steps in the script.

1	2	③	4	5
Disagree		Neutral		Agree

It was interesting to see how the child responded to the script.

1	2	3	4	⑤
Disagree		Neutral		Agree

Some parts of the script were not congruent with my philosophy or beliefs about learning.

1	2	③	4	5
Disagree		Neutral		Agree

The changes in behavior are worth the time I spend implementing the script.

1	2	③	4	5
Disagree		Neutral		Agree

I believe that implementing this script is the right thing to do.

1	②	3	4	5
Disagree		Neutral		Agree

The script does not work well for the environment for which it is intended.

1	2	3	④	5
Disagree		Neutral		Agree

There are easier ways to do the same thing the script intends.

1	2	③	4	5
Disagree		Neutral		Agree

The results of implementing the script are in line with the goals for the script.

1	2	3	4	⑤
Disagree		Neutral		Agree

Comments: *I like the idea of using the choice board. I think this helps. But, I often forget to check in to give Gabriel feedback. It is hard to do this when I am interacting with other children.*

Figure 12.4. Acceptability of Scripts Tool.

which behaviors are most concerning. They must also analyze whether targeting one behavior will affect other behaviors. Safety must always be the top priority.

Developing a Hypothesis Tool

Another essential element of an effective intervention plan is identifying the function of the targeted behavior (McLaren & Nelson, 2009). This can be done using the Developing a Hypothesis Tool in Figure 12.5. Behavioral support plans should be based on discussions about data collected through observation, interviews, and reviews of records (Todd, Campbell, Meyer, & Horner, 2008). Stakeholders should ask themselves what the behavior is used for. They should reflect long enough to have a sense of what the child gets or avoids by using the behavior. Stakeholders can then summarize the information into a hypothesis of the entire context influencing the behavior.

Purpose of This Tool	The purpose of this tool is to provide a format for reviewing the information in the behavioral support plan. Information gathered leads to a hypothesis or summary statement from which to build or evaluate interventions.
When to Use This Tool	This tool can be used to develop intervention plans or to evaluate assumptions of current intervention plans.
How to Use This Tool	This tool should be completed by a team of stakeholders. Stakeholders should discuss all data collected and come to a consensus on beliefs about the underlying function of the behavior and context of the behavior. As a group, stakeholders should complete the hypothesis or summary statement at the end.

Suggestions for Using This Tool

1. An essential part of intervention planning is to understand how to help the child learn replacements for challenging behavior. If the child is using a behavior to get or avoid something, the replacement should be acceptable to adults and children. It also should meet the same function as the challenging behavior. For example, a child can be taught to ask for a turn to play with a toy rather than simply taking the toy. Asking for a turn meets the child's purpose of getting the toy and the teacher's need for prosocial behavior.

2. Finding something that the child already knows how to do as a replacement for challenging behavior is very helpful; however, sometimes a new behavior or skill will be targeted as a replacement for challenging behavior. When it is necessary to teach the child the replacement behavior, the plan should allow time and provide guidance.

3. The hypothesis or summary statement should be compared with the intervention to determine whether the intervention

Developing a Hypothesis Tool

Directions: This tool should be completed by a team of stakeholders. Stakeholders should discuss all data collected and come to a consensus on beliefs about the underlying function of the behavior and context of the behavior. As a group, stakeholders should complete the hypothesis or summary statement at the end of this tool.

Child's name: *Shannon Bell*

Date: *11/7/09*

Completed by: *Jarod Bell (father), Karen Smith (teacher), Sean Fredrick (school psychologist)*

1. In thinking about the behavior of focus, what events or activities seem to indirectly make the child more likely to exhibit the behavior? What events set up the possibility that the challenging behavior may occur?

Classroom
- X Unpredictable schedule
- X Transitions
- X Too much sensory stimulation
- ___ Too little sensory stimulation
- X New room layout
- X Lack of preparation for change
- X New schedule
- X Home disruptions (Violence, crime, etc.)
- ___ Other (please specify):

Intrapersonal
- ___ Hunger
- X Fatigue
- ___ Illness
- ___ Preexisting limitations
- ___ Social responsiveness
- ___ Mobility
- ___ Language
- ___ Problem solving
- ___ Embarrassment
- ___ Medication changes
- X Temperament
- ___ Other (please specify):

Transactional
- ___ Specific person
- ___ History of home discipline
- ___ Exclusion by peers
- X Lack of familiar adult or peer
- X Unfamiliar person
- X Family disruptions (e.g., death, divorce, marriage)
- ___ Other (please specify):

2. At the time the behavior occurs, what events immediately appear to initiate the behavior?

Classroom
Classroom demands that are:
- ___ too hard
- ___ boring
- X confusing
- X long
- ___ teacher-directed
- X over stimulating
- X open-ended
- ___ Loss of toy or activity
- X Non-preferred activity
- X Non-engagement in activity
- ___ Other (please specify):

Intrapersonal
- X Too much sensory stimulation
- ___ Not enough sensory stimulation
- ___ Pain
- ___ Embarrassment
- X Difficulty attending
- X Extreme emotion
- X Difficulty with language
- ___ Other (please specify):

Transactional
- ___ Close proximity to others
- X Teasing or exclusion by others
- ___ Teacher correction
- X Loss of attention
- ___ Unfamiliar person
- ___ Adult redirection
- ___ Other (please specify):

Figure 12.5. Developing a Hypothesis Tool.

(continued)

Figure 12.5. *(continued)*

Developing a Hypothesis Tool *(continued)*

3. When the targeted behavior occurs, what does it look like?

Classroom	Intrapersonal	Transactional
____ Destroying property	____ Physical injury to self	_X_ Hitting
_X_ Destroying work of others	_X_ Extreme emotion	____ Biting
_X_ Disrupting routine	____ Painful thoughts	_X_ Kicking
_X_ Stopping activity	____ Self-stimulation	____ Spitting
_X_ Taking toy	____ Other (please specify):	____ Foul language
_X_ Unsafe use of toys and furniture		_X_ Taunting and/or teasing
____ Other (please specify):		____ Other (please specify):

4. What is the response to the child immediately after the behavior? What does he or she get or avoid?

Classroom	Intrapersonal	Transactional
____ Routine changed	____ Sensory stimulus obtained	_X_ Proximity to adult obtained
_X_ Activity stopped	____ Pain decreased or stopped	____ Proximity to adult avoided
_X_ Toy obtained	_X_ Emotions stabilized	_X_ Attention from adult
_X_ Preferred activity obtained	____ Other (please specify):	____ Attention from child
____ Other (please specify):		____ Time alone
		____ Other (please specify):

Hypothesis or summary statement:

When _____ *Shannon* _____ is _____ *tired or overstimulated* _____ and

(name of child)   (answers from Question 1)

_____ *classroom demands are confusing, too long or boring* _____, he or she is likely to

(answers from Question 2)

_____ *hit, kick, taunt* _____ in order to

(answers from Question 3)

_____ *gain attention and activities to stabilize emotions* _____.

(answers from Question 4)

really meets the same needs as the challenging behavior. If it does not, consider making changes in the plan.

4. Sometimes the hypothesis is wrong. It is important to test the hypothesis to know whether it is correct. This can be done by making small changes in the environment. For example, if the presence of a particular person seems to make it more likely that a behavior will occur, observations can be conducted when the person is present and when the person is not present. A comparison of the behavior under each condition helps to validate the hypothesis.

Evaluation of Plan Quality

Once stakeholders feel comfortable with the underlying assumptions of a behavioral support plan, they should evaluate the completeness and quality of the plan. Researchers have identified six concepts that should be included in behavior plans (Cook et al., 2007). The six concepts are

1. *Function of the behavior*: the purpose of the behavior for the child

2. *Specificity of the situation*: what happens before, during, and after the behavior

3. *Target behaviors and goal for new behavior*: specifically what the behavior looks like

4. *Methods for affirming or rewarding change*: feedback, information, or reward for change

5. *Strategies for addressing the challenging behavior when it occurs*: things to say and do

6. *Communication among team members*: regular ways to evaluate and change based on progress

The Evaluation of Plan Quality in Figure 12.6 provides questions for discussion to determine whether all elements are present in the plan.

Purpose of This Tool	The purpose of this tool is to provide feedback to the plan team when there are few changes in the targeted behaviors or progress has been stalled.
When to Use This Tool	This tool should be used when the stakeholder team receives data that indicate there is a need for change in the intervention plan.
How to Use This Tool	Stakeholders should meet to discuss all of the questions in this tool. Specific attention should be given to any *no* answers. Revisions to the plan should be based on an assessment of the effectiveness of the plan and the ability of the team members to implement the plan over time.

Evaluation of Plan Quality

Directions: Stakeholders should meet to discuss questions in this tool. Specific attention should be given to any *no* answers. Revisions to the plan should be based on an assessment of the effectiveness of the plan and the ability of the team members to implement the plan over time.

Plan for: _Shannon Bell_

Team members: _Jarod Bell (father), Karen Smith (teacher), Sean Fredrick (school psychologist)_

Date: _11/7/09_

Hypothesis or summary statement (from Figure 12.5)

When _____ _Shannon_ _____ is _____ _tired or overstimulated_ _____ and

        (name of child)   (answers from Question 1)

_____ _classroom demands are confusing, too long or boring_ _____ , he or she is likely to

                (answers from Question 2)

_____ _hit, kick, taunt_ _____ in order to

                (answers from Question 3)

_____ _gain attention and activities to stabilize emotions_ _____ .

                (answers from Question 4)

Function of behavior	Y	N
Does the hypothesis in Figure 12.5 match the underlying assumptions on which the plan was built?	X	
Does the hypothesis or summary describe the events that seem to make the behavior more likely even though they do not occur immediately before the event?	X	
Does the hypothesis clearly describe the challenging behavior so that everyone knows it when they see it?	X	
Have all of the observation, interview, and records data been considered in making judgments about the function of the behavior?	X	
Have you tested the hypothesis by making small changes in the environment or interactions?	X	
Specificity of the situation	Y	N
Is there consensus in the team regarding which elements of the environment seem to precede the behavior?	X	
Were there enough data to obtain team consensus about what tends to happen right after the child exhibits the behavior?		X
Have the environment, curriculum, schedules, and routines been modified enough to change the setting for the behavior?	X	

Figure 12.6. Evaluation of Plan Quality.

Evaluation of Plan Quality *(continued)*		
Target behavior and goal for new behavior	Y	N
Do all of the team members agree that they can identify the behavior when it happens?		X
Does this behavior happen in conjunction with other behavior? If so, do the behaviors typically happen in sequence? Does one predict the other?	X	
Is another behavior a safety issue that should be a higher priority than the behavior currently targeted?		X
Methods for affirming and rewarding change	Y	N
Have all stakeholders been involved in deciding on the methods to use in the intervention?		X
Are the methods easy for everyone to implement?	X	
Are there plans for responding to different responses from the child?	X	
Does the child seem to respond positively to the selected rewards or affirmations?	X	
Does the child need a reward that is more concrete?	X	
Are the rewards administered in the least intrusive way possible?	X	
Has the intervention been implemented for enough time to see change?	X	
Have steps been taken to assure that rewards are administered in a respectful, nonhumiliating way?	X	
Strategies for addressing the challenging behavior when it occurs	Y	N
Have consequences been included in the plan?	X	
Have steps been taken to assure that this child is not perceived as the "bad" child by children, families, and colleagues?	X	
Are the steps clear and easy to understand?	X	
Have plans already been revised based on unforeseen responses as the implementation is begun?	X	
Does the plan include steps for decreasing the level of support needed to sustain change?	X	
Communicating among team members	Y	N
Have scripts been written for each challenging situation?	X	
Do the scripts provide a place to document that stakeholders have implemented each step?	X	
Has each step in the script been implemented each time?		X
Have all team members been given access to all data for decision making?	X	
Have meetings taken place to discuss progress at all phases of the intervention?	X	

| Suggestions for Using This Tool | 1. One of the hardest decisions the team will make is whether the intervention has been in place long enough to see change. For some children, change takes place rapidly. For other children, change takes place at a slower rate. The intervention team must decide how long to implement the intervention before revisions are made. Frequent communication is needed for all team members to make decisions about the plan. |

2. Particular attention must be paid to the behavior or skill identified as a replacement for the challenging behavior. Teaching a child a replacement behavior for which they have no underlying skills takes time. The strategies must be based on an assessment of the knowledge and skills of the child. In addition, methods must be evidence based.

Conclusion

Plans that seem to work on paper sometimes do not work once they are implemented. Problems can arise for many reasons. Some of the more common sources of difficulties arise from the following:

- Incomplete or incorrect assumptions about the function of the behavior

- Mistaken judgments about the ease or efficiency of implementation

- Incomplete communication among stakeholders

- Inadequate planning for teaching new skills

All stakeholders should be involved in discussing modifications to the plan. Discussions should be informed by data obtained by observing, self-monitoring, and reviewing the plan. Stakeholders should use their knowledge of evidence-based practices and specific information about the child to make judgments about whether plans should be revised.

Rather than falling back into ineffective or punitive strategies for addressing challenging behaviors when plans do not work fast enough, teachers must make a commitment to the problem-solving process. Plans should be revised and implemented in systematic, consistent ways. When this happens, research shows that teachers and children will attain high levels of success (Cook et al., 2007; Scott, Liaupsin, & Nelson, 2001; Sugai & Horner, 2002).

References

Ainsworth, M.D. (1989). Attachments beyond infancy, *American Psychologist, 44,* 709–716.

Antrop, I., Buysse, A., Roeyers, H., & Oost, P. (2005). Activity in children with ADHD during waiting situations in the classroom: A pilot study. *British Journal of Educational Psychology, 75*(1), 51–69.

Atherton, J.S. (2005). *Learning and teaching: constructivism in learning,* Available: http//www.learning and teaching.info/learning/constructivism.htm, Accessed March 2009.

Avolio, B.J., & Yammorino, F. (2002). *Transformational and charismatic leadership.* Amsterdam, JAI Press, Elsevier.

Barnett, D., Bell, S., & Carey, C. (1999). *Designing preschool interventions: A practitioner's guide.* New York: Guilford Press.

Barnett, S., Lamy, C., & Frede, E. (2001). *Preschool classroom quality in Abbott districts 2000–2001* [CEER Supplementary Technical Report]. New Brunswick, NJ: Rutgers University.

Baumrind, D. (1966). Effects of authoritative parental control on child behavior. *Child Development, 37,* 887–907.

Baumrind, D. (1991). The influence of parenting style on adolescent competence and substance use. *Journal of Early Adolescence, 11*(1), 56–95.

Baumrind, D. (1996). The discipline controversy revisited. *Family Relations: Journal of Applied Family and Clinical Studies, 45,* 405–414.

Bell, S.H., & Barnett, D.W. (1999). Peer micronorms in the assessment of young children: Methodological review and examples. *Topics in Early Childhood Special Education, 19,* 112–122.

Bell, S.H., & Carr, V. (2004). Implementing individualized behavior plans. In S.H. Bell, V. Carr, D. Denno, L.J. Johnson, & L.R. Phillips (Eds.) *Challenging behaviors in early childhood settings: Creating a place for all children* (pp. 121–136). Baltimore: Paul H. Brookes Publishing Co.

Bell, S.H., Carr, V., Denno, D., Johnson, L.J., & Phillips, L.R. (Eds.) (2004) *Challenging behaviors in early childhood settings: Creating a place for all children.* Baltimore: Paul H. Brookes Publishing Co.

Berdoussis, N., Wong, A., & Wien, C. (2001) The learner as protagonist in a standardized curriculum. In C. Wien (Ed.), *Emergent curriculum in the primary classroom: Interpreting the reggio emilia approach in schools* (pp. 38–51). New York: Teachers College Press.

Berk, L.E., & Winsler, A. (1995). *Scaffolding children's learning: Vygotsky and early childhood education.* Washington, DC: NAEYC.

Bierman, K.L., Torres, M.M., Domitrovich, C.E., Welsh, J.A., & Gest, S.D. (2009). Behavioral and cognitive readiness for school: Cross-domain associations for children attending Head Start. *Social Development, 18*(2), 305–323.

Boat, M.B., Carr, V.W., Barnett, D., Nichols, A., Macmann, G., Pan, W., et al. (in press). Promoting change in preschool environments: A study of empirically-based teacher support. *NHSA Dialog.*

Bodrova, E., & Leong, D. (2005). High quality preschool programs: What would Vygotsky say? *Early Education and Development, 16*(4), 437–446.

Bohn, C., Roehrig, A. & Pressley, M. (2004). The first days of school in the classroom of two more effective and four less effective primary-grades teachers. *Elementary School Journal, 104*(4), 269–287.

Branson, D.M., & Bingham, A. (2009). Using interagency collaboration to support family-centered transition practices. *Young Exceptional Children, 12*(3), 15–31.

Bronson, M.B. (2000). *Self-regulation in early childhood: Nature and nurture.* New York: The Guilford Press.

Bryan, L., & Gast, D. (2000). Teaching on-task and on-schedule behaviors to high-functioning children with autism via picture activity schedules. *Autism and Developmental Disorders, 30,* 553–567.

Buck, G. (1999). Smoothing the rough edges of classroom transitions. *Intervention in School and Clinic, 34*(4), 224–229.

Burchinal, M.R., Howes, C., Pianta, R., Bryant, D., Early, D., Clifford, R., et al. (2008). Predicting child outcomes at the end of kindergarten from the quality of prekindergarten teacher-child interactions and instruction. *Applied Developmental Science, 12*(3), 140–153.

Burchinal, M.R., Peisner-Feinberg, E., Pianta, R., & Howes, C. (2002). Development of academic skills from preschool through second grade: Family and classroom predictors of developmental trajectories. *Journal of School Psychology, 40*(5), 415–436.

Burns, J.M. (1978). *Leadership.* New York: Harper & Row.

Buyse, E., Verschueren, K., Doumen, S., Van Damme, J., & Maes, F. (2008). Classroom problem behavior and teacher-child relationships in kindergarten: The moderating role of classroom climate. *Journal of School Psychology, 46*(4), 367–391.

Cameron, C., Connor, C., & Morrison, F. (2005). Effects of variation in teacher organization on classroom functioning. *Journal of School Psychology, 43,* 61–85.

Campbell, S., Shaw, D.S., & Gilliom, M. (2000). Early externalizing behavior problems: Toddlers and preschoolers at risk for later maladjustment. *Development & Psychopathology, 12,* 467–488.

Carr, E.G., Levin, L., McConnachie, G., Carlson, J., Kemp, D., & Smith, C. (1994). *Communication-based intervention for problem behavior: A user's guide for producing positive change.* Baltimore: Paul H. Brookes Publishing Co.

Carr, V., Johnson, L.J., & Corkwell, C.C. (2004). Developing centerwide support. In S.H. Bell, V. Carr, D. Denno, L.J. Johnson, & L.R. Phillips. *Challenging behaviors in early childhood setting: Creating a place for all children.* Baltimore: Paul H. Brookes Publishing Co.

Carr, V.W. & Boat, M.B. (2006). *Accelerating Learning Outcomes: Curriculum-based measures and teacher instruction in the ECE classroom.* Presentation to Cincinnati-Hamilton County Community Action Agency Head Start. Cincinnati, OH.

Casey, A.M., & McWilliam, R.A. (2007). The STARE: The Scale for Teachers' Assessment of Routines Engagement. *Young Exceptional Children, 11*(1), 2–15.

Chess, S., & Thomas, A. (1986). *Temperament in clinical practice.* New York: Guilford Press.

Chess, S., & Thomas, A. (1996). *Temperament theory and practice.* New York: Brunner/Mazel Publishers.

Cheung, S.K., & Kwok, S.Y.C. (2003). "How do Hong Kong children react to maternal I-messages and inductive reasoning?" *The Hong Kong Journal of Social Work, 37*(1), 3–14.

Cook, C., Crews, D., Wright, D., Mayer, R., Gale, B., Kraemer, B., et al. (2007). Establishing and evaluating the substantive adequacy of positive behavioral support plans. *Journal of Behavior Intervention, 16,* 191–206.

Copple, C., & Bredekamp, S. (2009). To be an excellent teacher. In C. Copple & S. Bredekamp (Eds.), *Developmentally appropriate practice in early childhood programs.* Washington, D.C.: National Association for the Education of Young Children.

Corsaro, W. (1985). *Friendship and peer culture in the early years.* Greenwich, CT: Ablex Publishing Corp.

Corsaro, W.A. (1988). Peer culture in the preschool. *Theory into Practice, 27*(1), 19–24.

Crone, D., & Horner, R. (2003). *Building positive behavior support systems in schools*. New York, London: Guilford Press.

Darling, N., & Steinberg, L. (1993). Parenting style as context: An integrative model. *Psychological Bulletin, 113*(3), 487–496.

Dauphin, M., Kinney, E., & Stromer, R. (2004). Using video-enhanced activity schedules and matrix training to teach sociodramatic play to a child with autism. *Journal of Positive Behavior Interventions, 6*(4), 238–250.

Denham, S., Mawson, T., Caverly, S., Schmidt, M., Hackney, R., Caswell, C., & DeMulder, E. (2001). Preschoolers at play: Co-socialisers of emotional and social compliance. *International Journal of Behavioral Development, 25*(4), 290–301.

Dewey, J. (1948, 1920). *Reconstruction in philosophy*. Boston: Beacon Press.

Dooley, P., Wilczenski, F., & Torem, C. (2001). Using an activity schedule to smooth school transitions. *Journal of Positive Behavior Interventions, 3*(1), 57–61.

Dreyfus, H.L., & Dreyfus, S.E. (1986). *Mind over machine: The power of human intuition and expertise in the era of the computer*. Oxford: Basil Blackwell.

Dunlap, G., & Liso, D. (2004). Brief #15: *Using choice and preference to promote improved behavior*. What Works Briefs.

Dunn, W. (2001). The sensations of everyday life: Empirical, theoretical and pragmatic considerations. *American Journal of Occupational Therapy. 55*(6).

Durand, V.M. (1990). Severe behavior problems: *A functional communication training approach*. New York: The Guilford Press.

Ehrhardt, K.E., Barnett, D.W., Lentz, F.E., Stollar, S.E., & Reifen, L. (1996). Innovative methodology in ecological consultation: Use of scripts to promote treatment acceptability and integrity. *School Psychology Quarterly, 11*, 149–168.

Elgas, P.M., & Lynch, E. (1998). Play. In Johnson, L.J., M.J. La Montange, P.M. Elgas, and A.M. Bauer. *Early childhood education: Blending theory, blending practice*, pp. 111–134. Baltimore: Paul H. Brookes Publishing Co.

Elias, C., & Berk, L. (2002). Self-regulation in young children: Is there a role for sociodramatic play? *Early Childhood Research Quarterly, 17*, 216–238.

Erwin, E., Brotherson, M., Palmer, S., Cook, C., Weigel, C., & Summers, J. (2009). How to promote self-determination for young children with disabilities. *Young Exceptional Children, 12*(2), 27–37.

Fantuzzo, J., Perry, M., & McDermott, P. (2004). Preschool approaches to learning and their relationship to other relevant classroom competencies for low-income children. *School Psychology Quarterly, 19*(3), 212–230.

Fudge, D., Reece, L., Skinner, C., & Cowden, D. (2007). Using multiple classroom rules, public cues, and consistent transition strategies to reduce inappropriate vocalization: An investigation of the Color Wheel. *Journal of Evidence Based Practices, 8*, 102–119.

Fudge, D., Reece, L., Skinner, C., & Cowden, D., Clark, J., & Bliss, S. (2008). Increasing on-task behavior in every student in a second-grade classroom during transitions: Validating the color wheel system. *Journal of School Psychology, 46*, 575–592.

Gay, G., & Haward, T. (2001). Multicultural education for the 21st century. *The Teacher Educator, 36*(1), 1–16.

Gleason, T.R., Gower, A.L., Hohmann, L.M., & Gleason, T.C. (2005). Temperament and friendship in preschool-aged children. *International Journal of Behavioral Development, 29*(4), 336–344.

Goncu, A., Patt, M., & Kouba, E. (2002). Understanding young children's pretend play in context. In *Blackwell Handbook of Childhood Social Development* (pp. 418–437). Oxford, UK: Blackwell Publishers.

Gonzalez-Mena, J. (2008). *Diversity in early education*. New York: The McGraw-Hill Co.

Gordon, T. (1974). T.E.T.: *Teacher effectiveness training*. New York: Wyden.

Gordon, T. (1989). *Teaching children self-discipline: At home and at school*. New York: Random House.

Greenwood, C.R., Horton, B.T., & Utley, C.A. (2002). Academic engagement: Current perspectives on research and practice. *The School Psychology Review, 31*, 328–349.

Grolnick, W.S., & Ryan, R.M. (1989). Parent styles associated with children's self-regulation and competence in school. *Journal of Educational Psychology, 11*(1), 56–95.

Hamre, B.K., & Pianta, R.C. (2001). Early teacher-child relationships and the trajectory of children's school outcomes through eighth grade. *Child Development, 72*, 625–638.

Harrist, A., & Bradley, D. (2003). "You can't say you can't play": Intervening in the process of social exclusion in the kindergarten classroom. *Early Childhood Research Quarterly, 18*, 185–205.

Hartman, A. (1995). Diagrammatic assessment of family relationships. *Families in Society: The Journal of Contemporary Human Services, 76*(2), 111–122.

Hemmeter, M.L., Ostrosky, M., & Fox, L. (2006). Social and emotional foundations for early learning: A conceptual model for intervention. *School Psychology Review, 35*(4), 583–601.

Hodge, D.R. (2005). Developing a spiritual assessment tool: A discussion of the strengths and limitations of five different assessment methods. *Health and Social Work, 30*, 314–323.

Holt, M., & Espelage, D. (2007). Perceived social support among bullies, victims and bully-victims. *Journal of Youth and Adolescence, 36*, 984–994.

Howard, T. (2001). Telling their side of the story: African American students' perceptions of culturally relevant teaching. *Urban Review, 33*(2), 131–148.

Howe, N., Rinaldi, C.M., Jennings, & Petrakos (2002). "No! The lambs can stay out because they got cozies" Constructive and destructive sibling conflict, pretend play, and social understanding. *Child Development, 73*(5), 1460–1473.

Howes, C., Burchinal, M., Pianta, R., Bryant, D., Early, D., Clifford, R., et al. (2008). Ready to learn? Children's pre-academic achievement in pre-kindergarten programs. *Early Childhood Research Quarterly, 23*(1), 27–50.

Hurley, E., & Allen, W. (2009). Culture and the interaction of student ethnicity with reward structure in group learning. *Cognition & Instruction, 27*(2), 121–146.

Hyson, M. (2008). *Enthusiastic and engaged learners: Approaches to learning in the early childhood classroom*. New York: Teachers College Press.

Individuals with Disabilities Education Improvement Act (IDEA) of 2004, PL 108-446, 20 U.S.C. §§ 1400 *et seq.*

Isaacs, S. (1933). *Social development in young children*. New York: Schocken Books.

Jewell, J.J., Krohn, E.J., Scott, V.G., Carlton, M., & Meinz, E. (2008). The differential impact of mothers' and fathers' discipline on preschool children's home and classroom behavior. *North American Journal of Psychology, 10*(1), 173–188.

Kagan, J. (1994). *Galen's prophecy*. New York: Basic Books.

Kagan, J. (1997). Temperament and the reactions to unfamiliarity. *Child Development, 68*, 139–143.

Kantor, R., Elgas, P., & Fernie, D. (1993). Cultural knowledge and social competence within a preschool peer culture group. *Early Childhood Research Quarterly, 8*, 125–147.

Keogh, B. K. (2003). *Temperament in the classroom. Understanding individual differences*. Baltimore: Paul H. Brookes Publishing Co.

Knoster, T.P., & McCurdy, B. (2005). Best practices in functional behavior assessment for designing individualized student programs. In A. Thomas & J. Grimes (Eds.), *Best practices in school psychology-IV* (pp. 1007–1028). Bethesda: National Association of School Psychologists.

Kochanska, G., Aksan, N., Prisco, T.R. & Adams, E.E. (2008). Mother-child and father-child mutually responsive orientation in the first 2 years and children's outcomes at preschool age: Mechanisms of influence. *Child Development, 79*(1), 30–44.

Kuhan, D., & Pease, M. (2008). What needs to develop in the development of inquiry skills. *Child Development, 26*(4), 512–559.

Ladd, G., Herald, S., & Kochel, K. (2006). School readiness: Are there social prerequisites? *Early Education and Development 17*(1), 115–150.

Ladson-Billings, G. (1997). *The dreamkeepers: Successful teachers of African American children*. San Francisco: Jossey-Bass.

Lara-Cinisomo, S., Fuligni, A., Ritchie, S., Howes, C., & Karoly, L. (2008). Getting ready for school: An examination of early childhood educators' belief systems. *Early Childhood Education Journal, 33*(4), 343–349.

Lawry, J., Danko, C., & Strain, P. S. (2000). Examining the role of the classroom environment in the prevention of problem behaviors. *Young Exceptional Children, 3*(2), 11–19.

Letiecq, B.L. (2007). African American fathering in violent neighborhoods: What role does spirituality play? *Fathering, 4*(2), 111–128.

Lewis, R. (2001). Classroom discipline and student responsibility: The students' view. *Teaching & Teacher Education, 17*(3), 307–319.

Lin, H., Lawrence, F., & Gorrell, J. (2003). Kindergarten teachers' views of children's readiness for school. *Early Childhood Research Quarterly, 18,* 225–237.

Logue, M.E. (2007). Early childhood learning standards: Tools for promoting social and academic success in Kindergarten. *Children & Schools, 29*(1), 35–43.

Maccoby, E.E., & Martin, J.A. (1983). Socialization in the context of the family: Parent-child interaction. In E.M. Hetherington (Ed.), *Handbook of child psychology: Socialization, personality, and social development* (Vol. 4, pp. 1–102). New York: Wiley.

Martin, R.P., Gaddis, L.R., Drew, K.D., & Moseley, M. (1988). Prediction of elementary school achievement from preschool temperament: Three studies. *School Psychology Review, 17,* 125–137.

McAloney, K., & Stagnitti, K. (2009). Pretend play and social play. *International Journal of Play Therapy, 18*(2), 99–113.

McClelland, M., Cameron, C., Connor, C., Farris, C., Jewkes, A., & Morrison, F. (2007). Links between behavioral regulation and preschoolers' literacy, vocabulary and math skills. *Developmental Psychology, 43,* 947–959.

McClelland, M., Morrison, F., & Holmes, D. (2000). Children at risk for early academic problems: The role of learning-related social skills. *Early Childhood Research Quarterly, 28*(4), 307–329.

McConnell, S. (2002). Interventions to facilitate social interaction for young children with autism: Review of available research and recommendations for educational intervention and future research. *Journal of Autism and Developmental Disorders, 32,* 351–372.

McCormick, K.M., Jolivette, K., & Ridgley, R. (2003). Choice making as an intervention strategy for young children. *Young Exceptional Children, 6*(2), 3–10.

McCormick, K.M., Stricklin, S., Nowak, T.M., & Rous, B. (2008). Using eco-mapping to understand family strengths and resources. *Young Exceptional Children, 11*(2), 17–28.

McLaren, E., & Nelson, C. (2009). Using functional behavior assessment to develop behavior interventions for students in Head Start. *Journal of Positive Behavior Interventions, 11*(1), 3–21.

McWilliam, R., & Kruif, R. (1998). *E-Quall III: Children's Engagement Codes.* Chapel Hill: Frank Porter Graham Child Development Center, University of North Carolina at Chapel Hill.

Mashburn, A.J. (2008). Evidence for creating, expanding, designing, and improving high-quality preschool programs. In L.M. Justice & C. Vukelich (Eds.) *Achieving excellence in preschool literacy instruction* (pp. 5–24). New York: Guilford Press.

Mendez, J.L., Fantuzzo, J., & Cicchetti, D. (2002). Profiles of social competence among low-income African American preschool children. *Child Development, 73*(4), 1085–1100.

Miller, L., Robinson, J., & Moulton, D. (2004). Sensory modulation dysfunction: Identification in early childhood. In R. Del Carmen-Wiggins & A. Carter (Eds.), *Handbook of infant, toddler and preschool mental health assessment* (pp. 247–270). New York: Oxford University Press.

Modry-Mandell, K.L., Gamble, W.C., & Taylor, A.R. (2007). Family emotional climate and sibling relationship quality: Influences on behavioral problems and adaptation in preschool-aged children. *Journal of Child and Family Studies, 16,* 61–73.

Morrison, R., Sainato, D., Benchaban, D., & Endo, S. (2002). Increasing play skills of children with autism using activity schedules and correspondence training. *Journal of Early Intervention, 26,* 89–97.

National Association of School Psychologists. (2006). *Tips for school administrators for reinforcing school safety.* Retrieved 3/28/09 from http://www.nasponline.org/resources/crisis_safety/schoolsafety_admin.aspx

Neilson, S., Olive, M., Donovan, A., & McEvoy, M. (1998). Challenging behavior in your classroom? Don't react, teach instead! *Young Exceptional Children, 2*(1), 2–10.

Nevin, J.A. (1996). The momentum of compliance. *Journal of Applied Behavior Analysis, 29,* 535–547.

New, R.S., & Cochran, M. (2007). *Early childhood education: An international encyclopedia.* Santa Barbara, CA: Praeger Publishers.

Nichols, A., & Barnett, D. (2004). *Procedures for coding instructional and caring contacts.* Unpublished manuscript, University of Cincinnati.

Okagaki, L., & Kiamond, K. (2000). Responding to cultural and linguistic differences in the beliefs and practices of families with young children. *Young Children, 55*(3), 74–80.

Ostrosky, M., Jung, E., & Hemmeter, M. (2002). Helping children make transitions between activities. *Center on the Social and Emotional Foundations for Early Learning, 4.*

Palmer, P. (1998). *The courage to teach*. San Francisco: Jossey-Bass.

Palmer, S., & Wehmeyer, M. (2003). Promoting self-determination in early elementary school: Teaching self-regulated problem-solving and goal setting skills. *Remedial and Special Education, 24*, 115–126.

Perlman, M., Garfinkel, D.A., & Turrell, S.L. (2007). Parent and sibling influences on the quality of children's conflict behaviors across the preschool period. *Social Development, 16*(4), 619–641.

Phillips, L.R., Hensler, M., & Cefalo, A. (2004). Seeing the challenge more clearly. In S.H. Bell, V. Carr, D. Denno, L.J. Johnson, & L.R. Phillips. *Challenging behaviors in early childhood settings: Creating a place for all children*. Baltimore: Paul H. Brookes Publishing Co.

Pianta, R.C., Hamre, B., & Stuhlman, M. (2003). Relationships between teachers and children. In W.M. Reynolds, G.E. Miller, & I.B. Weiner (Eds.), Handbook of psychology: Vol. 7—Educational psychology (pp. 199–234). Hoboken, NJ: Wiley.

Pianta, R. (1999). *Enhancing relationships between children and teachers*. Washington, DC: American Psychological Association.

Pianta, R., Howes, C., Burchinal, M., Bryant, D., Clifford, R., & Early, D. (2005). Features of kindergarten programs, classrooms, and teachers: Do they predict observed classroom quality and child-teacher interactions? *Applied Developmental Science, 9*, 144–159.

Pianta, R., & LaParo, K. (2003). Competence and classrooms: Key features of early schooling. *Education Leadership, 60*, 24–29.

Poland, S., Pitcher, G., & Lazarus, P. M. (2005). Best practices in crisis prevention and management. In A. Thomas & J. Grimes (Eds.), *Best practices in school psychology-IV* (pp. 1057–1079). Bethesda, MD: National Association of School Psychologists.

Polloway, E., & Patton, J. (1997). Strategies for teaching learners with special needs (6th ed.). Upper Saddle River, NJ: Prentice Hall.

Ponitz, C., Rimm-Kaufman, S., Grimm, K., & Curby, T. (2009). Kindergarten classroom quality, behavioral engagement, and reading achievement. *School Psychology Review, 38*(1), 102–120.

Powell, D., Burchinal, M., File, N., & Kontos, S. (2008). An eco-behavioral analysis of children's engagement in urban public school preschool classrooms. *Early Childhood Research Quarterly, 23*, 108–123.

Presley, R., & Martin, R.P. (1994). Toward a structure of preschool temperament: Factor structure of the Temperament Assessment Battery for Children. *Journal of Personality, 2*:3, 415–448.

Rogoff, B. (2003). *The cultural nature of human development*. New York: Oxford University Press.

Rothbart, M. (1989). Temperament in childhood: A framework. In G. Kohnstamm, J. Bates, & M. Rothbart (Eds.), *Temperament in childhood* (pp. 59–73). New York: Wiley.

Rous, B., & Hallam, R.A. (1998). Easing the transition to Kindergarten: Assessment of social, behavioral and functional skills in young children with disabilities. *Young Exceptional Children, 1*(4), 17–26.

Russell, A., Hart, C.H., Robinson, C.C. & Olsen, S.F. (2003). Children's sociable and aggressive behavior with peers: A comparison of the US and Australia, and contributions of temperament and parenting styles. *International Journal of Behavioral Development, 27*(1), 74–86.

Sainato, D. (1990). Classroom transitions: Organizing environments to promote independent performance in preschool. *Education and Treatment of Children, 13*(4), 288–298.

Sameroff, A., & Chandler, M. (1975). Reproductive risk and the continuum of caretaking casualty. In F.D. Horowitz, E.M. Hetherington, S. Scarr-Salapatek, & G. Siegel (Eds.), *Review of child development research, Vol 4*, 187–244. Chicago: University of Chicago Press.

Sameroff, A.J., & Fiese, B.H. (1990). Transactional regulation: The developmental ecology of early intervention. In S.J. Meisels & J.P. Shonkoff (Eds.), Handbook of early intervention (pp. 135–159). New York: Cambridge University Press.

Sameroff, A.J., Seifer, R., Baracas, R., Zax, M., & Greenspan, S. (1987). Intelligence quotient scores of 4-year-old children: Social-environmental risk factors, *Pediatrics, 79*(3), 343–350.

Sandall, S., McLean, M., & Smith, B. (2000). The Council for Exceptional Children's Division for Early Childhood (DEC) recommended practices in early intervention/early childhood special education. Longmont, CO: Sopris West.

Santos, R.M. (2001). Using what children know to teach them something new: Applying high-probability procedures in the classroom and at home In M. Ostrosky & S. Sandall (Eds.), *Teaching strategies: What to do to support young children's development*, Young Exceptional Children monograph series no. 3 (pp. 71–80). Longmont, CO: Sopris West.

Schön, D.A. (1996). *Educating the reflective practitioner: Toward a new design for teaching and learning in the professions.* San Francisco: Jossey-Bass, Inc.

Scott, T., Liaupsin, C., & Nelson, C. (2001). Behavior intervention planning: Using the Outcomes of Functional Behavioral Assessment. Longmont, CO: Sopris West.

Schick, L. (1998). *Understanding temperament: Strategies for creating family harmony.* Seattle: Parenting Press.

Smith, M., & Dickinson, D. (1994). Describing oral language opportunities and environments in Head Start and other preschool classrooms. *Early Childhood Research Quarterly, 9,* 345–366.

Spinelli, C.G. (1999). Home/school collaboration at the early childhood level: Making it work. *Young Exceptional Children, 2*(2), 20–26.

Stipek, D. (2002). *Motivation to learn: integrating theory and practice* (4th ed.). Boston: Allyn & Bacon.

Stipek, D., & Seal, K. (2001). *Motivated minds: Raising children to love learning.* New York: Holt.

Stormont, M. (2002). Externalizing behavior problems in young children: Contributing factors and early intervention. *Psychology in the Schools, 39*(2), 127–138.

Stormshak, E.A., Bellanti, C.J., & Bierman, K.L. (1995). The quality of sibling relationships and the development of social competence and behavioral control in aggressive children. *Developmental Psychology, 32,* 79–89.

Strain, P., & Hemmeter, M.L. (1997). Keys to being successful when confronted with challenging behaviors. *Young Exceptional Children, 1*(1), 2–8.

Stromer, R., Kimball, J., Kenney, E., & Taylor, B. (2006). Activity schedules, computer technology, and teaching children with autism spectrum disorders. *Focus on Autism and Other Developmental Disabilities, 21*(1), 14–24.

Sugai, G., & Horner, R. (2002). The evolution of discipline practices: School-wide positive behavior supports. *Child and Family Behavior Therapy, 24,* 23–50.

Talge, N.M., Donzella, B., & Gunnar, M.R. (2008). Fearful temperament and stress reactivity among preschool-aged children. *Infant and Child Development, 17,* 427–445.

Thomas, A., & Chess, S. (1977). *Temperament and development.* New York: Brunner/Mazel Publishers.

Thomas, A., Chess, S., & Birch, H.G. (1968). *Temperament and behavior disorders in children.* New York: University Press.

Thompson, R.A. (2009). Making the most of small effects. *Social Development,* 18(1), 247–251.

Thompson, S., & Rains, K. (2009). Learning about sensory integration: Strategies to meet young children's sensory needs at home. *Young Exceptional Children, 12*(2), 16–25.

Todd, A., Campbell, A., Meyer, G., & Horner, R. (2008). The effects of a targeted intervention to reduce problem behaviors. *Journal of Positive Behavior Interventions, 10*(1), 46–55.

Tomlinson, H., & Hyson, M. (2009). Developmentally appropriate practice in the preschool years—Ages 3–5: An overview. In C. Copple & S. Bredekamp (Eds.), *Developmentally appropriate practice in early childhood programs* (pp. 111–147). Washington, DC: National Association for the Education of Young Children.

Urban, J., Carlson, E., Egeland, B. & Sroufe, L.A. (1991). Patterns of individual adaptation across childhood. *Development and Psychopathology, 3,* 445–460.

Vygotsky, L. (1976). *Mind in society: The development of higher mental processes.* Cambridge, MA: Harvard University Press.

Walker, H.M., Stiller, B., & Golly, A. (1998). First Step to Success: A collaborative home-school intervention for preventing antisocial behavior at the point of school entry. *Young Exceptional Children, 1*(2), 2–6.

Walker, S., Berthelsen, D., & Irving, K. (2001). Temperament and peer acceptance in early childhood: Sex and social status differences. *Child Study Journal, 31*(3), 177–192.

Wallach, L. (1995). Violence and young children's development. *Emergency Librarian, 22*(5), 30–31.

Webster-Stratton, C. (2000). Oppositional-defiant and conduct-disordered children. In M. Hersen & R.T. Ammerman (Eds.), *Advanced abnormal child psychology* (2nd ed. , pp. 387–412). Mahwah, NJ: Lawrence Erlbaum Associates.

Webster-Stratton, C., & Reid, J. (2004). Strengthening social and emotional competence in young children – The foundation for early school readiness and success. *Infants and Young Children, 17*(2), 96–113.

Xu, Y. (2006). Toddler's emotional reactions to separation from their primary caregivers: Successful home-school transition. *Early Child Development and Care, 175*(6), 661–674.

Yarbrough, J., Skinner, C., Lee, Y., & Lemmons, C. (2004). Decreating transition times in a second grade classroom: Scientific support for the timely transitions game. *Journal of Applied School Psychology, 20,* 85–107.

Yuill, N., Strieth, S., Roake, C., Aspden, R., & Todd, B. (2006). Brief report: Designing a playground for children with autistic spectrum disorders—effects of playful peer interactions. *Journal of Autism and Developmental Disorders, 27,* 1192–1196.

Index

Information in figures and tables is indicated by *f* and *t*, respectively.